■ SCHOLASTIC

Teaching the Craft of Writing

Elaboration

by Lola M. Schaefer

D1315597

New York • Toronto • London • Auckland • Sydney
Mexico City • New Delhi • Hong Kong • Buenos Aires

Teaching *Resources*

Dedication

For young writers everywhere

Acknowledgments

I appreciate these teachers who shared their insights as well as samples of student work:

* ✳ Marolyn Krauss at Horizon Elementary School

* ✳ Michele LaFever and Carolyn Fletcher at South Adams Elementary School

* ✳ Jaime Brunson at J.E. Ober Elementary School

* ✳ Darla Kingrey and Ann Hollar at Horace Mann Elementary School

Thank you to my editors, Joanna and Sarah, who both continue to be a source of inspiration and support.

And, I offer my sincere gratitude to student writers, who willingly experiment and tell us what works best for them.

✳ ✳ ✳

Cover Design by Maria Lilja
Cover Illustration by Kristen Balouch
Interior Design by Sarah Morrow

Copyright © 2006 by Lola M. Schaefer
All rights reserved.
Published by Scholastic Inc.
Printed in the U.S.A.
ISBN 0-439-44402-0

2 3 4 5 6 7 8 9 10 40 11 10 09 08 07 06

Table of Contents

Introduction

For the past eight years, I have been a visiting writing coach in elementary and middle schools. During my residencies, the students and I create our own original pieces of writing from an initial idea through revision. During this three- to five-day writing process, we are constantly working on craft. Craft is the art of using tools and skills to produce meaningful text.

As I work with student writers, I envision that each of them has a writing backpack. Our job as teachers is to provide children with strategies that become life-long tools they can carry with them in these backpacks. How do we do this? We first create a non-threatening writing community where teacher and students experiment with words, side by side. Next, we offer students a rich environment of published literature, modeling, demonstration, practice (lots of practice), and a receptive audience.

What is so encouraging is that I watch student writers embrace these strategies and quickly improve in the craft of writing. Since writing is a form of self-expression, it only makes sense that they would want to know how to do the following:

- use and maintain a writer's notebook
- select and refine an idea
- organize for different purposes and genres
- add interest and information through elaboration
- develop a genuine writer's voice
- write strong leads that lure readers into the text
- create endings that satisfy readers
- revise the piece until it reflects their intent

I believe that students' attention and commitment are strong because they are practicing craft in the context of their own authentic work. Involvement is always more active when writers are able to self-select their topics. They have something to say that is important to them—something they believe and care about. The writing has a purpose and the strategies hold promise to help students realize that purpose.

Teaching craft is more a journey of discovery rather than a precise, step-by-step program. Student writers need to be immersed in a constant study of how other authors craft their work. They need to study published writing such as poetry, story, nonfiction, and memoir. They need well-focused mini-lessons that act as constant reminders of what craft is and what it can do. They need time to reflect, plan, draft, rethink, draft again, revise, and share.

Most important, our student writers need encouragement and support. Celebrate everything they write well. Then, watch your students express themselves in ways you never thought possible.

Chapter 1

What Is Elaboration?
Introducing Students to Elaboration

Elaboration is the detail or description that adds interest, information, and beauty to any text. Having details that add specific information has always been a trademark of good writing. That's why elaboration is an element of craft. Writers include details and descriptions to strengthen their writing—to share what's in their minds with their readers. They use specific images of places, people, actions, feelings, and dialogue to pull the reader deeper into their writing. Elaboration transforms everyday prose into art. It's the pizzazz that appeals to readers and paints pictures in their minds. Elaboration enables the author to share his or her intended meaning with an audience.

For these reasons, we can call elaboration the lifeblood of writing. It pumps energy and vitality into an otherwise lifeless form (the skeleton composed of basic organization and information), creating a heart-thumping, eye-dazzling, toe-tapping work that appeals to the reader's senses, heart, and mind. Since an author uses elaboration to paint vivid pictures, the reader is treated to an insider's view. He or she is taken behind the scenes, past the main idea, to meet the details and descriptions that make the meaning interesting and personal.

Today, elaboration is one of the criteria on all state and national standards for student writing. As teachers, we need to help students become aware of what elaboration is and the purpose for using it. Here is a simple introduction mini-lesson that I like to use with students that does exactly that.

Mini-Lesson: Defining Elaboration

Mrs. S.:   Does anyone know what the word *elaborate* means?

Usually, students shake their heads.

Mrs. S.:   Can you tell the difference between an elaborate sofa and a basic sofa at a furniture store?

Emma: Would one sofa be fancy and the other one be plain?

Mrs. S.: Yes. The basic sofa would be rather plain and simple. The elaborate sofa would have some interesting features. What could some of those interesting features be?

Emma: It could have fancy legs.

Mrs. S.: Yes. Detailed, carved legs would be an interesting feature. Can you think of anything else?

Will: It could have curved arms. There might be some carving on them, too.

Mrs. S.: Yes, it could have detailed arms with carvings. That would add interest. What other elaborate features can you think of?

Zoe: Instead of plain fabric, the elaborate sofa might have a pattern using many different colors.

Mrs. S.: That's right. The pattern would add interest to the sofa. Would you like to tell me now what you think *elaborate* means?

Emma: Does it mean fancy or interesting?

Mrs. S.: That's exactly what it means. *Elaborate* can also be a verb—an action word. To elaborate means "to work out in great detail, to add information, to make something ornate." Authors like to elaborate in their work. They add details that give more information. Since we are all authors, we want to add elaboration to our writing this year. Let's list on this chart paper the different ways we can do this.

I write the following on the chart paper, reading as I write:

ELABORATION

Authors add elaboration when they . . .

1. describe a person or place in detail
2. use specific vocabulary that paints pictures
3. show how something feels, smells, tastes, sounds, or looks
4. make a comparison between two different things (similes and metaphors)
5. use the exact thoughts or words of a character or person
6. describe how someone or something moves
7. show someone's feelings or emotions by what they do

We refer back to this list, both as readers and writers, throughout the year. As readers, we use the chart when we explore elaboration in literature. As writers, the chart helps us when we write personal narratives, work on showing rather than telling, and engage in peer questioning and revising.

Chapter 1 Review

- Elaboration is a trademark of good writing.

- Elaboration is the detail and description that an author adds to his or her writing.

- Elaboration pulls the reader deeper into the text.

- Writers elaborate in a variety of ways.

Chapter 2

Student Writers and Elaboration

Helping Students Develop Elaboration

As I work with student writers in various schools, I'm always impressed with their dedication to improving their writing. They are eager to learn strategies that will help them add interesting details to their writing. Students already know the difference between vague, lifeless writing and passages that grab their attention and leave them wanting more. When asked, these students say they want to craft writing that will knock the socks off their readers. Of course, why wouldn't they?! Every writer wants to be a strong communicator, someone who can make an impression on an audience.

When I work with teachers, I always recommend starting the year by modeling personal narrative for students. While remembering the emotional events of our lives, we can more naturally add specific details that will inform and interest our audience. Students enjoy identifying the elaboration in their teacher's writing. And, as they do, you will be helping them learn how to identify and celebrate it in each other's writing.

Mini-Lesson: The Difference Between Vague and Specific Writing

I like to demonstrate the difference between vague and specific writing by letting students tell me which details they appreciate in my own writing. This can be a quick mini-lesson for the introduction or reinforcement of using specific information and ideas. To begin the lesson, I write two short personal narratives on the overhead projector. Each personal narrative is about the same topic, but one contains more elaboration.

Here are two samples that I've used in the classroom.

#1   *Last week, I cleaned out my garden. It took a lot of hard work. I pulled out all kinds of plants and vines. I put them all in the wheelbarrow and took them out to the compost heap. Next, I cut back all my perennials. Finally, I tilled the soil several times. Now it's ready for spring.*

#2   *Last week, after the first hard frost, I cleaned out my garden. First, I pulled the tomato and pepper plants. Each one had to be banged against the wheelbarrow to loosen the tight ball of dirt that clung to the roots. Next, I grabbed handfuls of empty bean vines that had turned brown in autumn's air. But the most difficult plants to unearth were the brussels sprouts. I had to dig in my heels and lean backward before I could wrench them from the soil. In the late afternoon, I cut back all of my perennials until they all looked as if they had received a crew cut. Sweating, I pushed the loaded wheelbarrow to the compost heap and spread the plants to rot. When I returned to the garden, I tilled the soil several times until the mulch and dirt made a checkerboard with their rows. The garden is now hibernating, waiting for the warm sun of spring.*

After reading aloud the two narratives, the students and I discuss them.

> "I go back through my writing and highlight details. That way I know that I've included some. If I feel I don't have enough, I add some more."
>
> — 4th grader

Mrs. S.: Which piece of writing do you like more?

Vijay: I liked #2 better than #1.

Mrs. S.: Why do you like that one better?

Jason: You told us a lot more about what you did.

Laura: I could see what you did and how you did it.

Alison: You had more information in #2.

Sarah: It wasn't boring like #1.

Lin: You used better words in #2.

Mrs. S.: It appears that most of you think #2 is a stronger piece of writing. It definitely has more elaboration than #1. One way to make your writing stronger is by sharing information that no one would know unless you included it in your writing. Did I include any specific information in piece #2 that you wouldn't have known unless you read it?

Vijay: You wrote about banging the plants against the wheelbarrow to loosen the dirt around the roots.

Matt: The perennials looked as if they had gotten a crew cut.

Elena: I knew what kinds of plants you pulled.

Laura: You were sweating.

Lin: That part where the tilled rows made a checkerboard design.

Sarah: You spread the plants on the compost heap to rot.

M.J.: You dug in with your heels and leaned back to pull the brussels sprouts.

Mrs. S.: Which of these details did you enjoy reading the most?

My students usually say that they like the crew cut reference and my stance to pull the brussels sprouts.

Mrs. S.: I could add these details because I really did this, and I remember the different plants and what I did to clean out my garden. Since you weren't there, you wouldn't know unless I told you these things. How do you want to write? Like #1 or #2?

Students always tell me that they are going to write like the more detailed account. That's why I like to use this mini-lesson that contrasts two pieces of writing. Once we draw students' attention to vague, general writing, they immediately recognize it as boring. They want to mimic the use of interesting details—and they do!

Mini-Lesson: Celebrating Elaboration in Personal Narrative

This mini-lesson also helps introduce and reinforce the use of elaboration, but it focuses on students' personal narratives. As I've mentioned, it's wise to begin the year by writing personal narratives so that students can easily remember and include specific details in their pieces. Since they know exactly what happened during the important events of their lives, they have a rich background of information from which to draw.

I always encourage students to include details that the reader would never know unless they wrote those details. Here are some of the examples I use: *Don't just write, "We had a fun time at the ocean." Tell your audience exactly what you did that was entertaining, such as: "we jumped over waves taller than our dog Jake; we scooped floating seaweed and draped it across our heads and shoulders so that we looked like the creatures from the black lagoon; we buried each other in sand until only the tips of our noses, lips, and toes could be seen."*

As I'm hearing and reading student work, I take notes to remember pieces that have specific details. Later, I ask these students if I can make overhead transparencies of their work. Students are always excited to think a teacher will use their work in a mini-lesson for the class.

I begin by asking the student writer to come to the overhead projector and read his or her piece to the class. With the first reading, everyone becomes familiar with the topic and the style of writing. Before the second reading, I ask students to listen for elaboration in the work.

Mrs. S.: Listen this time for words or phrases that add information or descriptions that we wouldn't otherwise know. Think about which details you enjoy and why.

The personal narrative for this mini-lesson was written by a second grader.

My Snowy Day by Shanti

One Saturday, my sister, September, and I walked outside to play. When we got outside it was snowing again. September and I were feeling happy. We both love playing in the snow. We got on our warmest gloves, our coats, and our snow boots. We went back outside.

September and I made a snowman in our backyard. It was kind of medium sized. We put a scarf, a dark blue hat on it, and we had mittens on the end of stick arms.

Next we had a snowball fight. We both kept hitting each other in the face, but it did not hurt. Neither of us won the fight.

After awhile, we ran inside to warm up. We took off our boots and snowy clothes. We had hot cocoa. It helped to warm us up.

Mrs. S.: Thank you for reading your piece to us, Shanti. Now, students, can you mention at least three details or descriptions that you heard or saw in this writing?

Cleo: Shanti told us her sister's name—September.

Laura: She listed the different clothes and boots they put on.

Emma: She said the snowman was medium sized.

Vijay: They hit each other in the face, but nobody won the snowball fight.

Matt: Afterwards, they had hot cocoa.

Mrs. S.: Thank you. Shanti, the students found five different details that you added to your writing. This will help us stop and think about adding more information to our pieces as we write.

At this point, I usually stop and have the students mention their favorite detail(s) in the narrative. In Shanti's piece, most students say they enjoyed knowing that during the snowball fight, the sisters hit each other in the face and that no one really won. Then, of course, they add their own quick memories of past snowball fights. I like to see writers and readers/listeners making this kind of bridge. Making personal connections through words is one of the true purposes of writing.

Don't Criticize

Brenda Ueland (1891–1985), a writer and editor, taught writing classes in the Minneapolis, Minnesota, area for many years. She encouraged her students to write boldly and to be honest. She didn't believe in teaching through criticism, instead she tried to encourage better writing by finding the successes in her students' work. In *If You Want To Write*, Ueland says this about detail:

> . . . I wanted to free her [a student] into writing more about herself, to speak from herself and know that she was important. But I never told her this as a school-marmish criticism, saying: "You must be more careful to put in more personal details" . . . No, I didn't do that. Instead I just told her how good it was, how interesting and showed her places that proved it.

Extending the Mini-Lesson

At first, I recommend giving the student author only positive feedback for the details that he or she has added. After you have grown as a community of writers, you can extend this mini-lesson to include questions for the writer. Students always have authentic questions about their peers' work.

Looking at the student writer/reader, I ask: *Would you like to ask your classmates if they have any questions for you about this day or what happened?*

If the student writer/reader agrees, then I coach him or her on what to ask as shown below.

Mrs. S.:   Ask your friends what they would like to know about this day. You may decide to add a few more details after you hear their questions. It's up to you.

Shanti: Do you want to know anything else about this day?

Matt: When did this happen? Was it last month? Was it this month?

Elena: How did you make your snowman? Did you roll the snow or just pack it?

Jason: Was the snowman taller than you?

Lin: Where did you get the clothes that you put on the snowman?

You will need to watch your writer/reader carefully. You don't want to change the positive tone of this mini-lesson. The number of student questions should not exceed five. More than that and the student writer may feel overwhelmed and anxious. The student writer should answer each question as it is asked. I always offer the pen to the child to make brief notes with the new information on the overhead copy, or if he or she hesitates, I offer to be the note taker.

I close by asking the student writer to let us know when he or she has added information to his or her narrative by answering some of the other students' questions. It becomes a celebration time for revision because I always emphasize how much we look forward to seeing the revised work. This gives the student writer a purpose to revise. Most will add two or three details, simply because the requests came from a sincere interest on the part of their classmates. Remember, writers enjoy sharing their work with an attentive audience. (A lengthier example of this revision strategy appears in Chapter 6.)

Mini-Celebrations

As discussed previously, one way to reinforce elaboration in student writing is to take a few moments to notice what students have written well. For the first few minutes that they write, I like to travel around the room and look for mini-celebrations. If I read a great detail or description in their writing, I point to it and quietly say: "Bravo! This detail adds interest and life to your writing"; or "Great detail! I can actually feel that fur under my fingertips"; or "Writing the actual words that you spoke when you were frightened makes your writing so much more believable." I speak loudly enough that the writer and maybe the students on either side hear me, too. The carry-over from this mini-celebration is remarkable. Within minutes, other students are quietly pointing to different forms of elaboration in their own writing. My simple appreciation pushes the writer and nearby students to think and include more details. Not only that, but I'm also reinforcing the craft by speaking writer to writer. To keep this mini-celebration time positive, I only circulate for the first three or four minutes of the writer's workshop. That way, I'm not continually interrupting students as they work. The mini-celebrations are a brief time to recognize what students are doing well.

"Details make stories not boring."

— 2nd grader

Adding details is adding interest. Students do not want their writing to be "blah" or "boring." They want to express themselves with the most specific images possible. Through mini-lessons and modeling, we can show student writers the power of well-placed details. Through celebration, we show our appreciation of their efforts to include details that pull us into their writing.

Chapter 2 Review

- Students are eager to improve their writing with elaboration.

- Comparing samples of writing can help students identify the effects of elaboration.

- Celebrate elaboration by pointing out strong examples in students' writing.

- Offer mini-celebrations of elaboration to individual students during writing time.

Chapter 3

Read Like a Writer
Learning About Elaboration from Literature

One of the best ways to show students the purpose of elaboration is to read to them. Always select the best literature to read and reread. The first time we read aloud any book to students, the purpose needs to be pure enjoyment and entertainment. Even though time is always an issue in the classroom, we must provide enough read-aloud time so that we can revisit some books again and again. It is during these third, fourth, or fifth readings that we can encourage students to listen for simple, but important, details and descriptions. These interactions with published writing provide opportunities to explore characters' actions; thoughts, dialogue, and dialect; sensory images; show, don't tell; and other forms of elaboration.

Showing the Purpose and Value of Elaboration

The following mini-lessons use literature to show the purpose and value of elaboration.

Mini-Lesson: *When I Was Young in the Mountains*

First, I read the entire book to students. Remember, this is not the first time that I have read *When I Was Young in the Mountains* to them. Then, I go back and ask students to close their eyes while I reread the first two pages. In the beginning, Cynthia Rylant paints a picture of her grandfather coming home from the coal mine, covered in black dust. He would kiss his granddaughter on the top of her head with his lips, the only clean part of his body.

Mrs. S.:	Did you hear any words that painted a specific picture in your mind?
Cleo:	I liked "came home in the evening covered with the black dust of a coal mine."
M.J.:	"Only his lips were clean."
Will:	I could really see "he used them to kiss the top of my head."

Mrs. S.:   Why do you think the author took the time to tell us about her grandfather in these words?

Emma: She wants us to see her grandfather the way she saw him.

Lin: This is what she remembers of him.

Zoe: She liked that he took the only clean part and kissed her.

I repeat this process with three or four more spreads. Students enjoy picking out the descriptions and details. And, they are always more excited about the details that show an emotional connection in the story—the kinds of images with which they can relate. For instance, students always mention the kiss on top of her head, how her grandmother held her hand in the dark on the way to the Johnny-house, and how her grandmother cried at Peter's baptism in the swimming hole.

If you like, you can list the details that students mention on an overhead or chart paper and then go back and put a check in front of those that they appreciate the most. *Note:* The details students generally select as their favorites will be details that are centered on emotion. Point this out to them. The example below shows how I broach the subject with them.

Mrs. S.:   Authors show us emotion, rather than telling us about it. This is part of the craft of elaboration. We get to know the characters by what they say and do. Tell me some things you now know about the author's grandmother.

Students generally tell me that she was kind, helpful, considerate, protective (in the hoe and snake scene), proud, and loving.

Mrs. S.:   Did the author use those words when describing Grandma?

Adding Delicious Details

Poet and picture book writer Rebecca Kai Dotlich describes elaboration like this:

To make a sandwich you start with two plain slices of bread, but to make it delicious you add good things like cheese and pickles, tomatoes and turkey. Details are like that. To elaborate on an idea is to add words and details that fill the bread of the sandwich—what was once empty and bland becomes tasty with ingredients.

If you were an artist, you would use brushstrokes of paint and color. Being a writer, you use word-brushstrokes that create these details.

When I wrote the picture book Mama Loves, I wanted to create a mind picture of a city shopping day with a mama and her little ones. In just a few words, I tried to create that uptown, exciting environment, including details like cobblestone streets and chestnuts in brown bags. When I write poetry, I am careful and playful at the same time; I like to search for just the right word to place in my poems to create the detail that I think a reader is thirsty for. I put myself in the place of the reader and ask myself, what would make this line come alive for me? What would I want to know? When I read a novel or a poem that someone else has written, I eat up those details like bites of candy or cobbler. Details are everything!

To learn more about Rebecca Kai Dotlich and her poetry and picture books for children, visit her Web site: www.rebeccakaidotlich.com.

Zoe:	No, I didn't hear any of those words when you read the book.
Mrs. S.:	Then how do you know so much about the grandmother?
Alison:	Because of what she did in the story.
Shanti:	Her actions showed us what kind of person she was.
Mrs. S.:	You can do the same thing in your writing. Always let your character's actions and words show us something about him or her.

Mini-Lesson: *Davy Crockett Saves the World*

Another great book for illustrating elaboration is *Davy Crockett Saves the World* by Rosalyn Schanzer. Students in grades 2–4 sit spellbound through repeated readings of this tall tale. The story is jammed-packed with details and description. For instance, on the first page, the author writes how Davy could drink a river, comb his hair with a rake, shave with an ax, and run so fast that trees stepped out of his way.

This book elaborates through dialect, dialogue, and the descriptions of settings, people, and characters' actions. For a quick mini-lesson on the importance and value of elaboration, select any three spreads and read them twice to students. The first read is to reintroduce them to the great story. During the second read, have students listen for details. Then, record their offerings on chart paper. Later, go back and decide whether each detail is a description of a place or person, use of dialect, or information revealed through dialogue or action. To reinforce the idea that elaboration can be developed in many different ways, ask students to label the details they chose. (I use the elaboration list that is explained on page 7 of Chapter 1.) For example, even the names Rosalyn Schanzer uses are one form of elaboration: Davy's pet bear is named Bear Hug; his girlfriend's name is Sally Sugartree; and Davy climbs to the top of a mountain called Eagle Eye Peak.

The author also uses words like *baddest ball of fire, lickety-split, smithereens, hurrycane* (playing with language), *commenced, varmints,* and *discombobulated.* Certainly, some of these words add to the dialect, but even by themselves, they create images specific to this story. Vocabulary plays an important role in elaboration. The more specific the words, the better the picture that is painted in the reader's mind. (For more information about vocabulary and elaboration, see Chapter 4.)

Mini-Lesson: *Grandmother Winter*

Grandmother Winter, by Phyllis Root, is a book that celebrates the coming of winter with imagery that is gentle but specific. On one page, the author uses verbs to pull her reader deeper into the story: *"All spring Grandmother herds her geese as they gabble and squawk, honk and hiss, flapping a storm of feathers."* Phyllis Root also engages the senses when she describes the geese feathers with the lovely metaphor. Such specific references are preparing us for the journey into winter, and yet, they also provide concrete examples that students can understand.

After reading aloud this book one time, I then ask students to listen for action words that help paint pictures in their minds as I reread it. They have told me that the word *herds* is quite specific because it helps show them what Grandmother Winter is doing with her geese. They always laugh at the words *gabble, squawk, honk,* and *hiss.* These vivid verbs show them what sounds the geese are making—and they add spark and interest to a child's ear. The students love, absolutely love, the phrase "flapping a storm of feathers." During our discussion, they are actively engaged in Phyllis Root's writing. The kinds of details that she uses are the ones we want students to appreciate and mimic.

I usually guide students in finding their favorite descriptive phrase in this book and copying it in their writer's notebooks. The language in *Grandmother Winter* is the kind of language they enjoy because it is vibrant and presents specific images. Students need to celebrate words, and especially, the words that paint pictures in their minds and plant seeds of emotion in their hearts.

Mini-Lesson: *The Wanigan: A Life on the River*

Gloria Whelan's *The Wanigan: A Life on the River* is the beautiful account of an eleven-year-old girl traveling with her mother down the Au Sable River on a floating cookshack while her father and other loggers move timber down the river. The author takes you back in time to 1878 with her attention to detail.

After reading the entire book out loud to the class (which would take about five days of read-aloud time), I go back and find passages that paint pictures with the use of elaboration. For instance, on pages 86–87, Whelan describes a short walk on a parcel of land along the river:

With Bandit [a raccoon] in my arms, Jimmy and I waded onto the sandy shore. The land there had not yet been timbered. Instead of acres and acres of stumps, there were tall pines. We walked under the branches of the giant pines, their fallen needles soft under our feet, their fragrance all around us. A hawk with a red tail took off from an overhead branch. Deerflies buzzed around us. A crow whose caw was half bark and half cough scolded us.

Elaboration Must Follow the Story

Phyllis Root is the author of many critically-acclaimed picture books for children. She crafts stories that carry a whopping amount of emotion and elaboration. How does she accomplish that in so few words? Very carefully.

Here, Phyllis shares the role that elaboration plays in her writing:

For me, most stories start with a single thread, sometimes as simple as a single word or image. In my writing I follow those threads through twists and turns, tie them into knots, unravel them, start over again to find the one true thread of a story. Once I have found it, any elaboration to the story—sounds, rhymes, twists of plot—must serve that central thread.

If something doesn't follow the thread through in a true line from beginning to end, it must go, no matter how much I love it. There's joy in playing with a story and joy in cutting away anything unnecessary so that the true story shines through.

After I reread a passage like this with students, I have them describe how a "boring" writer might have said the same thing. You might think that such an exercise would be counterproductive to what we hope students will do in their writing. Not at all. Every time students compare strong writing and weak writing, it helps them clarify in their minds what they do and don't want to do in the future.

For the previous passage, a student might say the following: *I carried the raccoon to shore with Jimmy. There were lots of tall trees. We walked under them. The needles were soft and smelled good. A big bird flew out of one of the trees. There were a lot of bugs and a crow cawed.*

Students always laugh a little at the weakened version. That's what we want. We want them to hear bland writing and think that it's silly and ineffective. What a step in the right direction this is. If students can differentiate between strong and weak writing, they will start making conscious choices to add details and descriptions to their own pieces.

Mini-Lesson: Poetry and Sensory Description

Elaboration has everything to do with awakening the senses. We continually remind students to write what they heard, saw, smelled, tasted, or touched. (Let's hope not all five senses are engaged at all times; the writing can take on an artificial pretense. I always recommend that students use two or three senses in any one scene.)

Poetry is a great place to begin examining the use of sensory images. Due to its economy of words and emphasis on images, students can successfully identify this kind of elaboration with ease. One of my favorite poems to show the use of sensory description is "Invitation from a Mole" from *A Lucky Thing* by Alice Schertle. (She uses all five senses—beautifully, deftly!)

I copy the poem onto chart paper and read it with the students several times. Then, I ask them to tell me their favorite details. Here are some of their responses:

- "taste dirt on the tip of your tongue"
- "smell the sweet damp feet of mushrooms"
- "the cold face of a stone"
- "wear the earth like a glove"

Literature for Elaboration

Here are a few books that work well in grades 2–4. Select a couple to read again and again with your students, finding those details and descriptions that paint pictures in your minds.

- *The Butterfly* by Patricia Polacco
- *Canoe Days* by Gary Paulsen
- *The Girl on the High-Diving Horse* by Linda Oatman High
- *How the Elephant Got Its Trunk* retold by Jean Richards
- *Just Juice* by Karen Hesse
- *Nory Ryan's Song* by Patricia Reilly Giff
- *Owl Moon* by Jane Yolen
- *Runt* by Marion Dane Bauer
- *Thanksgiving in the White House* by Gary Hines
- *Three Pebbles and a Song* by Eileen Spinelli

My personal favorite, too, is "wear the earth like a glove," and, of course, I share that with the students. That line speaks about touch in such an unusual way. It makes a reader stop and think how closely a glove fits and how small the mole's tunnel is.

I continue our discussion to help students see how this poet takes readers into the meaning of the poem.

Mrs. S.: What does the poem ask readers to do?

Alison: It invites us to live like a mole.

Mrs. S.: How does the poem do that?

Will: The poem talks to us.

Emma: It tells us what to do.

Zoe: It tells us to touch and hear and taste and smell the same things that a mole does.

Mrs. S.: Does the way the poet wrote this make these experiences seem real?

M.J.: Yes. I even moved my tongue inside my mouth.

Jason: It made me think about what it would be like.

Mrs. S.: Which of her details do you think takes your mind underground with the mole?

Cleo: The detail about tasting dirt on your tongue.

Shanti: The one about smelling the feet of the mushrooms.

Vijay: I think they all do. I like her line about being in darkness because that's what would bother me the most.

> *"I go back and reread my story to see if it has details."*
>
> — 2nd grader

Next, I encourage student writers to find details that they want to copy into their writers' notebooks as examples of strong elaboration.

Placing excellent examples of the craft of elaboration in highly visible places is another form of support. I suggest that you post poems or excerpts from stories that have sensory descriptions in your classroom where students can go back and reread them independently. If we value details, then we show them, examine their use, and appreciate what they do for the meaning of our writing.

Chapter 3 Review

- Read elaboration-rich literature to students, and invite them to identify details or descriptions that paint pictures in their minds.

- Select writing examples that show emotion through elaboration.

- Ask students to identify their favorite details and descriptions.

- Have students label details as descriptions of places or people; specific and unique vocabulary; the actions, words (including dialect), and thoughts of characters; sensory images; and show, don't tell.

Chapter 4

Vocabulary
The Building Block of Elaboration

Writers are wordsmiths. Words are to wordsmiths as metals are to blacksmiths. It's amazing how many useful and beautiful works can be shaped with time, skill, and patience. Wordsmiths enjoy the meaning, sound, and uniqueness of words. They collect words, experiment with vocabulary, and surprise us with their choices. But most important, wordsmiths link words together to form art—food for the mind and heart.

I enjoy telling students that they are wordsmiths. It's a word whose meaning they want to explore. Once students realize the value of words, they can't get enough of them. They start mentioning new words they hear in the read-aloud or new words they find during independent reading. Students also want to be formally introduced to new words to expand their speaking and writing vocabularies. We can do this through direct instruction, for example, by demonstration and interactive mini-lessons that highlight rich vocabulary. But we must be careful not to rely on vocabulary workbooks or sophisticated word-of-the-day calendars as the only avenue to expand students' word repertoires. To be able to acquire new vocabulary and use it appropriately, student writers need to see and hear the words in context. So, it is a combination of strategies used in unison that creates wordsmiths.

Many students begin to list their favorite new words in their writer's notebook. They are proud to point out new vocabulary that they've included in their writing. Once you put this love of words into motion, it's almost impossible to slow it down, let alone stop it.

Mini-Lesson: Well-Chosen Vocabulary

Many classroom teachers already do a wonderful job of reading out loud to their students. To place even more emphasis on well-chosen vocabulary, I would suggest including as much poetry in your reading as possible. Children's poets take great pains to select the best words to create meaning. Since the form is relatively brief, students can really focus on the language. They can see that just a few words can paint a very specific picture in the reader's mind.

A Rich Vocabulary

In *Conversations*, Regie Routman writes about how we can help our students expand their vocabularies.

> While there is no one best way to ensure that students acquire a rich vocabulary, a combination approach that involves the following components seems to make the most sense.
>
> Students acquire many new words from reading widely, listening to stories, and talking about words (Smith and Elley 1994: Nagy 1988). While direct instruction has some impact on vocabulary growth, it is insufficient as the principal strategy for building an extensive vocabulary.
>
> Doing lots of reading seems to be the surest way to build a broad vocabulary. Just twenty minutes of daily reading can potentially lead to learning at least one thousand words per year (Nagy, Anderson, and Herman 1987).

This short mini-lesson can be used to introduce or reinforce well-chosen vocabulary use in writing. Post the poem "Paper Clips" by Rebecca Kai Dotlich (from *School Supplies: A Book of Poems*, selected by Lee Bennett Hopkins) on chart paper for the whole class to see. In this poem, Dotlich compares a paper clip to a tin creature that conquers pages with one bite. The poem is written as a metaphor and is packed with visual imagery. After I read the poem to my students at least three times, I lead a discussion about the word choice and the images that it creates.

Mrs. S.: Of course, we know that the poet is describing paper clips because the title tells us that, but then she compares a paper clip's properties to that of a creature. Which details or descriptions does she accurately use for both? In other words, which words or groups of words tell us what a paper clip, or a creature, is or does? (*Students really enjoy this mini-lesson. They can readily pull out vocabulary that specifically describes both the paper clip and the creature.*)

Sarah: "Tiny teeth."

Will: "Tin."

Zoe: "Slender breath."

Matt: "Silver pinch."

Jason: "Jaws."

Cleo: "No bigger than an inch."

M.J.: "Dragon grips."

Emma: "Conquer pages."

Lin: "One bite."

> "I make sure that I have lots of details listed in my plan. That way they will be in my writing."
>
> — 3rd grader

Mrs. S.: If you were to select just three words that are the most important to this poem, which would you select?

Here are two poems written by second graders who consider themselves wordsmiths.

Moon by Austin
The moon
  is like a diamond
     in the sky
When it shines
down
  down
    down
we all
go to sleep.

Flashing Lightning by Cassie
Roaring!
Crashing!
Hitting the ground
as it fights
to move
on its way
Boom!
Boom!
Bang!
As frisky as can be
Striking down
from the sky
Flashing at me
Boom!
Boom!
Crash!

Shanti:	*Teeth!*
Will:	*Grips!*
Zoe:	*Conquer!* I really like that one because one little paper clip can hold together a big mess of paper. I like the picture I get in my mind.
Mrs. S.:	That's great. Let's try some substitutions and see if we like the poem better. How about if the poem began "With their mouths they take slender breaths . . ."
Elena:	That sounds silly. It has to be teeth.
Matt:	Besides, paper clips don't have mouths, but their shapes do look like teeth.
Mrs. S.:	Let's try another. At the end of the poem we could say "but hold together lots of pages with one bite!"
Laura:	"Hold together" doesn't mean the same as "conquer"—it doesn't seem as strong.
Mrs. S.:	How about "lots of pages"—what do you think of that change?
Alison:	"Lots of pages" sounds like regular talk—not like poem talk.
Mrs. S.:	Do you think all of these words came quickly to the poet?
Lin:	I bet poets write their poems over and over.
Vijay:	They might start out with regular words, but after they think about it, they decide to use better words.

This mini-lesson really does make a difference. During the lesson, I often talk about author or poet intentions—that writers have an intended meaning and they select the best words to share that meaning with their audiences. I let students know that as wordsmiths, they need to make conscious decisions about the words they use. And, as I said before, students soon become excited about collecting words, experimenting with them, and surprising us with their choices.

Collecting Words

Many children come to school with limited vocabularies. We know that our daily read-alouds, their independent reading, and classroom conversations help expand their

Don't Fatten-Up the Writing

One point that I try to make with students is that a heavy use of adjectives and adverbs weakens writing. It takes time to show them that elaboration is not just inserting a color word here and an adverb there. (Children seem to come equipped with quite a repertoire of these two categories of words.) Used sparingly, of course, the correct adjective or adverb can add strong meaning to a piece of writing, but student writers need to know that precise verbs and nouns are the tools that create clear, concise writing.

In *Steering the Craft*, Ursula LeGuin shares her philosophy of how to limit the fat of adjectives and adverbs in writing.

> *Adjectives and adverbs are rich and good and fattening. The main thing is not to overindulge.*
>
> *When the quality that the adverb indicates can be put in the verb itself (they ran quickly = they raced) or the quality of the adjective can be put in the noun itself (a growling voice = a growl), the prose will be cleaner, more intense, more vivid . . . I would recommend to all storytellers a watchful attitude and a thoughtful, careful choice of adjectives and adverbs, because the bakery shop of English is rich beyond belief, and narrative prose, particularly if it's going a long distance, needs more muscle than fat.*

resources. Another component that can help students become aware of words is direct instruction; we can introduce students to new words and their meanings.

I always recommend that teachers begin introducing a word a week to their students. These are not long, complicated words but specific verbs or nouns that expand children's writing and speaking vocabularies.

Using Precise Verbs

Initially, I suggest introducing verbs. You will notice a distinct change in the quality of your students' pieces when they begin to use precise, active verbs. And, once you raise students' awareness of the power of precise verbs, they begin to make a conscious effort to select verbs that specifically describe the action they see in their minds. For students in grades 2–4, I suggest using verbs like *survey, crouch, project, jab, flail, hamper, blister, subdue, define, sprawl, discover, rely, whisk, unravel, stream, pounce, brood,* and *conquer.* I also suggest reserving a small area of wall space for these new and intriguing words.

On Monday, introduce the word. Sometimes, you may want to do this in game fashion, such as "Twenty Questions." This twenty-questions approach has been extremely

> *"I skip lines as I write my first draft. Then I go back and add details where I need them."*
>
> — 4th grader

Verbs Show What's Happening

For reinforcement on the power of specific verbs, copy excerpts from stories and have students identify the verbs that show the action. In these sentences from *Charlotte's Web*, E. B. White paints a picture of Wilbur's short flight.

"Wilbur <u>scrambled</u> to the top of the manure pile."

"'Very good!' said Charlotte. 'Now make an attachment with your spinnerets, <u>hurl</u> yourself into space, and let out a dragline as you go down!'"

"Wilbur <u>hesitated</u> a moment, then <u>jumped</u> out into the air. He <u>glanced</u> hastily behind to see if a piece of rope was following him to check his fall, but nothing seemed to be happening in his rear, and the next thing he knew he <u>landed</u> with a thump. 'Ooomp!' he <u>grunted</u>."

Have students underline or circle the action words that show what's happening. Don't be surprised when you see these words appear in their writing that same week.

---

successful, even in kindergarten. (Before inviting your students to ask the questions, you and a fellow teacher might want to demonstrate *how* to ask questions so students see how you *narrow* the possibilities.)

Before introducing the game, I write the word on a piece of tag board and put it in a gift-wrapped box. Then, I announce that I have a gift for students that will last a lifetime—a new word. I also reveal that the word is a verb. Then, I tell students that they cannot just guess the word, but they need to ask questions that lead them to the word. You have to be firm and insist that students don't try to guess the word during the questioning time. This is a time for them to be thinkers—to ask questions to get to the *meaning* of the word.

Here's a sample game for the verb *unravel*.

1. Can a person do this? No.
2. Can a car or vehicle do this? No.
3. Can an animal do this? No.
4. Can a machine do this? No.
5. Could a mountain or a river do this? No.
6. Can a thing made of fabric do this? Yes.
7. Could a sheet do this? Unlikely. No.
8. Could a sweater do this? Yes.
9. Would the sweater do this all by itself? No.
10. Would someone or something do this to the sweater? Yes.
11. Is the sweater better after this is done? No.
12. Is the sweater worse after this is done? Yes.
13. Does the sweater have marks on it? No.

14. Does it change shape? Yes, a little.

15. Does the word begin with a letter in the first half of the alphabet? No.

16. Does the word begin with a letter in the second half of the alphabet? Yes.

17. Does the word have one syllable? No.

18. Does the word have two syllables? No.

19. Does the word have three syllables? Yes.

20. Does the word have more than six letters? Yes.

After asking twenty questions, students can start to guess the word. I have probably demonstrated this approach in ten different settings, from grades K–4, and only once did students *not* guess the word.

Whether you use a game format or straight instruction to introduce a new word, students need to hear and see the word in context at least six more times that week. It's great when you can sneak the word into the morning message or into your own modeled writing. Students will discover the word and see it used in a meaningful context right away. Other engagements vary from discussions, using the word in sentences, sending a message that uses it to a neighboring classroom, posting a message or a sign with the word outside the classroom, or having students send messages to each other using it.

Proper Nouns

When discussing specific vocabulary with students, I also show the difference between a common noun such as *lake* and the proper noun *Lake Lanier*. Why have an audience guessing which lake, street, city, mountain, or canyon a writer means? It's helpful to begin a list like the one shown below to display in the classroom so students have a constant reminder to write the specific.

Common Nouns	Proper Nouns
kennel	Westview Kennel
river	Snake River
ocean	Indian Ocean
school	Horace Mann Elementary School
valley	Shenandoah Valley
hair salon	Curl and Twirl Hair Salon
street	Main Street
club	Cross-Country Ski Club
mountains	Appalachian Mountains
show	Home and Garden Show
cinema	Regal Star Cinema
cape	Cape Horn

Finally, post the word on the wall in a small area of the classroom designated for "WOW! Words," "Oooh-la-la Words," "Million Dollar Words," or "Wondrous Words." I recommend displaying only ten words at any one time. When the eleventh word is introduced, hang a zip-lock bag beneath the words and store the first word in it. That way, students have a record of the words to consult for spelling.

Precise and specific nouns can also be a part of these special words. Again, do not introduce extremely difficult words. Children in grades 2–4 need strong vocabulary that matches their experiences in the real world. Some nouns you might consider are *medallion, nozzle, catalog, bracket, pedestal, gesture, wharf, discipline, trowel, quarry,* and *vise.*

Use of these words is contagious. As soon as one child shares a piece of writing including one of the special words, other students become even more aware and consciously look for opportunities to use their new vocabulary, too.

Mini-Lesson: Precise Nouns and Verbs

Precise verbs and nouns add elaboration to writing. When a writer selects specific vocabulary, it creates detail. The reader can visualize exactly what the author is communicating. The meaning is picture-perfect!

This is how I present a mini-lesson on the importance of using precise nouns and verbs.

Mrs. S.: Tell me what picture you see in your mind when I say the word *person.*

M.J.: A kid.

Shanti: A teacher.

Alison: A bus driver.

Matt: My mom.

Will: My grandpa.

Zoe: A baby.

Mrs. S.: Now, tell me what picture you see in your mind when I say the word *infant.*

Zoe: My baby sister.

Vijay: A crying baby.

Elena: A sleeping baby.

Mrs. S.: Now, tell me what picture you see in your mind when I say "The infant moved."

Alison: A baby crawled.

Emma: A baby turned over.

Cleo: A baby wriggled.

Sarah: A baby moved her hand up and down.

Lin: A baby rocked.

Laura: A baby turned his head.

Mrs. S.: Now, tell me what picture you see in your mind when I say "The infant twisted her neck from side to side."

Jason: A baby turning her head from one side to the other.

Mrs. S.: Authors can place specific pictures in the minds of their readers by choosing just the right words. Let's try this again. Only this time, I'll give you a general or fuzzy picture. Then, you use specific words to make it clear. How else might an author say, "The bug bit?" Write what you see in your mind with precise words. (*When students are finished, I ask them to share their sentences.*)

Vijay: The cockroach chomped the dry bread.

Matt: The mosquito stung.

Elena: The ladybug chewed her dinner.

Will: The praying mantis tore her prey.

Cleo: The house fly tasted the hamburger.

Mrs. S.: Excellent choices. I saw the detail in my mind that you saw in yours. Let's practice one more time. How else could an author say, "The wind blew?"

Here are some of my students' responses:

- The breeze ruffled the leaves in the trees.
- The storm carried the trashcan across the road.
- The gust tore the tent apart.
- The wind scattered the dandelion seeds making a white ocean.

With all of this practice, students not only incorporate these precise words into their vocabularies, but they also become aware of the words that published authors link together. They read and listen like writers to see which words other authors use to paint pictures and to be precise. In fact, students might interrupt you during the read-aloud occasionally to ask you to repeat a word or to explain its meaning. This emphasis on vocabulary helps create wordsmiths. Once you have wordsmiths, you will have students who can find just the right words to elaborate their writing.

Chapter 4 Review

- Read out loud often to your students to expose them to new vocabulary.
- Provide a combination of strategies to expand student vocabularies.
- Offer a mini-lesson on the role precise language plays in elaboration.
- Introduce one precise verb or noun to your student writers each week, and use it in a meaningful context several times.
- Teach a mini-lesson that shows the value and meaning of specific vocabulary that paint pictures in the reader's mind.

Chapter 5

Show, Don't Tell
Give the Reader an Inside View

When writers elaborate, they take us deeper into their writing. We get an armchair view of who is speaking, what is taking place, and where it is happening. The craft of elaboration shows readers the sights, sounds, and emotions of another time and place, whether it be real or fictional. We want student writers to "show" actions and emotions in their writing. We want them to include comparisons that "show" size, color, shape, sound, taste, and other sensory features. "Tell" distances the audience because it provides only general descriptions. A "telling" piece lacks detail. It offers no lure to engage readers in the text. Like all writers, student writers want to enliven their writing and take their audiences deeper into meaning. "Show, don't tell" is one form of elaboration that helps them do just that.

 ## Mini-Lesson: Introducing "Show, Don't Tell"

"Show, don't tell" is one of the cardinal rules of good writing. Don't tell your readers that the mountains were magnificent. Show their magnificence through your description. Don't tell your audience that Ted was sorry. Show Ted's sorrow through his actions and words. Don't tell your listeners that it was cold. Show the temperature through what the people and animals do.

One of the easiest places to start with this concept is to remind students that writers paint pictures with words. We can write down on paper what we see in our minds. Here is a sample of a mini-lesson I use to introduce or reinforce that idea. Just as the mini-lesson at the end of Chapter 4 showed students the importance of specific word choice, this mini-lesson shows how important it is to paint exact pictures of actions in the mind of the reader. If the actions are vivid, then we should be able to act them out. The emphasis of this mini-lesson is not only on action but also on the details of motivation, or purpose for the action.

Mrs. S.: I'd like all of you to shut your eyes and listen to this sentence: *The boy went inside.* Now, tell me what you saw in your mind.

Elena:	I saw a boy about my age walking into his house.
Mrs. S.:	How did he walk? What door did he use? Was it the front or the back door? Was he carrying anything?

Students will have different answers to each of these questions. Since the sentence is vague, both in vocabulary and detail, they will envision their own images to create meaning for themselves.

Mrs. S.:	Let's look first at the verb *went*. *Went* is one of those general, telling words. It paints no picture in our minds. Listen to these sentences: *The dog went inside. The girl went inside. The repairman went inside.* My question as a writer about these sentences is *how*. How did each one go inside? Let's brainstorm some other words we could use for the word *went*.
Will:	*Walked* or maybe *ran*.
Zoe:	*Hurried!*
Emma:	*Jumped.*
Matt:	*Rushed.*
Mrs. S.:	All of those words are more specific and paint a better picture. They really show me how the boy was moving. I also like words like *hobbled, limped, bolted, crawled,* and *danced.* Now, I'd like to think about the noun *boy*. Are there any other ways we could say *boy* that would paint clearer pictures? These could be single words or phrases.
M.J.:	*Teenager.*
Cleo:	*Brother.*
Shanti:	*Tall boy.*
Vijay:	Or *unhappy boy.*
Mrs. S.:	I see that you're now getting some pictures in your minds as you're thinking about this. Let me write down the telling sentence. (*On chart paper, I write:* The boy went inside.) I have one more question. I know that earlier someone said she saw the boy walking into a house. What are some other places that he could be going?
Alison:	I know—school!
Cleo:	Or the toy store.
Will:	Maybe a restaurant.
Matt:	I think he's going to his friend's house.
Lin:	The video store.
Mrs. S.:	What good choices. Now, we need to stop and think and see a picture in our minds. Let me reread the sentence: *The boy went inside.* After I think a moment, I'm going to write down what I see. (*I close my eyes for a few seconds and think.*) Okay, I'm ready. (*On the chart paper, I write:* The third-grade boy hurried into the library to look for his sister.) Can you describe what you saw in your mind when I read my sentence? Let me repeat it: *The third-grade boy hurried into the library to look for his sister.*

Students will have similar responses such as: *I saw an eight-year-old boy rushing through the library doors, looking all around; I saw a boy with a worried look running into the town library and raising his eyebrows as he looks for his sister; I saw a boy about my size hurrying into the library.*

Mrs. S.:   Does anyone want to act out my sentence about the boy and the library?

I often have two or three students act out the most detailed sentence and then ask the other children to identify the similar features of their actions. I want them to know that a careful writer provides plenty of specifics that describe the action. I also want students to know that there is a direct correlation between "show" and acting. I believe that the drama part helps students see that when authors write, they have a motion picture going in their minds.

Mrs. S.:   Let's try that again. I'm going to think of a new picture to paint. (*I close my eyes and think for several seconds.*) I have a new picture in my mind. Let's see if I can put it in your mind by showing you with language. (*I write the following sentence on the board, and then read it aloud:* The prince crawled into the castle with his sword clutched to his side.) Can you describe what you see in your mind?

Students' responses will be quite similar: *I saw a hurt prince crawling through the open gate; I saw a prince crawling into the castle to surprise someone with his sword; I saw a prince crawling into the castle with his sword at his side and some blood on his shirt.* Again, I provide time for several students to act out the sentence.

Mrs. S.:   Now, let's see what kinds of pictures are in your minds today. Think for a moment to create your own image for the telling sentence, *The boy went inside.* Write it down, but be specific. Be sure to show what kind of boy, how he goes, and where he goes.

These are some of my students' responses:

- My brother ran into our house looking for me.
- The angry boy stomped into the principal's office.
- The second-grade boy rushed into his classroom for his coat.
- The toddler pulled away from his mother and ran into the toy store.
- The confused boy stumbled into the wrong locker room.

I close the lesson by saying: *Today, as you're writing, I hope you will stop and study the pictures in your minds, and then use language to paint those pictures for your readers.*

Mini-Lesson: Letting Emotions Paint Pictures

As student writers try to include feelings in their writing, they quite often write the following kinds of sentences:

- She was really frightened.
- He was angry.
- Boy, he was amazed!
- She was so sad.

We want to celebrate that students are including these emotions, because as we know, strong writing is more than just story or plot—it's the human connection made when emotional moments are shared between author and reader. The following mini-lesson is one way to help students show those feelings instead of just telling about them.

Mrs. S.: I've noticed in some of your writing that you're including the feelings of the people who you write about. BRAVO! Accomplished writers are always trying to show their characters' thoughts and feelings. This is another way we learn about the characters. Today, I want us to discuss how we can elaborate on these feelings and show our audience what we are thinking as we write. Please listen to this sentence: *The mother was so proud.* Now, tell me what you saw in your minds.

Students will have a variety of responses, such as: *I saw a mother standing and clapping; I saw a mother showing her award to people; I saw a mother pointing to an award and smiling.*

Mrs. S.: Why do you think you didn't all see the same thing?

Vijay: People show pride in different ways.

Elena: I didn't know why the mother was proud so it was hard to see a picture of her.

Mrs. S.: That's a good point. Can you tell me what your body does when you are proud?

Elena: I smile.

Will: I hold my head high and walk tall.

Jason: I call up people to celebrate.

Alison: My brother says I get a little puffed up.

Mrs. S.: My body does some of those same things, too, when I'm proud. The first sentence, *The mother was so proud*, is an example of a telling sentence. It tells us she's proud, but we really can't see it. We have to imagine what she's doing. I'm going to stop and think to see if I can imagine what this mother's body is doing to show her pride. (*I sit quietly for a few seconds and think.*)

Change Tell to Show

To practice writing that shows, provide a telling sentence each morning for a week on the chalkboard or overhead projector. Have students rewrite the sentence with specific vocabulary that shows. They enjoy this quick exercise, and the practice encourages them to think like writers.

Sample telling sentences:

The lady cried for a long time.

The men lifted it up.

The dog made a loud sound.

She looked at it.

The young girl sat in the middle.

It didn't look that good.

I have an idea. Let me write my show sentence for you on the overhead projector. (*I write:* Sarah's mother smiled and looked out over the audience as her daughter received the Good Sportsmanship Award.)

Mrs. S.:   Does anyone know what a Good Sportsmanship Award is?

Matt: Teams give it to people or kids for acting good whether they win or lose.

Lin: Kids who get that award are good sports. They never get mad at a call or if they lose.

Mrs. S.:   Exactly. Thank you for those explanations. Now, I'd like all of you to stop and think of a mom and how she would be showing her pride. Please write your own show sentence for the telling sentence: *The mom was so proud.*

If students look up from their paper when they've completed their sentences, I remind them to reread what they've written to see if it paints the picture that is in their mind. If it doesn't, they can take a few moments to revise their sentences. Some of the sentences my students have written are shown below.

- Brandon's mom stood and clapped when he took his bow.
- Leah's mom gave her daughter a balloon and a hug after the soccer championship game.
- Brittany's mom puffed up and smiled when her daughter said her first words.
- Kevin's mother clapped her hands and shouted when her son got an *A* in math.
- Jeni's mom called all her friends and told them about her daughter's science award.
- Ryan's mother almost burst out of her clothes when she found out that her son was on the honor roll.

Mrs. S.:   In your future writing, I hope you include descriptions of what people's bodies are doing to show their different emotions. Showing instead of telling will add elaboration to your writing

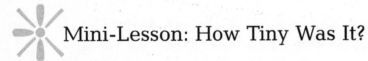

Mini-Lesson: How Tiny Was It?

As students add more description to their writing, they often will write these kinds of things: *The cat ran real fast. The castle was the biggest one in the kingdom. The river was really wide. Her hair was red, bright red.*

Holding several short mini-lessons on how to write comparisons will add "show" to your students' writing. I often begin a writer's workshop with this short explanation of how simile can add elaboration and paint pictures.

Mrs. S.:   I see that many of you are putting more description in your writing. I'm delighted to see that. Description adds details that will paint pictures in the reader's mind. Today, I want us to talk about some words that we use to describe—words like *golden, big, short, tall, fast, green, fragile,* or *loud.* We can show our readers and listeners just how loud, big, or red something is. Let's practice together. (*I write the following sentence on chart paper and read it aloud:* Hal's German Shepherd was really big.) Now, show me with your hands how big this dog was.

Of course, the students will have many different versions of the dog's size. Some will put a hand above their heads. Others will hold a hand at their chests. Still others might use both hands and show the dog's length to be as far as they can spread their arms.

Mrs. S.: It seems as if we have many different ideas. I'll try to write a comparison that will help us all understand just how big Hal's dog was. I'm going to compare his size to something we all know. Let me think for a moment. (*I close my eyes and think.*) I have something that I think will work. Listen to this sentence, please: *Hal's German Shepherd was the same size as our piano bench.* If you have a piano bench at your house, show me with your hands how tall that is.

Most of the students will be fairly close with their approximations, placing their hands at their waists or a bit lower.

Mrs. S.: Now, show me how long that is. (*Most lengths will be similar, suggesting two or three feet.*) That was fun. I want to try it again. Let me think. (*Again, I close my eyes and think.*) How about this comparison? Please, listen to this sentence: *Hal's German Shepherd is as long as my toy box.* Everyone who has a toy box, show us how long that is. (*Again, most of the students will show a similar length with their hands.*) Now, let's try this with something else. Listen to this sentence, please: *The hummingbird moved fast.* Tell me, what did you see?

Show Emotions with Body Actions

As extra support for your students, you might consider brainstorming sessions where you and they make lists of what their bodies do when experiencing the different emotions. I've done this in many classrooms with great success. For *fear,* my students have listed these responses:

> *I sweat.*
>
> *My heart beats hard and fast.*
>
> *I tremble.*
>
> *I can't speak.*
>
> *My legs feel wobbly.*
>
> *I get goose bumps.*
>
> *I gasp.*
>
> *I run.*
>
> *My tummy flip-flops.*
>
> *I scream.*
>
> *My eyes get big.*
>
> *I get a headache.*

If you make lists for at least four different emotions, it will raise your students' awareness of how to write about feelings with more elaboration. Other feelings you might explore are anger, disappointment, excitement, confusion, frustration, and joy.

Student responses will vary, but here's a sampling: *I saw a hummingbird flying off between the flowers; I saw a hummingbird zipping away from a house; I saw a hummingbird disappearing around the corner of a shed.*

Mrs. S.: Let me think of something to which I can compare the speed. (*I close my eyes and think.*) See if this sentence paints a more specific picture: *The hummingbird darted from flower to flower faster than the wind.* Another sentence could be: *The hummingbird raced from flower to flower faster than my eyes could follow.* What words did I use to describe how fast the hummingbird flew?

Shanti: Faster than the wind.

Will: Faster than your eyes could see.

Mrs. S.: Now, would you like to try? Let's rewrite this sentence: *The rabbit's fur was soft.* Before you write, think about all the soft things you could use in your comparison. Most writers wouldn't compare the fur of one animal to the fur of another animal. They would look for something completely different. For instance, I could write: *The rabbit's fur was as soft as a cloud of cotton balls* or *The rabbit's fur was as soft as my baby blanket.* Now, you try. Compare the softness of the rabbit's fur to something else to help show the reader just how soft it was.

Once Too Often

You might want to create a small list of comparisons or similes that are trite and overused. Post these in the room so students can avoid their use and try to be more original. Your list might begin with the following: *as light as a feather, beating like a drum, as tall as the sky, as bright as a star, as big as a house, as good as gold, as happy as a lark, as cold as ice, as old as the hills, as busy as a bee, as loud as a train, as wise as an owl, as big as a barn, as mad as a wet hen,* and *as slow as molasses.*

After students complete their work, I ask them to share their sentences. Here are some examples of their responses:

- The rabbit's fur was as soft as my baby brother's breath.
- The rabbit's fur was as soft as a ball of yarn.
- The rabbit's fur was as soft as marshmallows.
- The rabbit's fur was as soft as whipped cream.
- The rabbit's fur was as soft as my grandmother's crocheted afghan.

Mrs. S.: Writers like to compare. It helps them paint specific pictures. Tell me what could be as red as a tulip?

Emma: Lips.

Vijay: A sweater.

Alison: The sun.

Jason: A face or a tongue.

Sarah: A radish.

Mrs. S.: What could be as small as an eyelash?

> "Details can hook readers so they will want to read more."
>
> — 2nd grader

My students have come up with these comparisons: *pollen, an ant, a teensy sip, a comma, a whisper, a mistake.*

Mrs. S.: What could be as slow as a snail?

Their comparisons have included *an answer from a shy boy, the smile on a grumpy man's face, the opening of spring's first flower, our Internet connection, Mom getting out of bed.*

The more you do this kind of exercise with students, the more open their minds become. Within a few weeks, you will see these kinds of comparisons pop into their writing: *tip her over like a teacup, as difficult as losing a friend, as loud as a thousand crows, as light as a thought, as tiny as a raindrop, curved like the crescent moon, as golden as ripe wheat, as silly as a yard full of squirrels, as quiet as love.*

Helping students think about how to show will result in two things. First, after these mini-lessons, the class has a common language for "show, don't tell" and painting pictures in the reader's mind. This will help in peer critiques and teacher conferences. Also, with each reminder mini-lesson, students incorporate more show into their daily writing. And, when they do, they are eager to point out their accomplishments to one another and to you: *Listen, isn't this a good example of show? What do you think of this sentence? I think I painted a specific picture.*

Chapter 5 Review

- Writers show rather than tell the reader who is speaking, what is happening, and where it is happening.

- Describing what someone's body does shows the emotions that the character is experiencing.

- Using fresh similes and other comparisons adds elaboration to writing.

Revision

Adding Elaboration

As teachers present mini-lessons on the different craft elements, from ideas to voice, to organization, to elaboration, it's important to include revision strategies. During the writing of the first draft, authors are impassioned about what they want to say. They rush to get their basic ideas down on paper. It would be nearly impossible for them to remember and include everything they know or want to share on their topics. That's why most writers look forward to revising their work. It's a time to reflect on what is written and to improve on meaning.

Unfortunately, quite often I'm invited into classrooms where students show their first drafts to their teacher and receive this advice: *Go back and fix it.* The students return to their seats confused about what to fix and how to do it. Instead, we want to provide solid strategies that give purpose and direction to student writers. This chapter offers examples of these child-friendly revision strategies to add elaboration: peer questioning, spider legs and quick surgery. Introduce all of these to your students so each writer can decide which strategy works best for him or her.

Mini-Lesson: Peer Questioning

Peer questioning, one of the easiest and most effective elaboration revision strategies, can be modeled in front of the whole class. During this activity, a student writer asks peers if they have any questions about what he or she has written. (A simpler version of this mini-lesson is shown in Chapter 2.) While answering peer questions, the writer decides what additional information he or she would like to add. This strategy creates a need for revision. Since the student writer's peers have invested time and thought in his or her piece, the writer wants to add the information or ideas they requested and then share the improved piece.

To begin this mini-lesson, I first identify a student with a piece of writing that is solid but that could be stronger with some additional information. I ask that child's permission to make an overhead transparency of his or her work. The next day, I have the child stand at the overhead projector with the copy of the piece. Then, I ask him or her to read the piece aloud to the class.

The following mini-lesson features an excerpt written by Abigail, a third-grade student. She had completed an independent study of Venezuela and its people. Abigail wrote this piece to showcase some of her knowledge.

Hi, my name is Erika and I live in Venezuela. It's late July here and my birthday is today! We will be going to the waterfall and sleeping in a wigwam. Mama is buying stuff for the cake and my sisters and brothers and I have to pick fruit. We now have five buckets full of fruit and small branches. Mama is now home and she also brought ink and paper. Almazo and Andy have to fill two buckets full of water. Gina and I peel the fruit while Jenna breaks little twigs off the branches.

In three hours my guests will be coming. I invited three of my closest friends, my cousins, and Tia Tia. Mama is putting the flour in the bowl. Jenna is now done plucking twigs so she gets the logs from the basket and makes a fire. Mama is cooking the cake. It smells delicious!

Skipping Lines

One of my first suggestions when visiting a classroom is that student writers skip at least two or three lines as they write their first drafts. Whenever I ask students the purpose behind this, they know and offer these comments: *So, it's easier for us to read our first drafts. So we have a place to add information. If we have changes, there's room to do them. If we decide to move some of our piece, we can mark where we want that to go. Exactly!* It's for all these reasons that I recommend that we all skip lines during our first drafts.

Mrs. S.: Before we continue discussing Abigail's writing today, would anyone like to tell her what she did well—what you appreciate about her piece?

Bill: I like how you used names that sound as if they'd be the real names in Venezuela.

Anna: You told us when it was. It was late July.

Serge: All of your writing makes sense, and I can see people doing different jobs.

Vincent: You left me wanting to know what will happen at your party.

Leslie: I like how you wrote it as if you're Erika.

Randi: You were specific about what you were doing and what you were going to do.

Mrs. S.: Abigail, you received quite a bit of positive feedback on your writing. Congratulations! Now, I'd like you to read your piece again so the class can listen for spots where they might have questions—where they might want more information. (*Abigail reads her piece again.*)

Mrs. S.: Abigail, would you be open to adding more information—more details—to your story? (*She nods.*) Then, please read your first three sentences again and see if your classmates have any questions for you.

Abigail: *Hi, my name is Erika and I live in Venezuela. It's late July here and my birthday is today! We will be going to the waterfall and sleeping in a wigwam.*

Mrs. S.: Would you like to ask your classmates if they have any questions for you?

Abigail: (*smiling and looking at the class*) Does anyone have a question for me?

Carly: You say "the waterfall." Does it have a name?

Abigail: Yes, it's called Angel Falls.

Mrs. S.: Would you like to add that piece of information to your writing? (*Abigail nods.*) Would you like to make a note on your transparency, or would you like me to do that?

Abigail: I'll do it.

Angel Falls

We will be going to ~~the waterfall~~ and sleeping in a wigwam.

Student: You never told us where in Venezuela you live. Do you live in a city or out in the country?

Abigail: I live in a village. I'll add that.

in a village

Hi, my name is Erika and I live / in Venezuela.

Mrs. S.: Would you like to read your next three sentences and see if your classmates have any questions?

Abigail: Yes. *Mama is buying stuff for the cake and my sisters and brothers and I have to pick fruit. We now have five buckets full of fruit and small branches. Mama is now home and she also brought ink and paper.* Do you have any questions for me?

Carly: You say that your mama is buying stuff for the cake. What's the stuff?

Abigail: The cake is made differently than around here. She uses vegetables. Here, let me add that. (*Abigail crosses out the word* stuff *and adds the word* vegetables *above it.*)

Serge: You say that you and your brothers and sisters pick fruit. Can you tell us what kinds of fruit?

Abigail: Yes, the children pick apples, berries, oranges, and they also get those branches that Jenna uses later. Just a minute. (*Abigail crosses out the word* fruit *and above it writes* apples, berries, oranges, *and* twigs.) Any more questions?

Randi: When you say that Mama is now home and she also brought ink and paper, what else did she bring?

Abigail makes the correction shown below.

along with the veggies

Mama is now home and she also brought ink and paper/.

Abigail: Is that it? Are there any more questions?

Student: Do you want to tell us the names of the brothers and sisters?

Abigail: Sure. Their names are Gina, Andy, Almazo, and Jenna. I'd like to add those names here, but I don't know right now how I'll do that. (*Abigail places a caret after the words* brothers and sisters *and writes the names* Gina, Andy, Almazo, and Jenna *on the empty line above.*) Anything else? Okay, I'll read my next three sentences. *Almazo and Andy have to fill two buckets full of water. Gina and I peel the fruit while Jenna breaks little twigs off the branches. In three hours my guests will be coming.* Is there anything that you'd like to know?

Bill: Why are Almazo and Andy filling buckets with water?

Abigail: They use that water to wash the food and to water the plants. I'll add that. (*Abigail puts a caret after the words* full of water. *She adds* to wash the food and to water the plants *on the empty line above.*) Anything else?

No one has any more questions on this section.

Abigail: Ready for the next part? *I invited three of my closest friends, my cousins, and Tia Tia. Mama is putting the flour in the bowl. Jenna is now done plucking twigs so she gets the logs from the basket and makes a fire.*

Student: This isn't a big missing detail, but can you describe the bowl at all?

Abigail: Actually, it's a grass bowl. Let me add that one word. (*Abigail uses a caret again to insert the word* grass *before* bowl.) Any other questions?

Student: This isn't a question, but I forgot to say before that I like the word *plucking.*

Abigail: Thanks! Okay, here's the last of what I'm going to read today: *Mama is cooking the cake. It smells delicious!*

Mrs. S.: Abigail, you listed quite a few details for your piece. Now, you can decide if you want to add all of them to your piece or only some suggestions. Whatever you decide, we'd like to hear or see a copy of your revision. It can be soon, or you may want to wait until your whole piece is completed.

Every time students come to the overhead and ask for help from their classmates, they leave smiling, bubbling, and excited about rewriting the piece. *Always!* They love the attention and investment in thinking that their classmates offer. The interest in the writing is genuine. Students enjoy helping one another improve their pieces. They are craftspeople sharing their skills with one another.

As you may have noticed, I make it a point to ask the reader to share his or her revisions with us. When students have a ready audience to hear their revisions, it adds an immediate purpose that can't be beat. Inevitably, within minutes or hours, depending on the day's schedule, the student lets us know that the piece is revised and offers to read it.

Here's the revision that Abigail read to her classmates.

> *Hi, my name is Erika and I live in a village in Venezuela. It's late July here and my birthday is today! We will be going to Angel Falls and sleeping in a wigwam. Mama is buying vegetables for the cake and my brothers and sisters (Andy, Almazo, Jenna and Gina) and I have to pick apples, berries, oranges, and twigs. We now have five buckets full of fruit and twigs. Mama is now home and she also brought ink and paper along with the vegetables. Almazo and Andy have to fill two buckets full of water to wash the food and to water the plants. Gina and I peel the fruit while Jenna breaks little twigs off the branches.*
>
> *In three hours my guests will be coming. I invited three of my closest friends, my cousins, and Tia Tia. Mama is putting the flour in a grass bowl. Jenna is now done plucking twigs so she gets the logs from the basket and makes a fire. Mama is cooking the cake. It smells delicious!*

When Abigail finished, I didn't need to prompt the other students; they automatically raised their hands and expressed their appreciation.

- I like how you added the information that we asked about.
- I think your piece is stronger now. It has more details.
- I like what you've written. When can I hear the rest of it?
- Your revision made your piece a whole bunch better.

You can imagine how much Abigail now believes in the power of revision. She asked her classmates for authentic questions, answered them, and improved the quality of her piece. Plus, when Abigail read it back to them, they gave her positive feedback.

You will need to solidify this questioning approach by demonstrating it at least three or four times in a whole-group setting. From there, students are ready to read and listen to each other. I recommend pairs of children, no more than that. Always ask the writer to read the piece once all the way through and then reread while the listener thinks about questions he or she might have. Finally, the author reads two to three sentences at a time, and the listener asks questions.

As you saw from Abigail's demonstration, the whole group asked quite a few questions. You will need to monitor the number of questions according to the confidence and willingness of the writer. Abigail was involved and delighted to answer questions, but not all students have her attitude. Sometimes, I set a maximum of four to five questions for

> "I need help from a partner to add details. That person listens to what I've written and asks me questions. It's fun."
>
> — 3rd grader

the entire piece. When that number has been reached, we stop and let the writer return to his or her seat to decide which details to add.

It's also a good idea to set a minimum number of questions (such as three) when children meet in pairs. However, let students know that if both partners are willing, they may decide to ask and answer more.

Why should we teach our students how to ask questions about each other's writing? For one thing, it helps the writer add details. It improves the elaboration on their ideas. Secondly, students are reading to an audience for an authentic purpose, and in turn, the reader has an authentic purpose for listening well. It encourages high engagement from both. Most important, this strategy teaches students that as writers they need to ask themselves questions. We introduce a strategy to the whole group, have students practice it in pairs, and hope that through our guidance and reminders, students understand that *all* writers ask themselves questions while writing and then rereading their own first drafts.

Our main goal with all whole group mini-lessons is to plant seeds for the independent writer. By looking at how writers think, write, and revise together, we can create opportunities for dialogues that will cement these understandings in the minds of students. We are constantly moving them from instruction to independence, and scaffolding them along the way.

 ## Adding Elaboration with Spider Legs

During the revision process, another way to add more elaboration is with a strategy that many teachers call "spider legs." For this strategy, the student writer decides what information to add to his or her work. Spider legs works best when whole sentences of text are added to describe or explain a point in the writing rather than when a few words are added. These additions may be generated by the writer, or he or she may decide to include more information or ideas based on comments from writer friends.

For instance, a student might write quickly and say something like this: *When they opened their eyes, they saw a beautiful yard.* After rereading, the writer might want more elaboration. He or she might decide to add details that describe exactly what the yard looked like by asking the following questions: *Were there trees? If so what kind? Were there flowers? Do I want the names of any of them or their colors? Were there gardens? Grass? Fountains?*

During the revision process, the writer might expand the original sentence as follows: *Giant fir trees stood like a green wall on the right, separating the yard from the woods. A brick sidewalk twisted between flowerbeds and hedges, like a river flowing between hills of leaves and color. Hummingbirds and butterflies feasted on pink, red, and purple flowers.*

Instead of trying to write all this new information on the first draft, the student cuts a length of adding machine tape and writes #1 on it. This is one spider leg. In the text where the writer would like to add this information, he or she also writes #1. Then, he or she writes out the new information on the tape and staples or glues the spider leg of detail to the back of the page.

This student sample illustrates how spider legs can be used to add description to a page from a story.

> Margaret blinked. The girl was still there. Her filmy face and dress flickered in and out of the doorway, as if to say, *I'm here. I'm not. I'm here. I'm not.* Margaret didn't know what to do. She tried to take deep breaths and think. But she couldn't. #1
>
> "Help me," the ghost called.
>
> "W-w-w-what do you want me to do?" asked Margaret. She took a step back.
>
> "Follow me—to the well," said the ghost, and she put out her hand.
>
> Margaret didn't want to go. She was having all kinds of horrible thoughts. #2 She tried to stall, "W-w-why do you w-w-want to go to the well?" she asked, her voice weak.
>
> But the ghost turned, as if she didn't hear Margaret. ~~She moved out of the doorway and into the garden.~~ #3
>
> Margaret thought this was her chance to escape. She, too, turned and ran deeper into the house, toward the front door. Until . . .
>
> The ghost appeared before her—in the hallway. This time she held Margaret. #4 Margaret struggled to get away.

#1 Her chest was heavy like it was filled with stones. And her mind buzzed with worry.

#2 What will she do to me if I go? Will she hurt me? Will she push me into the well?

#3 She glided out of the doorway and into the rose garden.

#4 Her cold fingers pinched Margaret's arm and pulled her toward the door.

Some student writers may add one or two spider legs, while others will attach four or five. Again, this method is used to add lengthier details than just a word or two. Any smaller additions would still be written directly on the first draft using carets.

To teach the use of spider legs, I recommend that you write a short piece that lacks details. (You can write it on chart paper.) During a mini-lesson, read the piece out loud. Find at least two places where you, the writer, would like to add elaboration. Make the spider legs, write the new information or ideas, and attach them onto the back of the paper.

After you've added the spider legs, read the piece again with the new details. Ask students if they have any questions or suggestions. Then, you can make choices about which information to add and create new spider legs to include these details. I suggest leaving this large piece on display in the classroom as an example for students. Spider legs provide a concrete visual for them to see just how much elaboration they have added to their pieces.

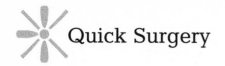

Quick Surgery

Another simple way to add lengthier elaboration is called "quick surgery," cutting open the piece. The piece below needs a little quick surgery to add details.

> *Last year my family and I drove to my Uncle Ray's house in the Rocky Mountains. This was a first for us. We'd never seen that kind of scenery.*
>
> *Uncle Ray lives in Golden, Colorado, but he and his family hike and camp all over the state. During our September trip, we loaded up all the camping gear and headed to Idaho Springs. That's where Indian Springs Resort is located. We stayed in the campground and did a lot of fun stuff.*
>
> *Now I can hardly wait to go back to Uncle Ray's house. Not only can I play with my cousins, but I just bet we'll have other exciting adventures, too.*

Quick surgery makes sense for two reasons. Many times, students will write up to an exciting moment such as this: *Last year my family and I drove to my Uncle Ray's house in the Rocky Mountains. This was a first for us. We'd never seen that kind of scenery.*

An audience will want to know more. They'll ask the writer to crack open this scene and tell them about the scenery: *What kind of scenery was it? What did you see? Were there mountains? Rivers? Did you see any bears?*

To accomplish this, the writer can delete the phrase *that kind of scenery*. He or she cuts along the lines separating the words *We'd never seen . . .* from *Uncle Ray lives . . .* Then, the writer can pull the piece apart.

Next, he or she tapes or glues the top part of the piece onto a larger piece of construction or writing paper. There is now space to add new details such as the following to the larger sheet of paper: *snow-covered peaks, mountain streams filled with sparkling rocks,* or *elk grazing in small pastures. It took our breath away!*

After completing the additions, the writer tapes or glues the rest of the piece that follows to the larger sheet.

> Last year my family and I drove to my uncle Ray's house in the Rocky Mountains. This was a first for us. We'd never seen that kind of scenery before.
>
> snow-covered peaks, mountain streams filled with sparkling rocks, elk grazing in small pastures. It took our breath away!

This particular piece has another spot where elaboration would add meaning. The writer again, could delete the words *did a lot of fun stuff* and cut the piece apart between the words *We stayed in the campground . . .* and *Now I can hardly wait . . .*

This will give the writer an opportunity to tell what they did that was fun, for example: *swam in a swimming pool filled with natural mineral water. The pool lady said that it was fed by hot spring water coming straight out of the earth! We took long hikes on trails that were so skinny we had to go single-file. At night, we sat around the campfire and told scary stories and listened to the coyotes howl.*

Uncle Ray lives in Golden, Colorado, but he and his family hike and camp all over the state. During our September trip, we loaded up all the camping gear and headed to Idaho Springs. That's where Indian Springs Resort is located. We stayed in the campground and ~~did a lot of fun stuff.~~ ℓ

swam in a swimming pool filled with natural mineral water. The pool lady said that it was fed by hot spring water coming straight from the earth! We took long hikes on trails that were so skinny we had to go single-file. At night, we sat around the campfire and told scary stories and listened to the coyotes howl.

Now I can hardly wait to go back to Uncle Ray's house. Not only can I play with my cousins, but I just bet we'll have other exciting adventures, too.

All these revision strategies—peer questioning, spider legs and quick surgery—provide opportunities to add needed details that will enhance student writing. Not only are they easy, but students also think they're fun. This reinforces the purpose and enjoyment of revision. Once you show your students the different revision strategies, hold them accountable. Some teachers I know hang a small chart with the names of five or six revision strategies listed on it. During writer's workshop, when a student uses one or more of the strategies, he or she initials them on the chart. This not only provides a quick visual to see which students are using which strategies, but it also can be a diagnostic tool for the teacher. If a strategy has few or no initials beside it, students might not understand the procedure or its benefits. At that time, you may choose to create some mini-lessons and re-introduce that revision strategy. Again, our job is to provide strategies that become life-long tools for these writers.

The Big and Small Details of Life

Joan Bauer is a novelist whose stories involve her readers in the emotional lives of fictional characters. Before Joan sits at her keyboard, she already knows these characters.

Life is made up of details. Some details we can see with our eyes like how hugely tall someone is, or the orange, pink, and yellow light gleaming from a sunset. Some can't be seen with the eye, but they're still important to know. When I write a story, I always think about my characters from the inside out. I need to know what their hearts are like before I put them into a story. By that I mean—what they care about, who their friends are, what their dreams are, what has hurt them, what has brought them joy. Bit by bit, detail by detail, I fill in their lives as I write a story. Sometimes I'll think about a small thing—a bird. Then I'll ask myself, what kind of bird is it? What kind of a chirp does it have? Would it flutter from branch to branch or would it hop? Or I'll think about a much bigger issue—what does it feel like when someone you trust has disappointed you? Do you cry, get angry, scream, or do you become silent and sad? All of these moments, big and small, go into writing. All of them are details. As a writer, I've learned to pause and look at the details in life and listen to the stories they tell.

To learn more about Joan Bauer and her approach to the craft of writing, visit her Web site at www.joanbauer.com.

Chapter 6 Review

- Students can add elaboration during revision.

- Model peer questioning with the whole class. Later, writers can use this strategy with a partner to improve elaboration.

- Encourage students to share revisions with an audience, and allow classmates to mention improvements they hear in a revised piece.

- Revising with spider legs helps students add lengthier details to a draft.

- Quick surgery gives student writers the opportunity to cut apart a draft and insert elaboration.

Final Thoughts: Enhance What's Already There

Young children describe in great detail the learning, play, and adventures that excite them. If they don't know the words to express just exactly what they've experienced, they coin words that fit their enthusiasm. So, we know that our students come to school with the ability to elaborate. Our job is not to extinguish that zest for explanation but to enhance it.

The first way we can do that is by modeling writing with authentic elaboration. One of the greatest teaching tools we have is our own writing. As we stand in front of students, thinking and writing, reading and experimenting, they are watching a real writer at work. If we write with a textbook style, they will assume that's what is expected from them. If we select writing ideas that inspire passion and enthusiasm in us, then our writing—and theirs—will be filled with those same emotions.

The literature we read aloud is another powerful tool. Good literature will contain elaboration that adds meaning and interest. It will brim with examples of show, not tell. The figurative language will paint wonderful pictures in the minds of our students. Read to them, celebrate the language, and talk about how the author crafts words into emotional moments.

In other words, give students permission to write what's already in them. Provide tools such as building vocabulary, incorporating similes and other comparisons, and using revision strategies that will sustain them through the process again and again. Write, read, listen to fellow craftspeople, and celebrate each of their successes.

Bibliography

Bauer, Marion Dane. *Runt*. New York: Clarion Books, 2002.

Dotlich, Rebecca Kai. *Mama Loves*. New York: HarperCollins, 2004.

Giff, Patricia Reilly. *Nory Ryan's Song*. New York: Delacorte Press, 2000.

Hesse, Karen. *Just Juice*. New York: Scholastic, 1998.

High, Linda Oatman. *The Girl on the High-Diving Horse: An Adventure in Atlantic City*. New York: Philomel Books, 2003.

Hines, Gary. *Thanksgiving in the White House*. New York: Henry Holt and Company, 2003.

Hopkins, Lee Bennett. *School Supplies: A Book of Poems*. New York: Simon & Schuster, 1996.

King, Stephen. *On Writing*. New York: Simon & Schuster Adult Publishing Group, 2000.

LeGuin, Ursula. *Steering the Craft: Exercises and Discussions on Story Writing for the Lone Navigator or the Mutinous Crew*. Portland, OR: The Eighth Mountain Press, 1998.

Paulsen, Gary. *Canoe Days*. New York: Bantam Doubleday Dell, 1999.

Polacco, Patricia. *The Butterfly*. New York: Philomel Books, 2000.

Richards, Jean. *How the Elephant Got Its Trunk*. New York: Henry Holt, 2003.

Root, Phyllis. *Grandmother Winter*. Boston: Houghton Mifflin Company, 1999.

Rylant, Cynthia. *When I Was Young in the Mountains.* New York: E. P. Dutton, 1982.

Schanzer, Rosalyn. *Davy Crockett Saves the World.* New York: HarperCollins, 2001.

Schertle, Alice. *A Lucky Thing.* San Diego: Harcourt Brace & Company, 1997.

Spinelli, Eileen. *Three Pebbles and a Song.* New York: Dial, 2003.

Ueland, Brenda. *If You Want to Write.* Saint Paul, MN: Graywolf Press, (1938) 1987.

Whelan, Gloria. *The Wanigan: A Life on the River.* New York: Alfred A. Knopf, 2002.

White, E.B. *Charlotte's Web.* New York: HarperCollins, 1999.

Yolen, Jane. *Owl Moon.* New York: Philomel Books, 1987.

SUSAN McCARTNEY

AMPHOTO BOOKS

AN IMPRINT OF WATSON-GUPTILL PUBLICATIONS

NEW YORK

This book is dedicated to Caroline

© DAVID CUDA

Susan McCartney, a Manhattan-based photographer, studied fine art and graphic design at Hammersmith College of Art in London and Cooper Union in New York. She refined her photography and vision at evening classes given by Richard Avedon, Alexey Brodovitch, Harold Kreiger, Walter Rosenblum, and Melvin Sokolsky. She has a BFA in photography from the School of Visual Arts. While getting established, she worked as a United Nations guide and at various travel and art jobs, and assisted briefly until becoming a professional photographer.

McCartney has shot assignments for such diverse clients and publications as British Airways, the British Tourist Authority, Caravan Tours, Club Europa, the Irish Tourist Board, Lan Chile Airlines, the *London Daily Mirror*, *The Economist*, *Glamour*, *House and Garden*, *Scholastic*, *Shell*, *Time*, *Travel/Holiday*, *Travel and Leisure*, the United States Army, the United States Postal Service, Varig Airlines, Warner Brothers Records, and *Woman's Day*. Her personal photographs have been featured in *Life*, *The New York Times Magazine*, *Nikon World*, and *Popular Photography*. She has shown and spoken about her work at the Smithsonian Institution, as well as on public television. Her stock photography appears in magazines and advertising around the world, and she has received awards from the Art Director's Club of New York and *Communication Arts* magazine.

McCartney conducts lighting workshops at New York City's School of Visual Arts. She has written two other books, *Travel Photography: A Complete Guide to How to Shoot and Sell* and *Nature and Wildlife Photography: A Practical Guide to How to Shoot and Sell*.

Half-title page: New York City's Central Park in snow. Nikon N90 in manual mode, 20mm F2.8 lens, Nikon SB-26 flash in TTL mode, ISO 100 slide film exposed for 1/250 sec. at *f*/2.8.

Title page: Mojave Desert road at dawn. Tripod-mounted Nikon N90 camera in manual mode, 20mm F2.8 lens, Nikon SB-23 flash in TTL mode, ISO 50 slide film exposed for 1 sec. at *f*/4–5.6.

All original diagrams created by Susan McCartney

Each photograph appearing in the Gallery is copyrighted in the name of the individual photographers. The rights remain in their possession.

Library of Congress Cataloging in Publication Data

McCartney, Susan.
  Mastering flash photography : a course in basic to advanced
  lighting techniques / Susan McCartney.
      p.   cm.
  Includes bibliographical references and index.
  ISBN 0-8174-4545-5 (pb)
    1. Electronic flash photography. 2. Photography—Lighting.
  I. title.
TR606.M38   1997   97-18999
778.7'2—dc21   CIP

Manufactured in Malaysia

1 2 3 4 5 6 7 8 9 / 05 04 03 02 01 00 99 98 97

Senior editor: Robin Simmen
Editor: Liz Harvey
Designer: Jay Anning
Production manager: Hector Campbell

CONTENTS

Acknowledgments

Six flash masters have let me include examples of their work in this book: Joe McNally, Michael "Nick" Nichols, Kenny Regan, Chip Simons, Danny Turner, and Theo Westenberger are very generous, and I owe them all a debt.

In writing and illustrating this book, I've called on many other people, among whom were the Collyns, Day, and Miller families; Jon Falk; Patricia and Wayne Fisher; Roger Gaess; Jeff Hirsch; Walter Lau; Phillip Leonian; Ray Ng; A.J. Nye; Lindsay Silverman; and Norman Stuessy. I am grateful to all.

I should especially like to thank Robin Simmen, Liz Harvey, and Jay Anning at Amphoto Books, who all had creative suggestions that contributed greatly to the final book.

INTRODUCTION

I believe that flash is a marvelous lighting medium; it is quick to use, much flash equipment is handy to carry, and most small flash units are reasonable in price compared to other forms of photographic lighting. With flash it is possible to freeze motion and to achieve other professional lighting effects with relative ease once you understand how. This book is intended to be a useful tool for anyone who wants to make the best possible flash pictures under different conditions whatever your current level of expertise as a photographer. To these ends, I've tried to be as clear and specific as possible in both my recommendations in the text and in the details give in the picture captions and the diagrams.

If you've just acquired a new electronic camera with a built-in or a separate flash and want to start pointing, shooting, and flashing immediately, you could start by reading Chapter 2 or 3. If you are an experienced photographer with a manual camera, you could begin at Chapter 8. But I do believe that Chapter 1 on flash fundamentals is important and that to truly master flash, you must sooner or later comprehend the underlying basics of lighting, even if you eventually choose to forget the details. Anyway, each chapter is self-contained: you can start reading the book anywhere that interests you. You can always refer backwards or forwards as needed later.

When you look at the pictures, you'll notice how often I use flash with other forms of light. For me, flash is as useful as a lighting adjunct—to bright or low sunlight, heavy-overcast skies, twilight, low-level indoor lighting, bright street lights—as it is the sole source of light at night or indoors. You can even use small flash for formal lighting in a studio once you know how. Learning to use small flash well can mean an easy transition to working with big professional flashes or strobe lights if and when you reach the point of needing a lot of light to get the effects you want.

Six of the world's top photographers, known as lighting masters, have been gracious enough to write about their various approaches to flash and to let me reproduce examples of their work in the Gallery. At the end of the book, you'll find a list of resources and an index.

SUSAN MCCARTNEY
New York City

While shooting the Rockefeller Center Christmas tree, I bracketed by varying the shutter speed (but never exceeding the flash sync speed) to affect both the background exposure and the overall mood of the pictures. The TTL flash fill hit the nearby snowflakes and stopped their motion. With my Nikon N90 in manual mode, a 20mm F2.8 lens, and my Nikon SB-26 flash, I exposed this winter scene on ISO 100 film for 1/30 sec.

Part One
BASIC FLASH

Fast films give a grainy, often bluish effect that is appropriate for some subjects. Flash fill often isn't needed for a good exposure, but it warms colors, adds sparkle, and lightens small shadows. To shoot these flowers, I used my Konica Off-Road point-and-shoot camera, its 28mm F2.8 lens, the closeup and flash-on modes, and ISO 1000 slide film.

*A*n easy way to improve your flash pictures is to study natural light, which you can do anytime, anywhere. If you look at any person or scene with your eyes closed to a narrow slit, you'll see approximately how the composition will translate to film. That image will almost always show more contrast, which is the difference between the brightest and darkest areas, than the open human eye sees.

Start by looking at bright sun falling at various times of the day onto faces, groups, objects, and even landscapes and city scenes. Hard sunlight always produces distinct shadows of different lengths at different times of day. Technically, any hard, direct light is called *spectral light* and can be glamorous or excessively harsh on people; its effects on animals, objects, and places vary.

When direct sunlight hits any subject from low and in front, it approximates the look of light from a built-in or on-camera flash. A hard light shone down from a moderate height from either side can be dynamic for portraits of the best-looking people, and can be good for some still-life subjects. A photographic light positioned this way is known as a *three-quarter light*. Low light shone from the side, called appropriately enough *sidelighting*, always emphasizes texture and is excellent for landscapes. Low lighting from behind the subject, or *backlighting* can create a halo effect around, for example, heads and flowers, and is good for some still lifes.

Toplighting, or high-noon sunlight from directly overhead, causes people's eye sockets to almost disappear and heavy shadows to form under noses and chins. Midday sun filtering down through trees or gaps in buildings produces intense bright and dark spots. This effectively "camouflages" landscape variations and makes streetscapes and building features hard to identify.

Diffused natural light, which occurs when clouds cover the sun, flatters many people and many other subjects. Flash is a small light source and can never be as soft as the illumination of a cloudy day. Nevertheless, you can diffuse it in a variety of ways.

When you shoot indoors, take a careful look at the hard or soft daylight falling on a person or object near a window. Close your eyes to slits once again, and consider the lighting contrast. Would adding light on the dark side help?

You should also practice "seeing" existing artificial light everywhere, which in photographic terms, is called *available light*. What is the difference, for example, between the light in a restaurant and the light in a hospital? Pay attention to the light in such places as stores, elevators, offices, schools, and factories, or outdoors at night. How does the available light affect people and objects?

Although you can't light a large space with one small flash, in this book you'll learn how to use flash to supplement low-level existing light. You'll also learn how to use both built-in flashes and flashes that detach to create many hard lighting effects, and to modify and soften some undesirable ones. When you know how to "see" light quality and understand how contrast affects images, you'll have taken a long step toward getting fine flash pictures.

The trick to shooting any sports picture is to anticipate motion. When I photographed some Little Leaguers playing baseball, it took me quite a few shots to record a ball being hit. The flash fill from my Nikon SB-26 flash in TTL mode highlighted the ball; the existing light was misty sunshine. Working with my Nikon N90 in manual mode, and a Sigma 80–200mm F2.8 lens set at about 100mm, I exposed ISO 100 slide film for 1/250 sec. at f/8.

Chapter 1
FLASH FUNDAMENTALS

This chapter might seem a bit technical to absolute beginners, but you don't need to learn it by heart, and being aware of some basics should help your first serious flash pictures. Refer back to this chapter from time to time as you become increasingly proficient. If you prefer to start shooting with a built-in flash immediately, skip to Chapter 2 and return to this one later.

But don't skip carefully studying your equipment manual(s) before shooting. And be sure to start slowly. An ideal way to learn with any type of camera and flash equipment is to photograph a willing human subject under peaceful conditions. Then achieve different effects using flash from varying distances and under many light conditions indoors and out, reshooting if necessary.

When you either work with a program camera and flash in which a built-in computer makes all the decisions or use a program setting, note the chosen mode (or variable settings used if these are options). You should also pay attention to the film speed and flash-to-subject distances you're using. Working this way will enable you to easily repeat effects that you like, and improve on those you don't. When learning how to operate advanced equipment, note the lens-aperture (*f*-stop), shutter-speed, and flash-setting variations you're using.

Finally, when developing new flash skills, don't forget your old ones. You should always aim for the best possible arrangement of the subject in the picture area, even when experimenting and testing. You'll also want to create a mood and express your point of view.

Types of Flash

Flash units comes in many shapes, sizes, and amount of light output, and can cost from less than $10 to thousands of dollars. The least expensive flashes are the tiny manual units built into focus-free snapshot cameras and the small manual flashes that are usable with just about any camera.

Automatic flashes, which are moderately priced, are still made and are still useful. These units work with all types of camera and are the generation between manual flash and computer-controlled flash. You must choose settings on the camera and flash within given guidelines; a sensor on the flash then determines accurate flash exposures. (Don't confuse automatic flash with the auto-flash setting/mode on program cameras. These control the flash output via computers built into the camera—and into the flash if it is detachable.)

Today almost all electronic point-and-shoot cameras manufactured have built-in flashes with output regulated by tiny, in-camera controls. Most entry and some midlevel, electronic 35mm single-lens-reflex (SLR) cameras incorporate a handy, computerized pop-up flash with exposure measured "through the lens" (TTL). Top-of-the-line elec-

On a bright, sunny day, TTL flash fill lightened the shadows on this jolly man as he worked in his sideshow booth. Here, I used my Nikon N90, a 28mm F2 manual lens, and my Nikon SB-24 flash. The exposure was *f*/5.6 for 1/125 sec. on ISO 50 film.

tronic 35mm SLR cameras are intended to interact with separate, quite powerful computer-controlled, or "dedicated," flashes designed for either on or off-camera use.

Almost all advanced-amateur and professional flashes have heads that you can angle so that you can "bounce," or reflect, the light from the flash. Some professional flashes are computer-controlled. The most powerful professional battery-powered flash units are manual, and have separate heads and battery packs. Exposure is most often determined by flash-meter readings. During use, such units are attached to big flash brackets or light-stands.

Advanced flashes, as well as the powerful professional flashes that run on continuous AC current (and often called "portable strobe" or "studio" flash), put out considerable amounts of light but work in basically the same way as the smallest manual flash.

Understanding Instruction Manuals

To get the most out of your flash, you should read and reread the instructions that come with it. This also applies, of course, to any camera. You'll be truly handicapped if you don't. If you acquire or own a good, brand-name camera or a TTL or automatic flash without instructions, contact the manufacturer for a copy of the manual. Quote the model and serial number. Don't buy any budget equipment—point-and-shoot camera or no-name flash—that doesn't come with a manual. When I teach lighting workshops, the biggest problem people have with learning to use flash well is that they don't know how to set and operate their units.

Some camera and/or flash manuals are basic, but all illustrate loading batteries, switching the unit on and off, activating a built-in flash, and attaching a separate flash to the camera hotshoe by means of the flash's hotfoot. Manuals for detachable TTL flash units also explain how to use the flash on a bracket by means of an optional TTL remote cord, an automatic cord with a sensor, or a PC/sync cord (see Chapters 10, 11, and 12 for more information).

Some manuals offer good suggestions for basic and advanced uses of flash. The manuals that come with top-of-the-line TTL flash units are thorough but can be confusing. This is because they include instructions for using the flash at many settings with many camera models. I carry my camera and flash manuals whenever I travel in case I need to vary my fairly standardized way of working. And until I've learned a new camera or flash, I also note its important settings on a file card for quick reference.

Battery Concerns

You'll soon learn that using flash "burns up" disposable batteries. So you should frequently change the batteries in a camera with built-in flash, or in detachable flash units. Even just turning on a flash after a few days of inactivity drains battery power because the storage capacitors in the flash have to be "formed up," or conditioned. When shooting fast-moving subjects with disposable AA batteries in my flash, I use a fresh set for every roll of film. This keeps the *flash recycle time*, or the recharge period needed between flashes, to a tolerable 7 to 10 seconds when the flash is being used close to full power. I

I made this shot of a classic camera and flash from the 1950s, an advanced 35mm SLR camera with a detachable TTL flash, and a good point-and-shoot camera with a built-in flash in a darkened studio. I set the lens aperture and shutter speed high enough to exclude any existing light. The main light was a slaved NVS-1 Vivitar 283 custom flash with a round reflector, which I fitted with a Norman grid. Two slaved Vivitar 283 units provided fill light. All the flash units were on lightstands. I aimed the gridded NVS-1 at the big flash reflector; I bounced the other 283 units off sheets of silver board spaced around the setup. I used a flash meter and Polaroid film tests to help me place the lights. Shooting with my Nikon N90, and a 55mm F3.5 manual macro lens, I exposed Kodak Ektachrome Professional EPR 64 slide film at f/8 for 1/60 sec.

mark tired batteries with an "X" and save them for non-photographic uses.

Today many small cameras use lithium batteries. I favor Radio Shack batteries and buy AA batteries in bulk packs. Eveready Energizer, Kodak, and Vartan batteries are fine, too. Avoid "bargain" batteries that can leak or otherwise harm expensive equipment. In tourist areas, such as Miami and British Columbia, photographic lithium batteries are often sold at ridiculously high prices. Some lithium batteries are hard to find outside of cities, and in remote places, you probably won't find these batteries for sale at all. So when you travel, keep spare batteries of all required sizes in your camera bag at all times.

Rechargeable Batteries and Battery Packs. I use convenient, fast-recycling, 6-volt (6V), rechargeable, lead-acid, gel-cell battery packs with my detachable flash units, except where there is no access to AC power to recharge the packs. The initial cost of a commercial or home-wired gel-cell pack is soon offset by savings on disposable batteries. (For more on battery packs, see Chapters 7 and 12).

Battery Testers. A basic, inexpensive (costing less than $30) battery tester from Radio Shack or electronics stores will save you frustration and money if you are a frequent user of disposable batteries. It can tell you if disposables, rechargeables, and 6V battery packs are still good.

Various manufacturers make batteries and battery packs.

Storing Battery-Powered Equipment. I once stored a Vivitar flash in a place where I didn't find it for a year. The batteries leaked, and the flash was corroded and not worth repairing. Always remove all batteries, and store them well away from any equipment that won't be used for a period of time.

Choosing Film

In order to take flash pictures, you need, of course, a camera, a flash (built-in or separate), and fresh batteries. The other essential is film. Many inexperienced photographers think a lot about equipment and little about film. I'm not suggesting that one film is better than all others; all the top-brand professional and amateur films made today are good. Naturally, I have favorite professional films and like some good amateur films, too (see below and page 13).

I do suggest, however, that whatever your equipment or current level of expertise, you choose name-brand, fresh-dated film and buy from a source that properly stores and refrigerates film.

Color Versus Black and White

Whether you shoot color or black-and-white pictures, your choice of film may be an artistic or a commercial decision, but it shouldn't be an unthinking one. You might like black-and-white images, but a client may require color prints. Great black-and-white slide (transparency) film is now available. Polaroid films give instant results for professional testing and gift prints, and can be manipulated for artistic purposes.

For the most part, photographers who shoot color for reproduction in print media choose professional color slide films. These films, which are also called "reversal films," currently produce the best possible color rendition; each has its own characteristics.

Good, amateur color slide films produce fine results. And in comparison to professional emulsions, their prices are lower and storage temperature is less impor-

tant—two factors to consider if you're taking a long trip to hot climates. Amateur photographers often start by shooting color with negative (print) films. The tremendous advantage that all negative films offer is that exposure isn't too critical—although it should be reasonably accurate. Also, professional and serious-amateur photographers can make black-and-white or color prints in a home darkroom, or use a custom lab. If you use a mini-lab, be aware that negative and print quality and good color can depend on choosing a reliable lab that always uses fresh chemicals.

Finally, keep in mind that today all types of film and prints can easily be scanned onto a computer for retouching or manipulation. (For a brief overview, see Chapter 10 on page 106.)

Film Speeds to Use with Flash

I ordinarily use ISO 100 film for flash pictures shot outdoors, or indoors in bright light. These general-purpose films are fine for outdoor pictures without flash, too. Many have fine *grain*, which is the pattern of particles that make up the image, and permit enlargements that contain excellent detail.

For low-lit indoor or outdoor scenes, you can use a medium-grain ISO 400 slide or print film. If you have an *f*/3.5 or *f*/4 lens, in many instances ISO 400 film will record some existing light, minimize the need for flash fill, and reduce contrast and dark backgrounds in flash shots. If you have a point-and-shoot camera with a zoom lens of *f*/8 or slower at the long end, always use ISO 400 film for your telephoto shots, or the flash won't be too effective. The smaller the *f*-stop, the more the flash range is reduced. ISO 400 film has moderate grain and is four times as sensitive to light as ISO 100 film, so it extends the range of flash. Keep in mind, however, that all flashes have strictly limited carrying power. For example, when you use built-in flash with any telephoto zoom, the flash can't light a dark scene beyond about 10 to 12 feet, even with ISO 400 film. (A few top-of-the-line zoom point-and-shoot cameras and all 35mm SLR cameras with built-in pop-up flashes permit adding a separate, more powerful flash for greater range.)

Use ISO 1000, ISO 3200, or faster films with flash only when you want grainy, moody effects. Superfast films look best for compositions without fine detail and aren't normally suitable for pictures of people in groups. The grain pattern obscures features, making them hard to read.

Color Slide Films. I shoot ISO 100 professional color transparency films (E-6 Process) for almost all flash pictures. I prefer Fuji Provia (RDPII) for most outdoor flash shots. I use Kodak Ektachrome 64 (EPR), which has a neutral color bias and excellent skin tones, for portraits and still-life pictures. Fuji Velvia is excellent for nature pictures. Kodachrome 25 and 64 are good when you need extremely fine detail. Agfa 1000 color slide film is great for grainy mood shots.

Color Print Films. Kodak Gold 100 and Fujicolor 100 negative films are the standard for small prints. Agfacolor 100

My French cousin drove me to photograph cows near her Normandy home. Shooting at sunset with my Nikon N90 camera in manual mode and mounted on a tripod, I metered off the sky. TTL flash illuminated the silhouetted cow, which stuck her tongue out for this shot, making it my top choice of several good frames. With a 20mm F2.8 lens, my Nikon SB-26 flash, and ISO 100 slide film, I exposed at f/5.6 for 1/4 sec.

film is reliable, and Konica makes a good, budget-priced ISO 100 color print film. All these films come with ISO 400 speeds, too. Kodak's Pro and Ektapress films are professional negative/print films that come with speeds of ISO 100, ISO 400, and ISO 1000 speeds. Ektachrome Pro film is available in all formats.

Ektapress 640 is a multiple-speed film designed for news photographers. You can expose it at speeds ranging from ISO 100 to ISO 1600 (ISO 640 is normal). The whole roll must be rated the same ISO speed and processed by a professional lab. Ektapress films come in 35mm format only.

Black-and-White Films. I use Kodak T-Max 100 and T-Max 400 for black-and-white prints. Recently I've fallen in love with Agfa Scala film; this ISO 200 film produces beautiful black-and-white slides with good grain and tonal range. Kodak Plus-X (ISO 125) and Tri-X (ISO 400) are fine, as are ISO 100 and ISO 400 films from Fuji, Ilford, and Agfa. Polaroid Polapan film (ISO 125) is an almost instant black-and-white slide film. To me, it has a slightly antique or warmish effect. Process this film in a few minutes with a Polaroid processor, but be careful when you handle it: Polapan scratches easily.

Processing and Storing Film

Process exposed film as quickly as possible. For critical color slides, use a professional lab to avoid possible *color shift,* or variation from ideal. Whichever film you use, if you can't process it immediately, store it—and store unused film, too—in a refrigerator.

How Flash Units Work

Small flashes incorporate electronic devices that boost 6V *direct current* (DC) drawn from disposable batteries or

I made this portrait on an overcast day, using my Nikon N90 in manual mode and a 35–80mm D zoom lens set at 70mm. The on-camera flash, in TTL mode, set at minus .7 (2/3 stop), and diffused with a Sto-Fen dome, added a subtle gleam to the girl's lips. It also produced eye highlights on both Megan and Hester, her beloved pet chicken. The exposure was 1/60 sec. at f/8 on Agfa Scala 200 black-and-white slide film.

rechargeable battery packs to a value of about 150–450V DC. (Precise voltage varies according to the size and design of the unit.) The high-voltage electricity is then stored in capacitors. When any flash is fired, the capacitors discharge through Xenon gas sealed in a glass or quartz flash tube. This causes the gas to *ionize,* or change its physical state, and emit a brief burst of white light. A signal from the camera usually triggers the flash, but other devices can trigger it, too.

A unique quality of Xenon gas is that it reverts almost immediately to its natural state after discharge and is then ready to be fired again. Unique, too, is the fact that the color of light emitted by ionized Xenon gas is close to white, which is the color of neutral (or photographic) daylight.

While shooting at a street festival celebrating the winter solstice, I selected my camera's program slow-sync mode. I handheld my Nikon N90 and SB-26 flash. The man's face appears sharp on the film because it was lit almost entirely by flash. Shiny mylar shreds blowing in the wind during the long exposure reflected enough existing street lighting to record as blur on film for a ghost effect. Here, I used a 35–80mm F3.5–4.5 zoom lens set at 80mm and ISO 100 slide film.

High-powered, professional flash units and AC-powered strobes all work on the same general principles as small flashes. All flashes and strobes, from tiny units built into cameras to the most powerful professional models, are designed to be used with daylight-balanced color films (and black-and-white films). You can easily blend flash and strobe light with daylight.

The Blazing Speed of the Light from a Flash

When film is exposed using daylight or continuously burning lights, together the shutter in the camera (sometimes it is part of the lens) and the lens aperture determine the length of the exposure.

When flash is used as the primary light source, maximum flash *sync speed*, or shutter-synchronization speed, and an appropriate lens aperture are set (by program or manually) so that the flash overpowers any low-level available light. Then the shutter is significant only in that it must be fully open when the flash peaks, otherwise part of the image will be blacked out. The duration of the flash burst alone determines the actual exposure time. (Distant artificial lights shining directly into a lens might record as bright spots in backgrounds, but shaded room or studio lamps will have almost no effect on a picture.)

With any flash unit, the burst of light rises, peaks, and falls in an extremely brief period. The average peak flash duration of a flash used at full power is about 1/350 sec. If a flash discharges at less than full power, extremely high flash speeds can result, rising to about 1/20,000 sec. with some small, adjustable flash units used on 1/32 power. At low-power, high-speed settings, flash range is reduced. As a result, you must use the flash extremely close to a subject.

For example, if you're using a Nikon SB-26 flash on full manual power, ISO 100 film, and a lens set at an aperture of f/5.6, the flash range is about 25 feet. If you cut back to 1/32 power, the *flash duration* is shortened to about 1/20,000 sec., and the maximum *flash range* is reduced to approximately 4 feet.

Computer-controlled, TTL built-in or detachable flashes incorporate devices that turn the flash off when the camera program or flash sensor judges that enough light has reached the foreground subject for a good exposure. Then, the exact flash duration depends on the amount of light that is put out. You can set high-quality computerized flash units in *manual mode* at varying power levels; in these situations, high-speed exposures are repeatable (see page 16).

How Flash Range and Power Are Rated

The light output of small, portable flash units is measured by a formula called the *guide number* (GN). The standard manufacturers' GN rating, listed in all flash manuals, measures the power and range of a flash, in feet (or meters), used in combination with ISO 100 film. (You can accurately calculate flash exposures by using GNs— see Chapter 8 on page 84.)

The higher any unit's GN with ISO 100 film, the more powerful the flash and the greater the distance the light can carry. Both tiny flashes built into point-and-shoot

▲ I shot this picture in the late afternoon when this Coney Island ride was in shade. The low shutter speed plus the TTL flash fill I chose meant that some movement recorded as blur. A slight ghost image is visible in front of the moving car. (I rarely use the rear shutter-curtain flash mode that throws blur behind moving subjects, because that fires the flash at the end of long exposures, and flash delay can cause missed moments.) Working with my Nikon N90 camera and a 20mm F2.8 lens, I exposed at f/11 for 1/8 sec. on ISO 50 slide film.

◀ I made this shot of a floor show in Tangier with my Nikon FM-2 and a Metz manual flash at 1/2 power. This image reveals the stopping power of flash: the dancer was moving very fast.

cameras and built-in pop-up flashes, have low power and range. Their GNs range from about 14 to 28 (in feet). One-piece, detachable flash units have GNs ranging from about 40 or 56 to 80 (in feet). Most advanced flashes with bounce heads have GNs of 110 to 130 (in feet). Handle-mount flashes have more power: their GNs are typically 160 to 190 (in feet). Faster films increase flash range, but only to a limited degree. (To convert feet into meters, divide the number of feet by 3.3. To convert meters into feet, multiply the number of meters by 3.3. For more metric information, refer to your flash manuals.)

Professional battery-powered flashes and strobes are measured in *watt-seconds* (WS), which are about double the power of GNs. In Europe, power is rated in equivalent *joules* (J). (See Chapter 10 on page 106.)

Don't worry. You needn't carry power ratings around in your head. But you do need to remember the maximum range of your flash with the film speed you've chosen.

Flash Recycle Time

The maximum frequency with which a battery-powered flash can be fired on full power is the *flash recycle time.* This varies from about once every 1½ seconds for a strobe drawing AC, to about once every 7 seconds for a small flash that uses alkaline batteries. Precise recycling time depends on the design of the flash and the type and state of the batteries.

For a typical adjustable 6V portable flash used on full power with fresh AA alkaline or lithium batteries, the usual manufacturer-claimed recycling time is around 5 to 7 seconds. Most manufacturers' claims for built-in and portable, battery-powered flash recycling times are optimistic. To allow a small flash to achieve its true full power, you should add a couple of extra seconds to the claimed recycle times whenever you shoot in order to avoid underexposed pictures. The use of a 6V rechargeable battery pack with a typical detachable flash unit shortens the recycling time considerably.

With a set of four new AA batteries, a Nikon SB-26 flash set at full power recycles in about 7 seconds. After you shoot a 36-exposure roll of film, the recycling time slows to about 12 or 15 seconds and finally to about 30 seconds. Three rolls of flashed pictures is all you can reasonably get out of one set of AA batteries. With my favorite 6V Underdog rechargeable gel-cell battery freshly charged, the recycling time is less than 2 seconds. After a couple of rolls of film, the recycling time slows to about 4 or 5 seconds, and I can get another couple of rolls out of it at slightly slower recycle times.

(Quantum and other manufacturers make superfast battery packs that recycle even faster. When you work with these high-voltage battery packs, you must be sure not to overheat your flash. Follow the manufacturer's instructions carefully.)

Flash Synchronization

In a computerized camera, the camera's *central processing unit* (*CPU*) sets the camera shutter to synchronize with the flash whenever the flash is activated. The CPU won't permit the shutter to exceed maximum sync speed. In 35mm SLR cameras used in *program modes* (P), the CPU will select the highest possible sync speed (often 1/250 sec.) in bright sun, and a moderate sync speed (usually 1/60 sec.) in low light. In low light, the 1/60 sec. sync speed might cut out too much background light. To compensate, choose an advanced camera mode or the simple-to-use *slow-sync mode* (SS). Many electronic cameras, including good point-and-shoots, now offer the useful SS mode or similar *night-portrait mode* (NP) or *museum mode* (MS). These sophisticated settings enable you to photograph someone or something silhouetted against distant lights in backgrounds beyond flash range.

Whenever you use flash, the synchronization of the camera's shutter is essential. The light from a flash builds, peaks, and falls off quickly, if the shutter isn't in sync with the flash at the critical moment, part of the light won't reach the image. The result will be either a black strip on a picture where the flash provided the sole light source, or a dark strip on a picture where the flash lightened shadows. With manual cameras, you must set flash sync by hand.

The newest program cameras, even when used in *manual mode* (M), will prevent the flash from firing if the shutter speed is accidentally set too high. For all SLR cameras with focal-plane shutters that travel across the picture area, you must learn the maximum flash sync speed. This might be as low as 1/30 sec., but most often it is 1/60 sec.; sometimes, though, the maximum sync speed is 1/90 sec., 1/125 sec., or 1/200 sec. (There is no minimum sync speed. You simply use any speed below

sync for special effects with flash combined with available light—see page 112).

Sync speed is marked in color or with an X on the shutter-speed dial of all older cameras. You can also find it listed in camera manuals. Make it a rule to check the shutter and set the sync speed (or below) whenever you attach or turn on a flash. (Most, but not all, medium-format cameras have leaf-type shutters that open and close in a circle, and sync at up to 1/500 sec.)

When fully charged and on full power, any manual flash or strobe unit puts out the same amount of light no matter what the tonality of the subject or its distance from the flash. Exposure is, therefore, predictable and exactly repeatable, and can be determined via a flash meter, Polaroid film tests, or a formula (see Chapters 6, 7, 8, and 10 for more information about automatic and manual flashes and strobes).

Flash Falloff and the Inverse Square Law

If you studied physics (I didn't), you've heard of the Inverse Square Law. This physical law states that the light from any single-point light source diminishes according to the square of the distance it travels. The law applies to a light source of any size, even the sun, although you can't see that. A single-point light can be any source that casts a single, hard-edged shadow: direct sunlight, a candle, a flashlight, or a low-wattage household bulb. It can also be any single photographic light source, such as a hot tungsten photoflood or a flash burst from a single tube of any size or power.

Let it forever be indelibly recorded in your memory that at 8 feet from any flash, a subject gets only 1/4 the light it gets at 4 feet, not 1/2 as much. At 16 feet from any flash, a subject receives 1/16 as much light as it does

I photographed members of the Chautauqua, New York, Literary Society using my tripod-mounted Nikon N8008 camera in manual mode, a 20mm F2.8 lens, and an attached Nikon SB-24 flash. Shade trees and the misty-morning sunlight made the scene contrasty. The TTL flash filled the shadows on the people enough to balance the foreground exposure with the light on the white house; light falloff is apparent on the women at the rear of the widely spaced group. The exposure on ISO 50 slide film was f/11 for 1/30 sec.

at 4 feet, and at 32 feet, it gets only 1/64 as much illumination as it does at 4 feet! If you remember the Inverse Square Law, you'll never waste film again by trying to flash subjects that are far out of range.

But there is one exception to the Inverse Square Law. When a light source is projected through special lenses, as spotlights or lighthouse beams are, light falloff is slowed. (For more information, see Chapter 9, "Teleflash," on page 93.)

Flash and Exposure

In addition to light falloff, all photographers must understand another flash principle: that programs controlling TTL-metered and automatic-flash exposures aren't completely foolproof. Small, light main subjects set against large, dark backgrounds; small, dark main subjects against large, light, bright, or highly reflective backgrounds; and spread-out groups of people are all hard to expose perfectly with flash. When you photograph such nonaverage situations, you can get the best possible flash results by moving in and grouping people close together so the important subjects fill the picture area. As you gain experience, you'll learn how to modify or supplement flash output for tricky situations.

How Flash Exposure Is Measured

All exposure readings measured by any type of metering device—whether built into the camera or handheld, including flash meters and the sensors controlling computerized flash units—are based on the subject being *average* in tone. In photography, an average subject is defined as one that reflects 18 percent of the light that falls on it; it is also called *average gray*. Kodak established this standard years ago, and 18-percent reflectance "gray cards" (made by Kodak and others) are still used as professional exposure aids today.

LIGHT FALLOFF

Today's electronic cameras used with built-in or added computerized flash units make getting good flash exposures simple for average situations. However, even the smartest computers can't control *light falloff*. The single most critical fact that all photographers must understand in order to shoot good flash exposures is light falloff. Even a tiny flash is quite bright when used close to a subject. But as the light travels, the illumination spreads out and rapidly falls off, or diminishes, until the light from the flash can't reach any farther or illuminate any part of the composition.

Everyone who fires a small flash at night from the bleachers at sporting events or at the tops of skyscrapers from ground level is doomed to black or blank pictures. No single flash can illuminate something that far away. Flash falloff is why so many flash pictures have dark or black backgrounds. Never entirely trust an auto flash setting. Learn the maximum range of your flash with your favorite film speeds.

To photograph the entrance to the MGM Grand Hotel in Las Vegas, I used my tripod-mounted Nikon N90 and an on-camera Nikon SB-26 flash for a time exposure. Exposing manually, I shot at f/4 for 1/2 sec. I added TTL flash fill as people within range walked by. Flash falloff is apparent but doesn't have a hard edge.

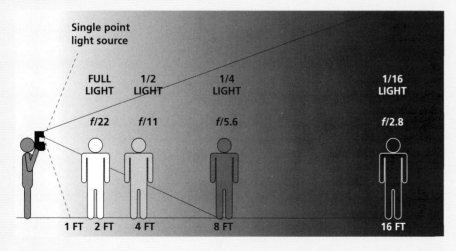

According to the Inverse Square Law, every time the flash-to-subject distance is doubled, the amount of light reaching the film is reduced by half. To compensate, you must open up the lens by two full *f*-stops (up to the maximum flash range). Rapid light falloff means that widely spaced subjects, far-distant subjects, or large areas can't be illuminated with a single flash, no matter how powerful.

With only a little practice, you can readily get good flash (and flash-filled daylight) exposures of average subjects and scenes with today's sophisticated camera metering systems and computer-controlled flashes. But even with electronic metering systems, flashes, and meters, flash (and other) exposure problems still arise when subjects are lighter, darker, and especially more contrasty than average.

Program Exposures and Flash

Program camera and flash combinations vary the shutter speed, lens aperture, and flash output according to formulas tested on many types of subjects. Program flash exposures are almost always good, and sometimes excellent, for average or midtoned subjects. But, as all types of meters and computerized cameras and flashes bias readings toward achieving overall average exposure, experienced photographers know that they can't rely on program exposures for non-average scenes.

For example, snow scenes are lighter than average. So using program settings often makes them come out gray and underexposed on film. And unusually dark subjects cause program settings and computerized flashes to bring up the tonal value to middle gray. This overexposes the subjects so that they look lighter on film than they should.

The most difficult exposure problems occur when the existing light is high in contrast, such as when dark subjects are backlit by bright sun on water. If both whites or bright highlights and blacks or deep shadows are present in the same scene, the photographer usually must bias the exposure to favor either the light or the dark elements, whichever are most critical. This is because film can't record the extremes of highlight and shadow detail that the human eye can. (All the films I know record shadow areas as darker than the human eye perceives them.)

Here, I bounced a Nikon SB-26 flash in TTL mode connected to a tripod-mounted Nikon N90 camera via an SC-17 remote cord out of a 42-inch white umbrella. The umbrella was about 3 feet away and aimed slightly down onto the subject. When all 19 shades of the Kodak gray scale are separated, the exposure is accurate enough for Agfa Scala ISO 200 black-and-white film. The scale works for color films, too.

▶ I metered off the deep-yellow leaves to avoid underexposing the snow in New York City's Central Park. The early-morning light was bluish; the TTL flash fill at minus .7 setting warmed the color of the leaves and whitened the foreground snow. Flash falloff is noticeable, but not hard-edged. Shooting with my Nikon N90 in manual mode, a 20mm F2.8 lens, and a Nikon SB-26 flash, I exposed at f/4 for 1/60 sec. on ISO 100 slide film.

▶▶ I photographed these flower sellers at the Seattle Public Market with my Nikon N90 in manual mode and a 20mm F2.8 lens. I aimed my Nikon SB-24 flash direct from about 5 feet, set to TTL fill mode to brighten the foreground and lower contrast. A Sto-Fen dome diffused the effect. The exposure was 1/60 sec. at f/8 on ISO 50 slide film.

Chapter 2

35MM CAMERAS WITH BUILT-IN FLASH

Can you make serious pictures with a handy camera that has a built-in flash? Yes, absolutely—if the camera has a good lens. But you must keep in mind that since built-in flashes are low-powered, you must make flash photographs from close distances. This limitation can actually be an advantage: it forces you to move in and make your pictures more intimate.

Tiny computerized flashes are built into just about all quality, electronic, 35mm rangefinder point-and-shoot cameras made today. Shutter speed, lens aperture, and flash output are all measured and controlled together, thereby making the process of getting good flash exposures of average-toned subjects simple. Small, sophisticated, through-the-lens-metered, pop-up type flashes are also built in to most entry- and midrange-level 35mm electronic single-lens-reflex (SLR) cameras made today. Pop-up flashes are a great way to start using flash, and in particular flash fill, in conjunction with daylight or existing light.

Avoid all the cheap snapshot cameras with built-in manual flashes; these are the so-called "focus-free" and disposable flash cameras. They have poor lenses, you have little to no control of exposures, and the results are passable at best.

Camera and flash manuals aren't intended to teach you photography. They simply show and explain how to use all the settings for the camera and the built-in or separate flash. Some manuals also make suggestions for using creative program options in different situations. Point-and-shoot camera manuals list lens apertures and flash ranges for popular film speeds (ISO 100, 400, and 1000). SLR cameras with built-in flash all have manuals that list maximum flash-to-subject distances.

Getting Started

If you are an absolute beginning photographer, you must first learn how to focus on a subject, and how to alter a composition while holding the subject in focus. Before you shoot your first flash pictures, understand that low-power, built-in flashes are designed to be aimed directly at the subject. You can't bounce, or reflect, the light of a built-in flash, nor can you diffuse it much. Learn to use *flash fill* with *general*, *portrait*, and other easy camera *modes* in sunshine, on gray days, in brightly illuminated interiors, and at night (see below). Your camera manual will help.

Fortunately, when computer-controlled flash, especially *through-the-lens* (TTL) flash, was invented, using flash fill became simple. This technique, which is also sometimes called *fill flash*, adds flash to augment the light falling on any low-lit or brightly lit subject without overpowering the existing light. Flash fill has a softer

I made this strictly grab (unposed) shot at an amusement park with my Pentax IQ-70 Zoom point-and-shoot camera and ISO 50 slide film. I used the flash-on mode and adjusted the 35–70mm F3.5–8.4 lens to 70mm.

20 REASONS TO USE SMALL FLASH

1. To get a picture of anything within flash range in low light or at night

2. To *stop*, or freeze, the motion of nearby moving subjects in low light

3. To *fill*, or lighten, facial shadows in sunlight that show up dark on film

4. To *open up*, or lighten, deep-set eye sockets in any portrait

5. To *warm up color*, or reduce the blue cast, of skin tones on overcast days

6. To emphasize any foreground subject on a gray, overcast day

7. To fill shadows on a close subject silhouetted against a sunset or sunrise

8. To lighten shadows or emphasize dark foreground objects in landscapes

9. To add light to foreground subjects in front of lit-up areas at night

10. To create motion effects by combining it with slow shutter speeds and moving subjects

11. To stop the motion of falling raindrops and snowflakes

12. To emphasize a texture, such as that of fur, feathers, cloth, wood, and artworks

13. To reveal black-on-black detail

14. To permit small *f*-stops with closeups in order to achieve the maximum zone of sharp focus

15. To add a *hairlight* or background separation to a portrait (used off-camera)

16. To add a bright *rimlight* behind a subject (used off-camera)

17. To brighten a dark corner of a room (used off-camera)

18. To correct the color of subjects in the foreground of rooms illuminated by fluorescent, tungsten, or industrial lights

19. To achieve formal lighting of portraits, groups, interiors, still lifes, etc., by combining it with additional flash units or strobes

20. To use in any way that helps you to arrive at your own "lighting look."

Flash fill used in the noonday sun almost completely eliminated the deep shadow under this ranger's Smokey Bear hat. Shooting in Olympic National Park with my Pentax IQ-70 point-and-shoot camera in flash-on mode and ISO 50 slide film, I set the camera's 35–70mm F3.5–8.4 zoom lens to 35mm.

quality than direct flash especially in daylight. In fact, flash fill can sometimes be so subtle that only an experienced eye can detect that the photographer used a flash. Working with flash fill is a favorite technique of mine, with either a built-in flash or a more powerful, separate flash unit.

For flash fill with a point-and-shoot camera, use *flash-on mode* in any light. With a 35mm SLR camera with a built-in flash, just pop up the flash to activate it. Built-in flash used as fill won't overpower daylight. Avoid using *auto flash mode*, especially for subjects at a distance. The flash will go off even if the subject is far beyond flash range (review Chapter 1). Although mastering flash fill isn't difficult, you should always carry and refer to your camera/flash manual(s). I still carry mine.

The look of pictures taken with small flash as the only light source is harsh in the hands of the unknowing. The photographs exhibit considerable contrast between the foreground and the dark background, as well as distinct shadows. If you want to avoid shadows, move subjects away from walls. But keep in mind that until quite recently, most photographs taken with portable flash contained this hard-shadow effect. Some of those photographs are masterpieces, and a hard-lighting look is currently in fashion.

35mm Rangefinder Point-and-Shoot Cameras

You'll soon discover that 35mm point-and-shoot cameras are easy to carry and fun to shoot, and can be used spontaneously. I stick to electronic/autofocus models that accept the full 35mm film format. The image quality of a sharp 35mm slide or negative makes big enlargements possible. You can, of course, experiment with a good *advanced photo system* (APS) format or an amateur Polaroid camera if you wish. Keep in mind that fine-art

By shooting at an angle to this red telephone booth, I avoided a flash hotspot on the metal. I used my Pentax IQ-70 Zoom point-and-shoot camera in flash-on mode, a 35–70mm F3.5–8.4 lens set at 35mm, and ISO 50 slide film.

Essential Point-and-Shoot Camera Features

Good, moderate-price, electronic point-and-shoot cameras offer a variety of features. These include such handy options as *flash-on/flash-off*, *redeye reduction*, and *closeup mode*. All of these facilitate camera operation and enable you to achieve different effects.

Autofocus. This saves you from getting many unsharp pictures in low light, and it is almost essential for flash pictures taken at night. But you should learn how to reframe autofocus compositions. Simply maintain focus by holding the shutter-release button halfway down so that the main subject isn't always centered (see your camera manual).

Autowinding. This feature makes rewinding film fast and convenient. It is now standard on all electronic cameras.

Bulb Mode. Some moderate-price point-and-shoot cameras offer *Bulb mode* (B). (The term "Bulb" comes from photography's early days when photographers squeezed a rubber bulb, which was connected to the shutter by a tube, in order to keep it open.) The B setting lets you hold the camera shutter open with your finger for long exposures. However, you'll discover that you must experiment with timing. And always mount your camera on a tripod when you use the B mode. You can combine this mode with flash-on mode (see page 23).

Closeup Mode. This setting, whose symbol is always a flower, permits you to focus within about 1 to 2 feet of a subject, depending on the camera or lens. I use the closeup mode for faces, pets, small objects, and flowers. With rangefinder point-and-shoot cameras, the lens doesn't cover precisely what you see in the viewfinder. This *parallax effect* is only noticeable with closeups, so when shooting them you must take care to place your subject within the bright *parallax-correction lines* in the viewfinder. If you don't, your composition won't record on film as you intended (see your camera manual). When using an SLR camera with a pop-up flash for a closeup, you won't experience a parallax problem; however, very large lenses or lens hoods can cause a shadowed area on the bottom of the film.

Computer-Controlled Flash. In electronic, rangefinder point-and-shoot cameras (which aren't necessarily expensive), the lens aperture, shutter speed, and flash output are measured together. This means that you don't need lessons in physics or math to compute flash exposures; you don't have to make any calculations. Simply set the flash-on mode, and then point and shoot at any subject within flash range.

Most point-and-shoot cameras suggest that you use print (negative) films, which are forgiving of slight exposure errors, but I've found that the cameras I like are accurate enough to use with color slide films, which demand excellent exposure. I made all the point-and-shoot pictures in this book with slide films. Judge the quality of the exposures for yourself.

photographers have exploited just about every camera and format ever made.

Give some thought to your choice. Good point-and-shoot cameras range from about $100 to more than $1,500. You can usually find a selection of less-expensive models in consumer electronics stores. If you buy a camera at a discount store, make your own decisions; the salespersons' recommendations might be influenced by their commission rate. Refuse "no-name" or "just-as-good" equipment. Reputable photo dealers get commissions, too, but most know the equipment and sell top point-and-shoots, which are accepted as professional tools today.

▲ Reflective signs can make graphic images. To shoot this sign in British Columbia, Canada, on ISO 50 film, I set the flash-on mode on my Pentax IQ-70 Zoom point-and-shoot camera and adjusted its 35–70mm F3.5–8.4 lens to 70mm.

◄ This nonreflective, historic-church model in a museum was easy to photograph with my Canon Sure Shot Panorama A-1 Underwater camera in flash-on mode, its 38mm F3.5 lens, and ISO 100 slide film. The problem was framing the image accurately, which isn't always easy to do with a point-and-shoot camera.

Flash-On/Flash-Off Control. Don't even think of buying a point-and-shoot camera without the flash-on/flash-off option. These settings let you, not the camera, control flash use. Without this absolutely essential feature, you won't be able to use flash fill in daylight, and you'll waste shots when subjects in low light are out of flash range.

Redeye Reduction. The *redeye-reduction mode* causes a low-level, pre-flash burst to go off before a main flash is fired. This pre-flash contracts the pupils of human and animal eyes somewhat in low light and allegedly reduces flash reflections from the back of the retina. But the mode does have some inherent problems: in practical use it doesn't get rid of much redeye, and worse, the delay in firing the shutter and main flash can result in missed shots. (I never use this mode.) In order to virtually eliminate redeye, I recommend either standing at an angle to your subjects or even better, using a detachable flash unit mounted high on a bracket.

Adequate Lens Speed
To achieve all the flash effects illustrated, it is important for you to choose a camera with a reasonably fast, built-in lens or a fast, separate lens. Lenses identified by low-number *f*-stops, such as *f*/1.4, *f*/2, and *f*/2.8, are considered fast. Lenses identified by apertures of *f*/3.5, *f*/4, and *f*/5.6 are considered moderately fast. And any lens with a higher-number aperture is slow. Fixed-lens *f*-stops and variable-aperture, maximum/minimum, zoom-lens *f*-

stops usually aren't marked on point-and-shoot cameras, but they're always listed in the manuals—although you might have a hard time finding them in the small print. Good detachable lenses have their speeds marked on the barrel.

The lowest-speed, fixed-focal-length lens that I would consider is an *f*/4. Fast and moderate-speed lenses permit the use of *slow*, or less sensitive to light, fine-grain films. When used wide open via an advanced program mode or manually, a fast lens lets any flash carry to its maximum range. Fast lenses also allow you to handhold your camera when shooting low-lit backgrounds while simultaneously adding program-controlled flash to foreground subjects within flash range.

Avoid Built-in Long Zoom Lenses
For practical flash photography with a point-and-shoot camera that has a built-in zoom lens, choose a camera with a moderate 2 to 1 zoom-lens range. Longer zooms built into most point-and-shoots are slow lenses, so you should avoid them. Point-and-shoot flashes don't have the power required to reach subjects at any distance unless fast and superfast films are routinely used. Zoom lenses with focal-length ranges of 35–70mm, 28–80mm, and 35–80mm zoom lenses and no slower than *f*/4 at the wide end and *f*/8 at the long end of the zoom are satisfactory. (If you want a practical longer zoom lens in a simple-to-use camera, see the information below on bridge cameras.)

Sophisticated Point-and-Shoot Cameras

Obviously, the most expensive point-and-shoot cameras have advantages: the sharpest, fastest lenses; a high number of autofocus steps; a wide range of shutter speeds; and a choice of program modes. These cameras are more durable than budget models, but they are also somewhat more complicated to use. Most of the best point-and-shoots offer the *slow-sync program mode* (SS); on some cameras, this mode is called the *night-portrait mode* (NP) or the *museum mode* (MS). The SS/NP/MS mode permits you to make flash exposures of nearby subjects combined with time exposures that record subjects beyond flash range.

Olympus makes unique *zoom-lens-reflex* (ZLR) point-and-shoot cameras, which are often called *bridge cameras*. Sized and shaped like camcorders, ZLR cameras come with noninterchangeable zoom lenses that show you exactly what the lens sees, just as 35mm SLR cameras do. ZLR lenses have adequate speed; a flash that pops up high is built into these cameras. The current top model, the IS 3-DLX, has a 35–180mm $f/4$–5.6 lens with a 5X zoom range (it costs around $1,000). This camera allows you to use a separate flash if more flash power is desired.

Professional point-and-shoot cameras are top-quality rangefinder cameras that you can operate either in program

▶ Here, fill light gave definition to the flashed area and warmed the color of the orange feed bucket in the overcast, bluish daylight. I used my Pentax IQ-70 Zoom point-and-shoot camera in flash-on mode, its 35–70mm F3.5–8.4 lens set at 70mm, and ISO 100 slide film.

▼ To shoot Miami's South Beach at night, I mounted my Pentax IQ-70 Zoom point-and-shoot camera and its 35–70mm F3.5–8.4 lens adjusted to 35mm on a tripod. I used ISO 50 slide film and both the flash-on and Bulb modes. I held the shutter release down briefly, making about six exposures at twilight at between 1/4 sec. and 1/2 sec. at $f/3.5$. This is the one I like best.

mode or with full manual control of lens apertures and shutter speeds. All of these cameras come with computer-controlled built-in flash. With some models, the lenses are interchangeable, and you can add a separate flash.

Weather-resistant and waterproof point-and-shoot cameras are great for use on and around beaches, pools, and lakes. They are also ideal for shooting on boats and in rainy, snowy, sandy, or dusty conditions. Remember to clean the glass that protects the lenses of all weather-proof cameras by wiping it with a facial tissue, such as Kleenex, or lens tissue before shooting. If you don't, out-of-focus water or dust spots might show on your pictures.

Waterproof point-and-shoots are designed to be used down to 15 feet or so, but my experience is that while the flash is fine used as fill at water level, a built-in flash isn't useful underwater. In seemingly clear pools and lakes, flash reflects bubbles and ordinarily invisible particles back into the lens, thereby obscuring the subject. In rivers and oceans, mud and sand magnify this problem. Serious underwater photographers use off-camera flash (see Chapter 12 on page 129).

Recommended Point-and-Shoot Cameras
The following descriptions of point-and-shoot models should help you make an informed decision when you choose a camera. But keep in mind that these camera models change frequently, so be sure to check current photography buying guides before making a purchase. (All models noted have glass lenses.)

Canon. The Canon Sure Shot cameras are all well-priced, with surprisingly sharp lenses. I currently own and like the Canon Sure Shot A-1. It has a 32mm *f*/3.5 lens and is waterproof to 16 feet.

Contax. The Contax T-VS camera, which has a 28–56mm *f*/3.5–6.5 lens and NP mode, and the Contax T-2 camera, which comes with a 38mm *f*/2.8 Zeiss Sonnar lens, are quality cameras. The Contax G-2 is a superb rangefinder camera that you can use as a point-and-shoot. It has a built-in flash and both manual and program controls; several lenses and a separate flash are options.

Konica. This company makes some great point-and-shoot cameras. I loved its now extinct water-resistant Off-Road model. Today's Konica Big-Mini Zoom TR camera, which has a 28–70mm *f*/3.5–8.4 lens, is good. The Konica Super-Compact Zoom camera has a 32mm *f*/3.5 lens and offers the *backlight-compensation mode*. You can use this option when bright light comes from directly behind a dark foreground subject. This situation can cause a silhouette effect in the final image. This mode opens up the lens, increases the flash output, or both, in order to ensure good foreground exposure.

Leica. This manufacturer's point-and-shoot cameras have quality lenses. You might want to consider the Leica Mini-II, with its 35mm *f*/3.5 four-element lens, or the Leica Mini-Zoom, which has a 35–70mm *f*/4–7.6 lens.

Minolta. Minolta's Freedom Zoom Explorer 70-EX camera has a 28–70mm *f*/3.5–8.4 lens and NP mode. Because this point-and-shoot camera comes with with my favorite 28mm focal length at the wide end of the zoom, I forgive its being a touch slow at the long end.

Nikon. I am a Nikon system user and once owned a handy Action-Touch water-resistant camera (this model is no longer made). The company's current Touch models include: the Lite-Touch, with a 28mm *f*/3.5 lens; the Zoom-Touch 500S, with a 35–80mm *f*/3.5–7 lens; and the Zoom-Touch 400, with a 35–70mm *f*/4–7.6 lens and SS mode. All of these point-and-shoot cameras represent value. Nikon's deluxe 28-TI model comes with a 28mm *f*/2.8 lens and offers full program operation plus manual controls.

Olympus. This camera manufacturer offers two outstanding point-and-shoot cameras. The Olympus Stylus is a slim, worldwide bestseller with a 35mm *f*/3.5 lens (and a bargain price). The Olympus IS-3 DLX, which has a 35–180mm *f*/4.5–5.6 lens, is at the top of the company's line of bridge cameras. This model is the only long-zoom-range point-and-shoot camera I would buy; you can add a separate TTL flash for even greater range.

Pentax. This manufacturer's point-and-shoot cameras are excellent. I own a five-year-old Pentax IQ-70 camera with a 35–70mm zoom lens (this model is no longer made). Today's Pentax IQ-Zoom 90-WR, which has a 38–90mm *f*/3.5–7.5 lens and is water resistant, and the compact Pentax UC-1 camera, which has a 32mm *f*/3.5 lens, are both fine choices.

Rollei. The Rollei Prego is a quality point-and-shoot camera with a fine 35mm *f*/3.5 Schneider Xenar lens and SS mode.

Samsung. The Samsung Maxima 77-i Zoom has a 35–70mm *f*/3.5–6.7 lens and offers backlighting compensation and B mode.

Yashica. The Yashica T-4 camera offers a high-quality 35mm *f*/3.5 Zeiss Tessar lens and backlight compensation. The Yashica T-4 Super model has the same lens and is weather-resistant.

Composing with a Rangefinder Camera
When you use any rangefinder camera, keeping the viewfinder pressed to your eye is a basic. Then the subject looks two-dimensional, as the final picture will. All rangefinder point-and-shoot models have small viewfinders, but don't worry. If you use this type of camera, you'll soon get used to the viewfinder. Become a Cyclops, and carefully frame subjects within the bright guide lines engraved on the viewfinder glass (they move when you move a zoom lens). It is hard to judge borders precisely with any rangefinder camera, so take care to avoid clutter around the edges of a composition.

The Parallax Problem and Rangefinder Closeups

As mentioned earlier, in any rangefinder camera, the viewfinder you look through when composing a picture is separate from the lens. And because it is off to one side or the other and is slightly above the lens, it doesn't "see" exactly what the lens covers. With normal and long-distance shots, this *parallax* effect isn't noticeable. But you must compensate for parallax error when shooting closeups. Locate the *parallax-compensation marks* in your viewfinder, and use them as guides (see your camera manual); otherwise, your subject will appear high and to one side—perhaps even partly cut off—in the picture area.

35mm SLR Cameras with Built-In Flash

Many good, electronic 35mm SLR cameras come with handy pop-up flashes. TTL viewing makes composing with reflex cameras easy, and lens interchangeability provides creative options. Also, SLR cameras enable you to

These tomatoes were a basically midtoned subject, so they presented no exposure problems. The flash fill from the pop-up flash on my Nikon N50 camera in program closeup mode gave definition and highlights to the fruit on an overcast day. I made this shot with a 35–80mm D zoom lens.

add a separate flash (which deactivates the built-in flash) if and when you need more flash power and versatility.

Although SLR cameras are bigger and a bit more complicated to use than most point-and-shoot cameras, a reasonably intelligent person can master the mechanics of photographing with an SLR in an hour. Read the camera manual, familiarize yourself with the features and easy settings, and carry the manual with you at first. It is essential to learn the maximum flash-to-subject distances for your favorite films. Then just pop up the built-in flash whenever a good subject is within flash range. The flash will provide fill to lighten shadows in sunlight or to brighten foreground subjects on gray days. Of course, the flash will fully illuminate subjects within flash range in low light or at night.

Essential Electronic 35mm SLR Camera Features

All 35mm SLR camera models with built-in, TTL-metered flash are made to appeal to photographers at every level, from beginner to professional. The majority of amateurs choose SLRs as their first serious camera. Look for the following features when you shop:

Built-in Pop-Up Flash. A built-in flash adds almost no weight to a camera, and it is always there. It can be useful out to 10 or 15 feet, depending on the film speed and lens aperture used. (With program exposures, the prevailing light conditions and lens-aperture setting affect the flash range. I consider built-in pop-up flash units most useful for adding flash to lighten shadows on faces. If you use a built-in flash a great deal, don't forget that it runs off the camera batteries, so be sure to carry extras. All electronic SLR cameras (and top-of-the-line Olympus bridge point-and-shoot models) permit you to mount a more powerful detachable TTL flash over the built-in pop-up flash.

Flash Sync Speed of At Least 1/125 sec. A sync speed of at least 1/125 sec. is the standard minimum with modern electronic cameras. A speed of 1/250 sec. is now the standard, and 1/300 sec. is currently the top speed for advanced SLR cameras with *focal-plane shutters*. (A sync speed of 1/500 sec. is the standard for medium-format cameras with *leaf-type shutters*.)

High sync speed is important when using flash to *fill*, or lighten, shadows in bright sunlight. A high sync speed permits the use of wide *f*-stops in bright light (via an advanced program mode or manually) without overex-

Shooting in a hard drizzle at dusk, I focused my tripod-mounted Konica Off-Road camera on the view from my New York City studio window. I held the shutter-release button down on this water-resistant, point-and-shoot camera for as short a time as possible (probably between 1/4 sec. and 1/2 sec.) and made three exposures. The bubble effect comes from the TTL flash hitting the closest out-of-focus raindrops. I used the built-in 28mm F2.8 lens, flash-on and Bulb modes, and ISO 50 film.

posing background areas. Wide apertures also extend the effective range of the flash in low light.

Depth-of-Field-Preview Setting. This feature *stops down* a program lens from the wide-open *viewing aperture* to the *taking aperture.* This setting helps you adjust the zone of sharp focus.

Range of Modes. Full program mode (P); user-controlled but easy options, such as *landscape* (L), *sport, portrait,* and SS (or similarly named) *modes;* and *manual mode* (M) are all useful on entry-level cameras. Intermediate-level SLR cameras offer M mode and various P modes, as well as *aperture-priority mode* (A) and *shutter-priority mode* (S).

With the A mode, when you choose a desired aperture for creative reasons, the camera sets an appropriate shutter speed (but not above flash sync speed). Conversely, with the S mode when you select a desired shutter speed for creative reasons, the camera transmits a signal to program lenses only and sets the correct aperture. With the M mode, you choose both the aperture and shutter speed for creative reasons but can still enjoy the benefits of TTL-metered flash.

Easy-to-Use Controls. Any SLR camera should have well-marked external controls, whether you prefer traditional numbered dials or *liquid-crystal-display* (LCD) readout screens. Ideally, shutter speed, aperture, and correct or over-and-underexposure-indication and frame numbers should be clearly visible on a panel that is readable when your eye is to the viewfinder. Such easy-to-read and easy-to-use controls are available in top-of-the-line camera models.

Opt for a camera with a minimal number of settings that require holding down two buttons simultaneously. All of these features will help you operate your camera and flash and make creative decisions much more quickly.

Advantages of TTL Metering

Today's electronic 35mm SLR cameras offer TTL metering. A sensor close to the film plane measures all the light reaching the film. An in-camera computer then adjusts lens aperture and shutter speed and precisely determines the needed flash or flash-fill output. TTL metering accurately exposes most subjects. The exceptions are non-average-toned and high-contrast subjects, which require you to think and, possibly, to bracket exposures. Here are some tips for the first few times you use TTL flash.

In Sunlight. Stand as close as possible to your subject. Remember, flash range is reduced in bright sunlight because the camera program must set small lens apertures.

On Gray Days. To emphasize close foreground subjects, use flash fill with ISO 100 film. To minimize the amount of flash needed, use ISO 400 or 1000 film.

In Bad Weather. Protect cameras that aren't water resistant. I use either clear plastic bags taped tight or plastic cling wrap. Use fast film and the flash-on mode. Try the SS mode or the B mode, too.

With Bright Backlighting. Select an ISO 100 or slower film. Stand close for portraits so the fill light can balance the existing backlighting. Use the flash-on mode, or activate the pop-up flash to add flash fill.

With Bright Lights at Night. Mount your camera on a tripod. Choose the SS mode. Pose people so they're silhouetted against the bright lights; have them stand as still as possible in order to minimize *ghosts*, or blurred moving images. If the SS mode isn't available, try the flash-on mode combined with the B mode.

While Panning. When you *pan*, or follow, a moving subject, use a long SS (or B) exposure in order to achieve blur-plus-sharpness effects. Flash fill "stops," or freezes, both slow-moving silhouetted subjects and parts of fast-moving subjects, such as cars.

In Near Darkness. Work close to your subject to reduce the risk of overexposing small light subjects, such as light-skinned faces, that are against dark backgrounds.

Program Camera Modes and Built-in Flash

Simple modes are designed to make it easy for inexperienced photographers to make creative decisions. Beginners can change the camera's shutter speed and aperture to suit the subject. If they use a flash, they contribute to varying flash output also. These basic modes include *general*, *portrait*, *landscape* (L), and *closeup modes*. Some entry-level SLR cameras also offer a *sport mode*.

The A and S Modes, as well as full creative control with manual settings (M mode) are available on all advanced and professional electronic 35mm SLR cameras. The SS flash-fill mode (or similarly named program setting) is also offered on a few good point-and-shoot cameras and most entry-level program SLR cameras. Advanced program modes can be useful to even experienced professional photographers when light is changing fast.

Aperture-Priority Mode. On SLR cameras, the A mode enables you to control the lens opening for creative use of depth of field.

Auto Mode. This mode is the cause of more bad flash pictures than any other. In some shooting situations, you might be surrounded by people merrily flashing at impossibly distant subjects. They're using flash with the *auto flash mode*, which is standard on inexpensive point-and-shoot cameras and appears on a few good cameras, too. Don't imitate these individuals.

Bulb Mode. In the B mode, the camera shutter stays open as long as you hold down the shutter-release button, thereby making time exposures possible. At night, combine the B mode with the flash-on mode for subjects within flash range; precise timing isn't critical with exposures of several seconds at night, but you must use a tripod for sharp backgrounds.

Closeup Mode. Use this mode, which is indicated by a flower symbol, in conjunction with the flash-on mode for frame-filling flash pictures; shoot from the minimum distance you can focus a point-and-shoot camera. Closeup mode is good for photographing flowers, small pets, and big insects, as well as for copying small objects.

You can also shoot frame-filling faces (though you may get large noses using this mode for human portraits). When shooting closeups with a rangefinder camera, remember to compensate for parallax by using viewfinder marks. And when shooting closeups with SLR pop-up flashes, you should fire-test flashes to be sure that the light doesn't overshoot your intended subject, or that lenses or hoods don't cast a shadow. If available, choose the A mode and a small f-stop for the best results with flash closeups.

Flash-On Mode. Select this simple, useful setting with point-and-shoot cameras to add computer-controlled flash fill to any subject within flash range, in any light. In bright sun or on gray days, the flash-on mode puts out just enough light to "open up" dark shadows on faces. The mode also adds highlights to deepset eyes, a shine to dark fur or feathers, and definition to close landscape features. At night, use the flash-on mode only if your subject is within flash range. And if it is, be sure to work as close as possible to it in order to avoid black backgrounds. With an SLR camera, pop up the built-in flash, and use the same techniques.

Flash-Off Mode. This point-and-shoot mode is useful for photographing distant scenes when nothing interesting is within flash range. In low light or at night, it forces the camera to make long exposures. Be sure to use a tripod when working in this mode.

Landscape Mode. Similar in effect to flash-off mode, the intermediate-level L mode sets a small aperture and slow shutter speed for maximum depth-of-field. Mount your camera on a tripod for this mode to avoid blurred images in low light.

Manual Mode. On dedicated/TTL SLR cameras, the M mode, which is an advanced mode, permits you to control all camera settings. TTL-metered flash fill is also still possible with this mode.

Portrait Mode. This intermediate-level mode selects wide-open lens apertures to throw backgrounds out of focus.

Redeye-Reduction Mode. With point-and-shoot and SLR cameras, this flash mode puts out a pre-flash burst that causes people's pupils to contract. This in turn reduces the red effect caused by flash reflecting off the retina. Unfortunately, in my experience, this mode never eliminates redeye. In fact, it often makes people blink just in time for the second flash that takes the picture. Minimize the chances of redeye by photographing your subjects at an angle.

Shutter-Priority Mode. On SLR cameras, the S mode allows you to choose the shutter speed. Keep in mind, though, that this mode requires a *dedicated* lens that allows the camera to set the *f*-stop. One superfast dedicated lens might be more useful to you than two or three moderate-speed auto lenses.

Slow-Sync Mode. This advanced but simple-to-use flash setting is featured on some point-and-shoot cameras and many electronic TTL SLR cameras. The SS (or NP or MS) mode is a more precise alternative to the B mode because it meters low-lit backgrounds, sets a slow shutter speed, and then adds flash in order to illuminate dark foreground subjects. Use the SS mode to photograph your loved ones in front of the Sphinx in Egypt, the Space Needle in Seattle or the Acropolis in Athens, all of which are illuminated with floodlights at night. The SS mode also works well in low daylight.

Selecting a 35mm SLR Camera

Choosing one SLR camera brand over another isn't going to make you a better photographer, no matter what the manufacturers claim. To find a camera that is right for you, handle different brands and models. Ask some questions: Are the controls easy to understand and operate? Is the camera going to satisfy my needs a year from now? Do I want a better lens than the basic zoom lens included in the camera kit? Do I like the optional separate flash and other accessories? Finally, check current photo buying guides for model updates.

Canon and Nikon are known for their top-of-the-line SLR camera systems, which professional photographers use. The companies' entry- and intermediate-level models with built-in flash accept most of the accessories that the professional models do. Beginners might want to consider Nikon's N50 camera. I own one and like it. The Nikon N70 is advanced electronically, with plus or minus adjustment of the TTL-flash output; I don't care for the pictograph controls. (My workhorses are advanced/professional-level N90s.) Canon's EOS-Elan II, A-2 and A-2E cameras all have built-in TTL flashes. The Elan is respected; the professional-quality A-2E is excellent. All these cameras accept separate dedicated flash units.

COPING WITH REDEYE

The vampirish-looking eyes that appear in some color flash pictures of people are caused by light reflecting off blood vessels at the back of the retina. Unfortunately, this problem, which most often occurs in flash pictures taken from a distance, can't be completely prevented via the use of built-in flash. But the *redeye-reduction (pre-flash) modes* found on some cameras and flash units sometimes help. To almost completely eliminate redeye, you must do what professionals do: use a detachable flash mounted high on a bracket (see Chapter 5 on page 54).

If redeye occurs, minimize its ugly effect in small color prints by retouching. Stipple the red area with a fine-point black marker. You can also get a *cyan*, or blue-green, redeye-retouching marker at photo stores. On black-and-white prints, the effect is white eyes (white pupils). Retouch black-and-white prints by stippling them with Spot Tone, a retouching fluid available at photo dealers. Important slides ruined by redeye can be scanned onto a CD-ROM disc by Kodak, and then retouched in minutes by a computer-literate person with an appropriate graphics program.

Because the flash is centered over the lens, group pictures, like this one, made in low light with a 35mm camera with a pop-up flash almost always show redeye. Using the camera's redeye-reduction mode might help, but in my experience it usually hasn't. Try standing at an angle to or above your subjects if possible. Professionals always mount a separate flash high on a bracket for group shots.

To minimize the redeye effect in group shots, professional photographer Wayne Fisher puts a detachable flash on a bracket. Here, he's using his Canon EOS-1 camera, and a Canon 430-EZ flash on a Stroboframe Quick Flip bracket.

Canon and Nikon both offer a huge variety of lenses, separate flashes, and accessories.

Minolta also makes excellent, innovative cameras. The 400-si is a good beginner's choice. The 700-si is a solid, midrange model; I've used it, and I can recommend it. Minolta's basic zoom lens is sharp. Later you can add Minolta's detachable flash, the 5400-xi, which you can operate in cordless TTL mode from the 700-si. (This is currently the only true cordless remote TTL flash on the market.)

(As mentioned earlier, the Olympus IS-3 bridge camera is a viable reflex-camera choice for a beginner who doesn't need lens options. The IS-3 offers a detachable flash.)

Pentax is respected for rugged, budget-priced mechanical cameras and point-and-shoot cameras. The Pentax PZ 70 model is a good, entry-level electronic 35mm SLR camera. The Sigma AS-300N and the Yashica 300 cameras are also reliable entry-level 35mm choices. (You can expect to pay between about $400 and $1,000 for an entry-level to midlevel electronic 35mm SLR or bridge camera with a built-in flash and a moderate zoom-range lens.)

Choosing First Lenses for Entry-Level 35mm SLR Cameras
Before you buy any lenses for flash work, you should give some thought to how and what you shoot most. Do you shoot primarily portraits indoors? Groups of people? Landscapes? Interiors? Still-life arrangements that you want to be ultra-sharp? Wildlife or sports? Rock groups and entertainment? Nature closeups? All of these subjects call for different ideal lens choices. And be aware that if you photograph from a distance with flash, you must buy the fastest possible telephoto or zoom lens or lenses because of rapid flash falloff. Although name-brand zoom lenses are sharp, most still aren't quite as sharp and none are as fast as the very best single-focal-length lenses.

A program camera selects a moderate lens aperture for good depth of field and the maximum sync speed when the pop-up flash is in closeup mode. Program exposures are best when used with midtoned subjects. I made this cat portrait with my Nikon N50 in closeup mode, its maximum sync speed of 1/125 sec., a 35–80mm D zoom lens, a pop-up flash, and ISO 100 film.

My favorite lenses are: a 20mm for landscapes and cityscapes, a 28mm for groups and location portraits, a superfast 50mm for general low-light shooting, and an 80mm for portraits. I carry 35–80mm and 80–200mm telephoto zoom lenses whenever I travel (with the exception of a basic 35–80mm zoom lens, all of my lenses are f/2.8 or faster). I use a 300mm f/2.8 telephoto lens for wildlife subjects and sometimes for landscapes.

Zoom Lenses. Camera manufacturers often sell their basic, autofocus 35–70mm or 28–80mm zoom lenses with cameras as part of a kit. These zoom lenses are perfectly acceptable in terms of optical quality, though slower and not as physically rugged as top-of-the-line lenses. Apertures are usually f/4 to f/5.6, which are just fine for beginning flash. Zoom lenses are convenient, but they certainly aren't required for flash photography. In my experience, flash is usable with everything from the widest of wide-angle lenses to all but the most extreme telephoto lenses. (Using flash with long telephoto lenses requires special techniques—see Chapter 10 on page 106.)

Dedicated Lenses. Some have a mini-computer built-in, and some have an internal motor. They operate fast in low light with dedicated/TTL cameras and flash units. Today manufacturers, including Canon, Minolta and Nikon, offer special dedicated lenses (each brand uses different designations). Look into dedicated lenses if you are serious about flash photography. The increase in both autofocus speed and flash-exposure accuracy makes them worth the price difference.

Fast Lenses. The faster the lens, the better the autofocus works in low light and the greater the potential maximum flash range. Fast lenses are usually of the finest quality, which is always a critical factor if you intend to make big enlargements. Serious photographers should opt for the fastest and best lenses they can afford no matter which first camera model they choose.

How fast is fast? Many single-focal-length lenses have maximum apertures of f/1.4, f/2, or f/2.8. Some top-of-the-line zoom lenses have an aperture of f/2.8 at all focal lengths. An adequately fast zoom lens for flash is in the f/4 or f/4 to f/5.6 aperture range. Fast lenses have just two drawbacks: they are heavy and expensive.

Wide-Angle Lenses. I use wide-angle lenses for getting close to people and conveying a feeling of intimacy, which I strive for in my pictures. (These lenses don't noticeably distort features unless used closer than about 3 feet to the subject or at the edge of a composition.) Wide-angle lenses are "musts" for shooting landscapes and interiors. In terms of flash, the great advantage of wide-angle lenses is that if you work close the reduced flash-to-subject distance means you can choose smaller apertures and get greater depth of field than is possible with standard or long lenses.

Manual Lenses. If you own an old manual lens that fits your electronic SLR camera (as my old Nikkor lenses do),

These women were very close when I flashed; the touch of fill light brightened the umbrellas and offset the bluish daylight. I made the shot with my Konica Off-Road weather-resistant, point-and-shoot camera in flash-on mode, its 28mm F2.8 lens, and Agfa ISO 1000 slide film.

you can use them for TTL-metered flash exposures. Select the camera's A mode. The chosen lens aperture won't show on the camera's LCD panel or be visible in the viewfinder screen, but the shutter speed will be adjusted electronically, and the flash output will be regulated by the in-camera CPU controls. Set a small aperture—for example, *f*/11 is safe with ISO 100 film—whenever you use the A mode, to add flash fill in sunshine. If you don't, the subject will be overexposed because an electronic camera can't select a shutter speed higher than flash sync when the flash is activated.

Minimizing Pop-Up Flash Problems
Apart from the standard warning about not exceeding the flash range, you should also be aware of several potential problems when shooting with a built-in, pop-up flash. The following suggestions will help you avoid them.

Use a Separate Flash with Big Lenses or Big Lens Shades. These devices can prevent some of the light from a pop-up flash from reaching the intended subject. This shows up as a quarter-moon-shaped shadow in the bottom of a picture. If you often have this problem, switch to a separate flash.

Don't Shoot Extreme Closeups with a Built-In Flash. When working with a built-in flash, you shouldn't use a *macro,* or closeup, lens or *extension tubes,* which are inexpensive rings that you insert between the camera body and lens and that permit close-focusing with any lens. If you do, the illumination from a pop-up flash will probably over-

shoot your subject, leaving it wholly or partly unlit. Use a separate flash off-camera for closeups. (For more on flash closeups, see Chapters 5, 6, and 7.)

Built-In Flash Can't Do Everything. Some subjects are hard if not impossible to photograph well with built-in flash. These include:

- Anything beyond maximum flash range
- Flat art behind glass
- Computer and television screens (use slow shutter speeds)
- Glassware and shiny objects
- All-white or all-black objects
- White objects on black backgrounds
- Black objects on white backgrounds
- Tiny subjects
- Distant wildlife and sports subjects
- Extreme closeups.

For approaches to photographing these subjects, see Parts 2 and 3 of this book.

When Not to Use Flash. Never use flash when it could distract someone performing a dangerous task, or at events where all photography is forbidden. You can't sneak flash pictures. And don't photograph people—with or without flash—who are liable to respond angrily.

Chapter 3
FAVORITE SUBJECTS

As subjects, people have fascinated photographers—and been a major source of income for professionals—since almost the beginnings of the art. Think of Victorian albums and early travel scenes featuring exotic peoples. From the 1930s to 1970s, magazines like the old *Life* ran classic picture stories about people in peace and war, as well as then-contemporary fashion, lifestyle, and entertainment images. Now, much advertising and many magazines are devoted to personalities and celebrities.

Good "people" skills are basic to photojournalism, travel, and fashion photography. Most pictures in newspapers are still of people, and sports and music-business photography are about people, too. Corporations, indus-

trial companies, and public-relations firms use many pictures of executives, managers, workers, and conferences in annual reports, promotional brochures, and increasingly on the World Wide Web. The market for up-to-the-minute, model-released stock (existing) photographs of people of all ages, races, and types doing things that represent life is huge worldwide.

The business of recording milestones in the lives of "average" people feeds thousands of professional wedding, portrait, and school photographers annually. Billions of people all over the world shoot family pictures, and when these are done well can be much, much more than snapshots.

Making high-quality pictures of people involves psychology, a good eye, a sensitivity to mood, and the ability to approach someone close or to sense when to recede into the background. Ideally, the aim is to always make an image that conveys a feeling of intimacy to viewers.

Using Small Flash for People Photography

Just a few years ago, most amateur cameras were strictly used for snapshots. That was before the days of mini-computers controlling the interaction of the aperture, shutter speed, and flash output. Now, any photographer who is comfortable being close to people, has an eye for a good composition, and an understanding of how to use flash fill with existing light can make quality images of almost any human subject. I even know of a magazine photographer who shoots people assignments with a point-and-shoot camera.

To successfully use flash for people photography, you must be aware of the most basic rule of photographic lighting: The light source should be close to the main subject. So, much of the secret of lighting people well with a small built-in flash—or any small flash used on-camera—is to move close to your subject. If possible, use the flash as *fill*, or supplemental, light. If a tiny flash is your sole source of light at night, you'll be able to achieve acceptable light quality on people only if you shoot extremely close.

I'm assuming here that you are familiar with the flash basics discussed in the previous chapters, and that you're using a modern, fully-electronic camera with a built-in or on-camera computer-controlled or dedicated/TTL flash that turns on or pops up even in bright light. (Inexpensive flash cameras used on auto-flash settings don't do this.)

If your SLR camera with pop-up flash permits changing lenses, use a good-quality, reasonably fast lens with an aperture no slower than *f*/3.5 or *f*/4 aperture. In low light, use the *aperture-priority mode* (A) to set the lens wide open in order to maximize flash range. You can use a manual lens with through-the-lens (TTL) flash using the A mode also (review Chapter 2 and your camera manual).

Everyone likes to take pictures of family occasions. I made this shot of a new second lieutenant being "pinned" on graduation day at West Point. Working with my Nikon N90, a 20mm F2.8 D lens, and my on-camera Nikon SB-26 flash in TTL mode, and ISO 100 film, I metered off the family members and manually exposed for 1/250 sec. at *f*/8. Flash fill lightened the dark side of the scene.

Using Flash Indoors or in Low Daylight

Program-camera settings can make pictures taken in low daylight look like night pictures when you add flash as fill. Generally, programs used with flash select *handhold-able*, or quite fast, shutter speeds, which cut out most existing light. To avoid this, put your camera on a tripod and choose the *slow-sync mode* (SS), which slows shutter speeds (your camera might have a slightly different name for this mode). Other preventative options are to use the *Bulb mode* (B), or to choose a slow shutter speed in the *shutter-priority mode* (S) or *manual camera mode* (M).

With all of these methods, you can set low shutter speeds that record low-lit backgrounds beyond the flash range. The TTL flash fill that you add takes the slow shutter speeds into consideration and doesn't overexpose foregrounds. With fast-moving subjects, such as small children, you are likely to get some ghost images.

Approaching People

People who feel comfortable photographing family, friends, and strangers take the best pictures of them. You aren't stealing anyone's soul when you record them on film. And if you ask your subjects' permission before shooting, you'll generally get a positive response. If you don't, simply say thanks and move on.

If you photograph enough strangers, you'll soon learn how people indicate through their body language and expressions if they're willing to be approached. When I'm shooting outdoors in places where people congregate or near backgrounds where I want to include a person or several people, I stand around a great deal with a camera in my hand but without taking any pictures. I smile often, approaching only the people who smile back or send some other kind of positive message. I don't get too many rejections.

Styles of People Pictures

When you start to seriously photograph people, you should think about the kind of pictures you want. This decision might influence your style of lighting.

Documentary-Style People Pictures

Documentary-style, unposed or *set-up* (photographer-arranged) shots of interesting or dramatic happenings are used in newspapers and news magazines. Portraits of relaxed-looking people in interesting places are used in magazines and books, and sometimes by businesses and corporations. Professional models, actors, and good-looking people are photographed for the people illustrations used for a great deal of advertising, while elegant models are needed for much fashion and beauty photography. Take a look at some current magazines for the latest styles. Formal portraiture and meeting and event photography are needed for business or corporate public-relations brochures. Of course, weddings are shot for individual clients.

Documentary-Style Unposed Pictures. Flash is highly suitable for documentary photography, the truly unposed pictures of people made when a photographer finds—or waits for—marvelous moments and spontaneous emotions of people going about their lives, and captures them on film. This is

A large umbrella shaded this hot-dog seller and the interior of his cart were shaded from the sun. The bright existing light meant that the TTL flash fill was minimal. It added eye highlights as well as some shine to the metal cart, but the small flash hotspots didn't cause under-exposure. Here, I worked with ISO 100 slide film and my Nikon N50 in general program mode and a pop-up flash, and set my 35–80mm F3.5–4.5 zoom lens at 35mm.

the classic style of big-time magazine photojournalists, the most serious of whom spend days, weeks, months, or even years working on a given project. Some freelance photographers make a point of hanging out at places where they are likely to see celebrities, or listen to police and fire calls on short-wave radios in order to get leads. Many newspaper and magazine photojournalists start their careers this way. (For whatever reason, wedding photographers call their unposed pictures "candids.")

Documentary-Style Set-Up Pictures. Because of the time constraints that newspaper and magazine photographers face, they sometimes must create "real-looking," posed situations in a hurry. Flash is often the most appropriate light. Photojournalism skills can be polished at events that are accessible to beginners, including political meetings, parades, parties, weddings, graduations, and school and college sporting events. A great deal of activity takes place at all of these.

Some amateur photographers keep a camera close at all times to produce an ongoing essay on a person. They might record a child's growth, or a partner's emotions, or a grandparent's activities. These photographers are members of the family of photojournalists, too.

When you use any small flash to lighten shadows in a bright backlit scene, it is important to work as close as possible to your subjects or the flash fill might not be strong enough to balance the foreground and background exposures. I shot this picture from water level at about 3 feet from the woman and child as the West Virginia late-afternoon sun was shining toward me. I used my Canon Sure Shot A-1 camera, which is waterproof to 16 feet and has a 32mm F3.5 lens, in flash-on mode and ISO 100 slide film.

LENSES FOR PEOPLE PICTURES

For most studio-type portraits and pictures of children, use a lens with a focal length of 70mm or 80mm or the long end of a zoom-lens range. Either choice will enable you to fill the frame with the head and shoulders, without distorting the subject's features. Depth of field is shallow, throwing distracting backgrounds out of focus. Shooting frame-filling portraits means that flash fill will be effective even at the small apertures at the long end of most built-in zoom lenses.

Wide-angle lenses and short-end zoom-lens settings, of, for example, 35mm or 28mm, enhance many location portraits and documentary pictures. Wide-angle lenses and zoom settings provide depth of field sufficient to let you frame people close enough for a good size, and at the same time show backgrounds in reasonably sharp focus. Avoid possible distortion by keeping your subject(s) in the center 2/3 of the picture area.

Working with my Pentax IQ-70 Zoom point-and-shoot camera in flash-on mode, I zoomed in for this frame-filling portrait of a happy graduate. The flash fill in the bright noon sunshine lightened the shadow area under the mortarboard. I set the Pentax's 35–70mm F3.5–8.4 zoom lens at 70mm and used ISO 50 slide film.

I made this photograph of a little girl in a flower market with my Nikon N50, in program mode, with a 35–80mm F3.5–4.5 zoom lens. I used TTL flash fill from the camera's pop-up flash on this drizzly day. The exposure on ISO 64 film was 1/60 sec. at f/5.6.

In stormy weather, I made my host sail closer than he liked to this Connecticut lighthouse so that it appeared large in the frame. Flash fill emphasized the foreground subject in the scene. I used my Konica Off-Road weather-resistant, point-and-shoot camera, its 28mm F2.8 lens, the flash-on mode, and ISO 50 film.

Portraiture

Portraits can be of individuals or groups, and made indoors or outdoors against real backgrounds. Portraits can also be shot in a studio setting against plain walls or white or colored *seamless paper*, which is also called *no-seam paper* or just *seamless*. It comes in 9-foot-wide, 36-feet-long rolls, and easy-to-carry half-width rolls. Seamless comes in white, black, grays, browns, and blues, as well as many other colors and tints. You can purchase seamless through photo dealers, mail-order houses, and catalogs (see "Resources" on page 142).

Location Portraits. Location portraits are made at sites carefully selected to complement the subject. People's homes and workplaces are often good locations. Of course, you can find wonderful location-portrait sites in streets, gardens, or gorgeous landscapes, especially when you travel (see "Quick Tips for Using Flash Outdoors" on page 40). In such places, flash is often useful for augmenting the existing light.

For location portraits, pose your subjects in a spot that doesn't overpower them. A pattern of bricks, for example,

is far too strong for most portrait backgrounds. Pay attention to unwanted objects in the background. If you notice an ugly or otherwise unappealing element, change your angle or ask your subject to move. In sunlight, expose for backgrounds, and add flash fill from up close to open up shadows on faces, in deep eye sockets, or under hats.

In good location portraiture, the subjects are obviously aware of the photographer's presence but seem unconcerned by it. The aim is often just as much to make a graphic image that symbolizes something about a profession or place as it is to make a revealing likeness of an individual. For example, you might want to photograph a truck driver with his rig against a background of a crowded highway interchange. Magazine stories about people (often called editorial illustrations), some pictures made for corporate and industrial clients, and fine-art portraits are often photographed this way.

Studio Portraits. The studio portraitist's primary aim is to get a good likeness of the subjects and, usually, to please and even flatter them. The exception is when you shoot

I photographed this toddler in a garden in low, late-afternoon sunlight. I set the TTL flash at minus .3 and bounced it out of a LumiQuest device for a subtle fill effect to suit the subject. Working with my Nikon N90 in manual mode, a 35–80mm F3.5–4.5 D zoom lens set at about 60mm, and a Nikon SB-26 flash, I exposed for 1/125 sec. at f/4 on Ektachrome 64 professional slide film.

portraits of well-known personalities for publication; a gutsy, fresh approach might be more important than flattery. A built-in flash alone is too harsh a light for flattering studio portraits, but it can be a useful adjunct if your studio has a window that lets in plenty of indirect light—but not direct sunlight. Use flash as fill light to reduce facial shadows around the subject's eyes and chin, and minimize wrinkles and contrast. If you place a person at least 3 or 4 feet from the nearest wall, the weak shadow from a built-in flash used as fill should fall well below the picture area and not record on the background. For comparison purposes, shoot any type of portrait with and without added flash to see which effects please you most. You might be surprised at the improvement that flash fill can make.

The approach that you use for studio/indoor portraits works for location portraits, too. Simply include more of the landscape, room, or office in the composition. Working with a wide-angle lens helps.

Photographing Children and Teenagers

No one is in a better position to shoot good pictures of children and teenagers than parents or those who spend a great time with them. You can't make a baby or toddler do anything at any given moment, but wonderful expressions and amusing action can happen at any time. These moments can be as short-lived as a rainbow, so keep a camera close at hand. Get down to the children's level when you photograph to meet them at their eye level. For formal portraits, think about the colors and tones of clothing and backgrounds. I prefer neutral surroundings for small children to emphasize their beautiful skin quality.

Children up to about age 12 are easy to photograph because most aren't self-conscious in front of the camera. For formal pictures, don't "over-groom" your subjects or be too fussy about perfection in their dress; this will probably cause the children to stiffen up. The best approach of all is to photograph them when they're absorbed in a game, sport, book, pet, or group of friends.

When you photograph teenagers, getting their respect is a must. Don't make yourself "uncool" in their eyes by trying to be one of the gang. If the teens are interested in photography—and many are—you've got it made. Shoot while holding their attention by explaining exactly what you're doing. Keep in mind that many teenagers are

among the very small group of individuals who are attractive enough to be photographed with hard light. So you can use flash as the sole source of light.

Photographing Men and Women

When you photograph adults, suggest that they wear their favorite clothing. Pay attention to their grooming. For "working" portraits, make sure that your subjects' attire, such as overalls and uniforms, is clean and wrinkle-free. Also, have people actually do what they're supposed to, not just pretend. If you photograph people at work, have them actually talk on the telephone, sign the letter, or read the law book. An alternate approach is to have them look at the camera as if they were interrupted while cooking, painting, hammering, or reading an X-ray.

Mature men and women are the people with most of the power in professions and trades, business and finance, education and scholarship, the arts, and of course, in the home. Careful posing can minimize any physical defects. For example, have large people sit behind a table or desk, with their hands placed in front of them. Photograph

I made this shot just as the fire captain rushed to be included in the group of volunteer firefighters. The flash fill opened up the facial shadows that the bright afternoon sun caused. Here, I used my Canon Sure Shot Max in flash-on mode, the camera's 35mm F3.5 lens, and ISO 50 slide film.

someone with a prominent nose from directly in front. Large ears call for a three-quarter angle; have the subject's eyes look directly into the camera.

Hardly anyone wants to magnify wrinkles, so place senior citizens in shade. Other options for seniors are to shoot on an overcast day, and to combine windowlight with flash fill. Don't use direct flash during senior sessions. Pay close attention to thick-lens eyeglasses; have your subjects move their heads so that reflections are minimized. Try using a flashlight at the flash position to help visualize where the flash will fall.

Most older subjects look their best when animated. So do whatever it takes to get them to smile, laugh, or talk as you keep your eye against the viewfinder and your finger on the shutter-release button. You always want to be ready to capture the relaxed moment.

Flash fill is helpful for lightening the deep shadows over eyes that the fluorescent lighting so common in offices, schools, and hospitals causes. Flash fill also corrects the greenish color of fluorescent lighting on subjects within flash range, which is a problem on color slide film.

Outdoors, *backlighting*, or the low-angled sunlight coming from behind your subjects, can rim their hair with light and look romantic. To use a built-in flash with strong backlighting, you must stand extremely close to your subjects, within 3 or 4 feet.

This picture of a cook in her kitchen is one of three grab shots that I made at twilight with my Konica Off-Road point-and-shoot camera, which has a 28mm F2.8 lens. I wanted to record the light outside the window as the blue it was, not as underexposed black. I knew from experience that a Bulb exposure would allow some available light to record on the ISO 50 slide film. After setting both the Bulb and flash-on modes, I handheld my camera while pressing down the shutter release for between 1/4 sec. and 1/2 sec. for each exposure. The flash fill corrected the color of the kitchen lights.

To show some movement in this portrait of participants in New York City's St. Patrick's Day Parade, I selected a slow shutter speed. I added the on-camera TTL flash in fill mode; the flash was softened via a Sto-Fen diffuser placed over the head. With my Nikon N90 in manual mode, a 28mm F2.8 lens, and a Nikon SB-24 flash, I exposed at f/8 for 1/15 sec. on ISO 50 slide film.

HANDLING REFLECTIONS

When you photograph people who are wearing eyeglasses, ask them to angle their heads slightly or turn sideways from the lens; then shoot from above or below the subject. For a formal portrait, ask your subjects to turn their heads away, but aim their eyes directly into the lens. Then add flash fill. A small glint on eyeglasses doesn't spoil a picture. In situations that you can't control, try to wait for eyeglass wearers to turn their heads away from the lens slightly.

These approaches minimize eye-obscuring reflections and reduce the chances of redeye showing up in the shots. If you must use flash at a distance from people, try the flash redeye-reduction mode. This puts out a "pre-flash," which in theory causes the pupils to contract, thereby lessening the redeye effect. I find that this mode often makes people blink as you take the actual photograph. To minimize the chance of losing a good flash picture because your subject blinks at the critical moment, shoot several frames.

Family celebrations offer great opportunities for people pictures. I shot from a low angle in afternoon sun to isolate this couple against the sky. Flash fill lightened the shadows, and the vantage point minimized flash reflections in the eyeglasses. Working with my Pentax IQ-70 Zoom point-and-shoot camera, I adjusted its 35–70mm F3.5–8.4 lens to 70mm, set the flash-on mode, and shot ISO 100 slide film.

Photographing Groups

Celebrations, such as weddings, graduations, and reunions, are the perfect opportunities to get group pictures spanning generations that can become heirlooms. Good group flash pictures call for careful arrangements. People must all be about the same distance from the flash for proper overall flash exposure.

Suppose, for example, you're using a program camera and a computer-controlled flash (any type), and you want to photograph three friends. If the first friend stands 4 feet from the flash; the second friend, 4 feet behind her and 8 feet from the flash; and the third friend 8 feet behind the first friend and 12 feet from the flash, only the first friend in the front of your composition will be properly exposed. The second friend will appear dark and somewhat underexposed in the frame. The third friend in the back of the image will be very dark—almost totally underexposed—because any program flash starts to cut off as soon as it hits the first person.

To compensate for this, photograph the three friends standing close together. Pose them side by side about 4 to 6 feet from the flash. All three friends will be well exposed in the resulting photograph (if your equipment is working correctly) because all are at about the same distance from the flash.

Business Situations. A safe approach to shooting formal business groups is to arrange people by height, no more than two rows deep, with the most important people front and center. Ask everyone to look into the camera except those who wear eyeglasses. Remember, you should ask those individuals to turn their heads slightly right or left, and look at the lens.

Make it routine to take several pictures of any group-the more people, the harder it is to make everyone look attractive at the same time. I ask businesspeople to look serious. For any other type of group, I try to make some at least smile by talking the whole time that I'm taking the pictures. At the end of a group shoot, some people relax and fall into interesting or revealing poses. A few extra frames taken at this point can make the difference between an average group shot and an interesting photograph.

Parties. These occasions are made for flash photography. You'll take a lot of pictures. Tips for photographing people at parties: Stand close to minimize contrast and yawning dark backgrounds. Allow enough time between shots for your flash to fully recycle, or you'll get underexposed images. At discos and Halloween parties, and on other fun occasions, try using SS flash fill with a handheld camera. The resulting impressionistic blur combined with sharpness and ghost effects might convey the feeling of the party perfectly.

Performances. Small flash units won't carry to a distant stage, and might even disturb the performers and the audience. Try shooting without flash using fast film. Better yet, get permission to shoot during rehearsals. You can also shoot portraits of performers and groups when an event is over.

It might be possible to secure advance permission from the artists or the management—preferably both—in order to photograph. When you work in a theater, shooting from in the wings can be fine. If you're allowed to shoot during any actual performance, try and get what you want in as few shots as possible to minimize the chance of creating a disturbance.

Photographing Pets

I approach pets the same way I do small children. I get down on the pets' level, and try photographing them against a neutral background. Grass, wood, or leaves are

Flash fill from a pop-up flash brightened this double portrait and lightened facial shadows. The existing daylight was sufficient enough to prevent a redeye problem. I set my Nikon N50 in general program mode, and used a 35–80mm F3.5–4.5 zoom lens at about 50mm and ISO 100 slide film.

good backdrops. Using a contrasting background in a vivid color can sometimes work for an animal portrait. Never expect a pet to do anything it doesn't want to.

Flash improves many pet pictures. Even when used at some distance, flash can add highlights to deep-set eyes even on dull days, or give shine or texture to dark fur or feathers. To diffuse the flash when working close to pets, thereby slightly softening its effect and background shadows, tape a piece of thin tracing paper or white plastic cut from a grocery bag over a built-in flash head. For a separate flash head, you can use either of these home-made diffusers or a commercial diffuser.

Keep in mind that all diffusers reduce the light output from all flashes. So when working at any distance greater than about 5 feet with small flashes and about 10 to 12 feet with detachable flashes, use the flash direct. This will maximize its effectiveness.

Quick Tips for Using Flash Outdoors

Although the L mode on cameras turns off a flash, flash can be surprisingly useful for landscape and cityscape photography in either bright sun or low light. Use wide-angle lenses or zoom settings, and work as close as possible to rocks, bushes, mailboxes, or whatever catches your eye. The trick is to set the overall exposure for the background via the S mode and maximum sync speed in bright light, or the A mode in low light. Of course, you can use the M setting if available and desired. Then simply use flash as fill light to emphasize nearby landscape or cityscape features within the flash range.

Adding Flash to Landscapes. You can never illuminate an entire landscape with flash, but you can use flash fill on a nearby shadowed rock or clump of flowers. Flash fill can lighten the tone of a dark tree trunk or fence, brighten a sign, or add highlights to a close dog, horse, or cow, or you can paint a dark landscape with flash (see page 52).

Photographing Wildlife. Some city or suburban wildlife is accustomed enough to people to be lured by food to within flash range. It is illegal to feed wildlife in national parks, but some people do anyway. So you might get lucky and have a hopeful chipmunk or deer come within range cf your small flash. Never, ever try to lure bears, bison, or other potentially dangerous animals within range of a small flash.

Shooting Sports with Flash. If you have the option when photographing sporting events, use the A mode and set a wide-open lens aperture. If you don't have those options, load ISO 400 film in your camera. When you shoot sports indoors or in low outdoor light, adding flash is useful only when the action comes within 6 feet with a built-in flash, and 10 to 12 feet with a separate flash. For greater distances, use the fastest possible film, with an ISO rating of 1000 or higher. Remember the inevitable flash falloff, and don't waste flash in situations where it can't possibly reach the subject.

Another good approach is to choose the *sport mode* if available and add flash fill. Note that with program settings, flash fill is most effective at the wide *f*-stops needed in low light; you might get your best flash results in poor weather. The speed of the flash can stop people or animals running or jumping, for example, if they are within flash range when you shoot in low light. For sporting events, take symbolic and team portraits before or after games.

Stopping Action. Proceed as you do for shooting sports. Once again, low light offers the best opportunities because wide lens openings maximize the flash range. In this type of light, conventional flash modes provide most of the illumination of subjects within flash range, and you'll get sharp, stopped images. You can successfully use flash for such subjects as (close) moving cars or bicycles on night-lit city streets; moving rides at fairgrounds; or the action at pool halls, bowling alleys, or health clubs.

Blurring Action. To blur action in low light, use the SS mode if available, or use slow shutter speeds selected in the S or M mode and add flash fill. *Pan*, or move the camera, in the same direction and speed as the moving subject. The combined sharpness and blur effects can be interesting.

First try this using the program SS flash mode (if available) with ISO 100 film. Any part of the picture illuminated only by flash will record as sharp on film, while the background will be blurred. It takes practice to get repeatable effects, and you shouldn't expect all such pictures to be great.

I posed a beloved pet on a shaded garden bench and made squeaking noises to get its attention. I focused on the animal's eyes, then reframed the image while holding down the shutter release halfway. Flash fill from my Canon Sure Shot Max, which has a 35mm F3.5 lens, in the flash-on mode added eye and nose highlights. According to the dog's owners, this picture, one of a whole roll, truly caught their pet's spirit.

Flash in the Rain. When you shoot in rainy weather with equipment that isn't water-resistant, protect your camera and flash by covering all but the lens with plastic wrap. I sometimes shoot protected by a long-handled, 48-inch photographic umbrella resting on my head and clamped under my left arm! Moisture can harm electronic equipment. Focus, for example, on damp streets, moist flowers, or wet rocks in the foreground of misty seascapes. Flash fill stops close raindrops, and brighten reds and yellows when you're shooting these warm colors in rain.

Low light in bad weather records somewhat blue on color film. Using flash will brighten all colors but especially reds and yellows on overcast or rainy days. If you're photographing people in bad weather conditions, such as rain or snow, flash will "warm up" bluish skin tones and make them look more natural.

Flash in Snow. Once again, you should protect your camera and flash if they aren't water-resistant when you shoot in inclement weather conditions. Remember that batteries slow down in the cold, and keep spare batteries—and your camera when you aren't using it—close to your body for warmth. Flash stops most falling snowflakes beautifully. Try and include something midtoned in scenes to avoid underexposure of snowy landscapes.

Backlight compensation or "plus" (+) and "minus" (-) camera and/or flash settings (where available) are often used in conjunction with a "Select" or "Set" button. These settings alter program exposures to compensate for compositions and subjects that aren't average in tone overall. (For more information, see your camera and flash manuals for specifics about your equipment, as well as Chapters 10 and 11.)

I shot this picture of a young man in the surf on a rainy evening on Long Island, New York. I determined exposure by taking a reading off the sky with the in-camera meter on my Nikon N90, which was in manual mode. I mounted the Nikon SB-26 flash on the hotshoe and aimed the flash, which was in TTL mode, directly at the subject while shooting handheld. Autofocus with a 20mm F2.8 lens helped because the foreground subject was dim against the gray sky and sea. The existing light came from the rear, so no ghosting occurred. The exposure was *f*/4 for 1/4 sec. on ISO 100 film.

Part Two
INTERMEDIATE FLASH

To shoot this closeup of a tulip, I mounted my Nikon N90 camera, which was in aperture-priority mode, on a tripod. A small *f*-stop, *f*/16, was chosen for maximum depth of field. If you don't stop down the lens, even a good TTL flash will overexpose closeups. Here, I aimed my Nikon SB-26 flash, attached by an SC-17 dedicated cord, from the side with my left hand. I used a 105mm F3.5 manual macro lens and ISO 50 slide film.

*A*fter you've used camera-controlled programs or point-and-shoot modes for a while, the next step is to learn how to use advanced camera and lens modes. You can set the aperture-priority mode and shutter-priority mode on your camera while retaining the benefits of TTL flash exposure. But true control comes when you can set your program camera manually.

How Lens Aperture Affects Flash Exposures

Lens apertures always affect how much light reaches the film and are one of the factors, along with flash power and film speed, that determine flash range. A large (or wide or low number) aperture, such as f/4, maximizes flash range. Conversely, a small (high number) aperture, such as f/16, reduces flash range considerably.

Moderate to extreme wide-angle lenses (35mm, 28mm, 20mm, 18mm, or even wider) have good to excellent depth of field (zone of sharp focus from front to back) even at wide-open apertures. Using smaller lens apertures than about f/8 or f/11 isn't desirable with small flash for anything but closeups (because of the reduction in flash range). So, if you want both good depth of field and good flash range, use wide-angle lenses. (Some people worry about the flash coverage of wide-angle lenses; I don't, as the pictures in this chapter show.)

Moderate and long telephoto lenses (and zoom lenses at the telephoto end) have shallow or extremely shallow depth of field when used at wide apertures, and only moderate depth of field when used at small apertures. This makes it easy to throw distracting backgrounds out of focus, but for flash to be effective, you must always use small-aperture telephoto and long zoom lenses at close distances, or with fast film, or both. Flash isn't effective when used with telephoto lenses beyond the indicated range for the selected aperture and film-speed combination. Remember, flash can't do everything.

How Shutter Speeds Affect Flash Exposure

When a camera shutter is synchronized with peak flash output (which is taken care of when TTL flash is used on a dedicated camera intended for it), the shutter speed visibly affects only that part of a picture beyond flash range. Camera programs always set a high shutter speed, often 1/250 sec., on sunny days to avoid overexposing backgrounds. A moderate shutter speed, almost always 1/60 sec., is set when you use flash on overcast days or at night. The intent is that backgrounds won't show blur caused by camera shake, but the effect is that flash often cuts out available background light, thereby making low-lit day pictures look like night pictures.

The *slow-sync mode* (SS) works by setting slow shutter speeds to record low-lit backgrounds combined with flashed foregrounds. I think this is the single most useful simple camera program; in fact, it is the only one I use.

Using Flash with Aperture-Priority Mode

Selecting the *aperture-priority mode* (A), when shooting with flash is appropriate in several situations. First, it comes in handy when you work with wide-angle lenses or the wide end of zoom lenses set at a moderate or small lens opening when you stand close to a subject you want to flash, but also want the background to be in sharp focus. The A mode is a good choice when you want the flash to be effective to the maximum possible distance, too. Simply select the widest aperture with any lens.

The aperture-priority option is also the right mode to choose whenever you use a manual lens on a dedicated camera. And you should also select it whenever you use

TTL flash for closeups or extreme closeups. By setting a small or minimum lens aperture, you'll prevent overexposure. This results because programs can't activate and shut off a flash instantaneously.

In all of the above situations, the camera will select what it judges to be an appropriate shutter speed. If you choose a wide lens aperture in bright light, the LCD screen or viewfinder indicator in your camera might show an error or overexposure signal. If this happens, you must reduce the lens aperture because you can't set the shutter set above maximum sync speed (or part of the light from the flash won't reach the film).

Using Flash with Shutter-Priority Mode

The camera shutter opens and closes to admit light. This factor, along with the lens aperture, controls the amount of light reaching the film, or the "exposure" of all pictures made in daylight or under continuously burning artificial lights. Shutter speeds also control motion effects and blur on conventionally exposed pictures. Fast (high number) shutter speeds stop motion, while slow (low number) ones record moving subjects as varying degrees of blur. When you combine extremely long time exposures (of several minutes) with small lens apertures, moving figures may actually disappear and not record on film at all.

A top-of-the-line program SLR camera might have a shutter-speed range from a high of about 1/2000 sec. or even 1/8000 sec. to a low of 30 seconds. Usually, you can't combine flash and the highest shutter speeds (see Chapter 10 on page 106 for exceptions when flash power is reduced). Maximum shutter speeds usable with full-power flash are 1/300 sec. or 1/250 sec. on all top 35mm electronic and manual SLR cameras. Entry-level program cameras sync at about 1/125 sec. or 1/200 sec.

Choose the *shutter-priority mode* (S) only with dedicated lenses or the camera won't be able to set an appropriate lens aperture. You should also use it when you want to know which shutter speed you're using to control motion and blur effects. As good as program SS mode is, you have no control over it and can never be sure of repeating pleasing effects.

For example, set the S mode to photograph a waterfall. Select different slow shutter speeds, from 1/30 sec. to 1 second, to vary blurred water effects. At the same time, add TTL-metered flash fill. The speed of the flash burst—a minimum of about 1/350 sec—will "stop" the motion of water droplets within flash range, as well as produce blur and sharpness effects that are possible only with flash and slow shutter speeds. You'll soon learn which speeds to set for effects that you like.

You can also apply this technique to *panning*, or following a moving subject. For example, if you set slow shutter speeds, pan with bike riders on night-lit city streets, and add TTL-metered flash as fill light, the flash will "stop" all or most of the cyclists' motion within its range. The background, which is out of flash range, will record as bright streaks on film. Vary shutter and pan speeds to achieve different effects. Be aware that you might get some *ghost*, or overlapping, images, especially if the street lighting is bright (see "Rear Shutter Curtain Sync" on page 114).

Chapter 4
DETACHABLE FLASH UNITS USED ON-CAMERA

If you own a *dedicated*, or computer-controlled, SLR camera with built-in flash but have been hesitant to add a separate flash because you thought it might be complicated to operate, relax. Most compact dedicated flashes have only a couple of controls and can be used on- or off-camera, while retaining all the benefits of computer-controlled flash exposures. Using advanced flashes with simple program camera modes can even be easy. Set the "TTL-fill" mode, and aim the flash directly at the subject.

All flashes dedicated to specific cameras have a *hotfoot* with several retractable, metal electronic contacts. The foot slides and locks onto the camera *hotshoe* over the viewfinder. The shoe has metal receptors that receive and transmit information between the camera and the flash. A detachable TTL flash physically connected to a camera by the hotshoe (or used off-camera connected to it by a dedicated cord—see page 54) deactivates any built-in flash.

Advantages of On-Camera Detachable Flash

The primary advantage any detachable flash has over any built-in unit is more power. Increased power gives greater flash range or the creative option of modifying flash effects. Compact dedicated-flash units that throw light directly forward typically have *guide numbers* (GNs) of about 56 to 66 (based on ISO 100 film, and measured in feet). This is 50 percent to 100 percent more power than the average built-in unit's GN of about 28 to 40. Just about all camera manufacturers offer a compact dedicated flash. Sunpak is a well-respected independent maker; its flash units can be dedicated to most camera brands and are well-priced.

Detachable flashes with heads that angle or swivel—some even zoom with different lenses—are bigger than compacts and have GNs in about the 80 to 130 range. They're designed to be used both on- and off-camera. A

Shooting a story on the Santa Clauses who raise money for charity in New York City during the holiday season, I got off a subway train to follow two Santas. As I stood with my Nikon N8008 camera and Nikon SB-24 flash in hand, I spotted another Santa in the moving train drifting slowly toward me. I grabbed only one shot. I aimed my on-camera flash, which was diffused with a LumiQuest bounce device, at a 45-degree angle to the train window. Working with my camera in manual mode and a 28mm F2 manual lens, I exposed ISO 100 slide film for 1/15 sec. at f/4.

GN of 120 with ISO 100 film is average for a top-of-the-line detachable unit when used with a 50mm standard lens, which is four times the power of a built-in flash. Metz is a well-known independent maker of such units that have *modules*, or adapters, for many camera brands.

More flash power means that you can choose smaller lens apertures—via the *aperture-priority mode* (A) or *landscape mode* (L) camera programs, or manually—than you can with built-in flash units. This, in turn, means increased depth of field in flash pictures. And greater flash range means that the effectiveness of the flash with telephoto or zoom lenses is increased. Another benefit of more power is that modifying the light from a flash becomes practical. To soften shadows quite effectively when using a compact detachable flash unit or an adjustable flash aimed straight forward, tape thin white fabric or plastic over the flash head. Another option is to use a frosted-plastic diffusing dome. Sto-Fen makes a small, neat one that slips snugly over a flash head and soften shadows quite effectively. Of course, the diffusing dome reduces the flash range, so I don't use it for any subjects beyond about 10 to 12 feet.

Metering through the lens aimed at the sky and working in aperture-priority mode, I deliberately underexposed this shot of a U.S. Army Band drum major by 1/2 stop. The program set the maximum flash sync speed, which on my Nikon N90 is 1/250 sec. Direct TTL flash from my Nikon SB-26 flash set at minus .3 filled the shadowed face and gave the bearskin a sheen. I adjusted my 80–200mm F4–5.6 zoom lens to about 120mm and exposed at f/16 on ISO 100 slide film.

Advantages of Compact Flash

Compact, detachable dedicated flashes marketed by manufacturers for their cameras are relatively inexpensive (about $100). Mid-price, compact dedicated flashes permit you to make some adjustments and cost two to three times as much (about $200–$300).

The most sophisticated, adjustable TTL flash units designed for on- or off-camera use have heads that you can angle in order to bounce light off ceilings, walls, reflectors, or bounce devices. Some top-of-the-line dedicated flashes, when used with appropriate cameras, permit you to adjust the programmed flash and flash-fill output (already quite accurate in most situations) for special situations. Such flashes cost more than their less complex counterparts (about $350-$500).

Even the nontechnical-minded find compact units easy to operate. The usual controls are just "On/Off" and "TTL/Manual." You simply attach the unit to your camera hotshoe, turn it on, set it to "TTL" mode, then shoot in the way you would with a built-in or pop-up flash.

Compact flash units are rugged and easy to carry. You can leave one on a camera—it alters the weight and balance very little—and it is ready whenever you need it. This is a help when you walk along city streets or hike in the country. I like compact flashes because they don't look too professional. I use one whenever I want to look like a harmless tourist and blend into the background.

I own two compact units that aim light directly at the subject when used on-camera: Nikon SB-23s, which have a GN of 66. For the most part, I use these flashes to fill shadows on faces in sunlight. Sometimes, however, I use them to warm foreground color on gray days, too. Background shadows caused by a flash unit aimed directly at a subject are rarely a problem outdoors. Compact flashes can also be used advantageously to emphasize close foreground elements in landscapes.

I came across this cow skull on a red board in Cameron, Arizona. The compact Nikon SB-23 flash that I used in TTL mode lightened the deep shadow to the right. I used my Nikon N90 in aperture-priority mode and a 28mm F2.8 D lens, exposing at *f*/16 on ISO 100 slide film.

Independent Brand Dedicated Flashes

Two independent manufacturers make compact, adjustable modular flash units for use on or off dedicated cameras: Metz and Sunpak. Metz (or Mecablitz), a German company, makes top-quality flashes dedicated to most brands. Owners of European-designed cameras favor Metz especially. Leica, Contax, and Hasselblad SLR users are probably already aware of compact and handlemount Metz flashes. Most models are sophisticated and can be dedicated to top-of-the-line Japanese cameras, too.

Sunpak flashes are well priced, and the company offers a wider range of amateur and professional dedicated and other units than any other manufacturer. Sunpak provides reliable service, too. Experts consider Sunpak electronics excellent. Most Sunpak flash units are quite rugged and simple to operate.

To help you choose a flash that is right for your needs and budget, get a complete list of camera manufacturers', Sunpak's, and/or Metz's flashes either from dealers or directly from the distributors or manufacturers (see "Resources" on page 142).

Salespeople in consumer-electronics stores might try to convince you to buy a cheap flash. But keep in mind that bargain-priced goods often aren't bargains. In my lighting workshops, I've been shown "no-name" flashes that melted at the foot when fired rapidly and an adjustable flash that fractured at the angle. A worst-case scenario would be a flash that shorted and damaged the electronics of an expensive Canon, Minolta, Nikon, or some other dedicated camera. Believe me, this can happen. Buy an inexpensive flash unit for a manual camera if you wish (see Chapter 9 on page 93). But for electronic cameras, stick to manufacturers' flashes or purchase one made by Metz or Sunpak.

▲ For this shot of a snowy churchyard in Wiltshire, England, I metered the existing light off the gray tombstones. The on-camera flash in TTL mode hit the foreground and brightened what little color there was in the scene. With my Nikon N90 camera in manual mode, a 20mm F2.8 lens, and my Nikon SB-26 flash, I exposed for 1/60 sec. at f/4 on ISO 100 slide film.

◄ Here, I metered off this New York City clockmeister's face to avoid underexposing the clock. I mounted my Nikon N90 camera and 28mm F2.8 D lens on a tripod, and put my compact Nikon SB-23 flash in TTL mode. The exposure on ISO 100 slide film was 1/15 sec. at f/8.

Wanting blur, I handheld my Nikon N90, which was in manual mode, to shoot this night parade in New York City's East Village. I metered off the middle-gray sidewalk and added TTL flash via my Nikon SB-26 flash. Working with a 20mm F2.8 lens and Fuji Sensia 100 slide film, I exposed for 2 seconds at f/2.8.

Advanced Adjustable Flash Use

In some circumstances, even the best of programmed flash exposures don't or can't give you exactly the effects you want. The biggest problems for programmed flash exposures occur when there is high contrast in a scene, and, especially, when small but important subjects or objects are much brighter or darker than the background. In these situations, some top-of-the-line dedicated flash models permit you to activate a "Select" button in order to decrease or increase TTL programmed flash exposures in 1/3- or 1/2-stop increments. This invaluable control is what makes these expensive units worth every penny to creative advanced and professional photographers.

If you think that one day you'll want to use advanced flash features, you can buy a top-of-the-line model and use it with the simple "TTL flash fill" setting and camera program modes at first. Gradually, you'll learn how to use the advanced flash settings. Note that your program camera must have adequate computer power to take full advantage of advanced flash units. Check with the manufacturer for camera and advanced flash compatibility.

Camera makers and independent equipment manufacturers offer several types of advanced dedicated/TTL flash units designed to be used on- or off-camera. The most versatile flashes are bounce units that angle in the middle and rotate. You can aim the flash sideways as well as upward; you can also flip the unit so the flash pattern conforms to vertical shots. Some small detachable flashes have heads that rotate inside the flash, thereby permitting bounce effects.

FILLING SHADOWS WITH ON-CAMERA DETACHABLE FLASH

When shooting in sunlight, you can eliminate unappealing close shadows by filling them in with flash. The process is uncomplicated because compact dedicated flashes have only two controls: "On/Off" and "TTL/Manual." With the flash locked in place on the camera hotshoe, turn the camera on, and select the desired mode (refer to your camera manual). Next, check that the flash power switch is on. If you're using a simple compact flash, set the mode switch to "TTL." If you're working with an advanced flash, you must set it to "On," and both the "TTL" and "Fill" icons must show on the flash's LCD screen.

Bounce adjustable flash off a white card at the subject if you wish. Stand well within the maximum flash range for the flash and film, and shoot (camera computers judge how much flash fill is needed).

For this shot of a vendor in a shaded booth in bright sunshine, I chose a small f-stop, f/16, to produce a saturated background. I used TTL flash at the plus .7 setting to fill the shadow area inside the booth, my Nikon N90 in aperture-priority mode, a 35–80mm F3.5–4.5 zoom lens set at about 50mm, my Nikon SB-26 flash, and ISO 100 slide film.

Direct Flash

Getting good flash exposures with a dedicated SLR camera that you've set to a program mode and combined with a dedicated TTL flash used on-camera and aimed directly at the subject is as simple as using a point-and-shoot camera with a built-in flash. Even the newest of beginners doesn't need to fear this approach. Remember, a compact flash unit ordinarily has only two controls, "On/Off" and "TTL/Manual."

I often use my advanced bounce-flash units on-camera, aimed directly at my subject. Direct flash permits me to work at maximum flash range, and I often like the look of direct flash used as fill light. When you work under pressure, the simpler the setup, the easier it is to think about the pictures—and not worry about your equipment.

A handy flash-range indicator that works only when the flash head is aimed straight forward shows on the LCD screen of my Nikon SB-26 flash units, as well as on Canon and other top-of-the-line flashes. To minimize redeye and reflections when pointing any flash directly forward, use the same techniques that you use with a built-in flash (see Chapter 3 on page 32).

Diffused Flash

Sometimes when you use direct flash, you want a *slightly* softer effect. To achieve this, you need to diffuse the flash. Commercial diffusers are translucent domes that come in various shapes and fit snugly over most flash heads. I use the plastic Sto-Fen dome (which costs less than $20). These diffusers produce a fairly soft light quality when used with flash aimed direct.

You can also make your own diffusing dome. Simply lightly sand the top of a plastic slide box. Then attach it over a flash head with tape. Placing white margarine tubs over flash heads works, as does diffusing with white tissue over the flash head.

Be aware that top-of-the-line adjustable TTL flashes have a range indicator bar that shows on the flash LCD screen only when you point the head straight forward. Using diffusion reduces flash range, so to be safe you should deduct 50 percent from the indicated maximum flash range when using a Sto-Fen dome or any other diffusing material over a TTL flash not aimed directly at a subject.

Bounce Flash

You can angle adjustable flashes that bend in the middle to "bounce," or reflect, light. These units were designed for on-camera use, thereby enabling amateur photographers to easily take flash shots of such occasions as children's birthday parties. The flashes also were meant to be aimed at the low, white ceilings found in most homes so the light would reflect softly down onto the scene.

These first bounce flashes worked so well that news photographers soon adopted them. Since low, white ceilings usually aren't available on news occasions, some clever photographer folded a 3 x 5-inch white file card and angled it over his flash. This meant that flash could be bounced anywhere, even outdoors. White file cards are still used to bounce flash. You can also cut a sturdy card from white or silver artists' illustration board. Several commercial bounce devices are options, too.

Of the commercial bounce cards available on the market, one has become a standard for professional photographers. The vinyl-covered LumiQuest is inexpensive (it costs less than $20), folds flat, wipes clean, and can be attached to most flash heads via thick rubber bands. (Vel-

Keeping your camera and TTL flash turned on and set for the prevailing light will enable you to capture unexpected moments. For this shot of a "climbing" cow, which I made in Wiltshire, England, I used my Nikon N90 in aperture-priority mode, a 20mm F2.8 lens, and my Nikon SB-26 flash. I exposed Agfa Scala 200 slide film at f/11.

To photograph this woman seated for a tea ceremony in Japan, I determined the exposure via a flash meter. I rotated the flash head, which was on the manual setting, and bounced the flash out of a 42-inch white umbrella mounted on a stand to the left and aimed down onto the subject. I bracketed by varying the *f*-stop. With my Nikon FM-2 manual camera, a 28mm F2 manual lens, and my Nikon SB-24 flash, I exposed for 1/60 sec. at *f*/4–5.6 on ISO 64 slide film.

cro patches come with the LumiQuest, but I dislike sticking Velcro onto a good flash head.) I use the most basic LumiQuest bounce cards; models that diffuse as well as bounce light reduce the flash range too much for me.

Mid-price bounce-flash units don't have many controls. You can use them on-camera aimed directly at the subject just like a built-in or compact flash. Be sure the flash is set to TTL mode when shooting. Some adjustable flashes have an LCD screen on the back. If yours does, be aware that the screen must show a "TTL" icon (symbol) and a "Fill" icon together whenever you use flash as fill in daylight. (Each flash unit is different, so study the manual that came with your flash to learn settings and icons.)

Keep in mind that bouncing light always reduces flash range. As a result, when bouncing light you must get a minimum of 50 percent closer to subjects than when using direct flash. You can comfortably photograph people, groups, room interiors, or landscape elements from a distance of about 12 feet. Remember, LCD range indicators on advanced flashes don't operate when flash heads are angled. Bouncing flash is a good—but not perfect—way to eliminate the dreaded redeye effect and eye-obscuring reflections in glasses. It solves most of these problems; however, shooting slightly down on people or having subjects angle their heads is still helpful.

Bouncing Flash for Soft Effects

Bouncing flash off low, white ceilings or walls can soften flash shadows a great deal. But this approach uses a lot of power and might cause a color shift on color films, and is the reason why professional photographers tape white bounce cards to flash heads almost universally.

Effective flash fill in sunlight is possible at up to about 12 feet from your foreground subject when you use bounce flash as fill with general camera programs. (Flash range is always reduced when you shoot in sunlight because you or the camera program must select small lens apertures, or the backgrounds will be overexposed.)

Suppose that you want to shoot direct flash exposures of people silhouetted against bright sunrises, sunsets, or water. In these situations, you must cut the flash-to-subject distance to a maximum of about 5 to 7 feet. This will enable you to achieve a correct balance between the foregrounds and backgrounds.

Bouncing Flash Off Ceilings. This old technique still works when the ceiling is low and white or nearly so. Just remember that the light will come off the bounce surface at the opposite angle to the surface it hits, like a billiard ball. Be careful not to overshoot your subject. For example, if you bounce a flash forward and angled off a 16-foot ceiling, the light will travel about 20 feet in each direction. With ISO 100 film, this distance is beyond the range of some bounce units even when set at maximum lens aperture. Use a white bounce card here. Another caution: Bouncing flash straight up at ceilings can result in deeply shadowed eye sockets.

Bouncing Flash Off Walls. Some flashes are designed to let you rotate and angle them on-camera. When you use these units to bounce the light into a corner of a room with white walls and a low, white ceiling, a very soft effect is produced. But this technique is useful only when the ceiling isn't too high or the wall too distant.

Walls can be useful bounce surfaces: the effect is sidelighting, or strong light on one side. Keep in mind, though, that any colored wall will absorb light and reduce flash distance. Also, a bright-colored wall will cause a corresponding strong color tint in color pictures.

Bouncing Flash Off Large Surfaces. When you want the softest possible bounce light, bounce your flash off a big surface. If white walls and ceilings aren't available, you can use circular, folding fabric reflectors. These reflectors, which are ordinarily white on one side and silver or gold on the other, are used by many advanced photographers who work outdoors.

Moderate-size reflectors are easy to pack and carry (prices start at about $40). Big round and oblong reflectors designed to spread light over a standing figure are useful in studios, too. Fashion photographers often use reflectors to aim light from the sun back at models, but you can bounce flash or strobe off the reflectors as well. You can hang portable reflectors on walls, tripods, or lightstands; you can also tape them up anywhere you want in order to bounce light back at a subject.

Another option is to get some white, silver, and gold artists' illustration boards. These come in 20 x 30-inch sheets (which cost about $2 to $3 each) and make good reflectors. Keep in mind, though, that they are less portable than commercial reflectors.

You might also want to buy big, silver "space blankets," which are made of thin mylar and are designed to keep backpackers and hunters warm. These blankets (which cost about $3) are highly reflective, are readily available at sporting-goods stores, and fold to nothing. To use a space blanket as a reflector, simply tape or hang it from a wall or ceiling—or anywhere really—and bounce flash off it from a few feet away. The resulting wide spread of bounce light provides a good imitation of daylight in photographs. Finally, white sheets or shower curtains hung anywhere make great reflectors.

For this baby portrait, I used TTL flash with a LumiQuest bounce device to soften the light. With my Nikon N90 in aperture-priority mode, a 35–80mm F3.5–4.5 zoom lens set at 70mm, and my Nikon SB-26 flash, I exposed at *f*/11 on ISO 100 slide film.

TAKING PRECAUTIONS WITH BOUNCED FLASH

When you work with bounce flash, you have to keep some important points in mind as you shoot. First, avoid using auto or program camera modes. They fire any attached flash whenever it is turned on in low light, even if the light can't possibly reach the subject. You'll find that you don't often use certain settings on advanced adjustable TTL flashes. To avoid accidentally changing settings when I shoot, I put black masking tape over the buttons or slides I'm not using.

Any bounce flash must always have something within range to bounce off. I've often seen people attempting to bounce flash off dark cathedral ceilings far out of any flash unit's range. Believe it or not, I've even seen bounce flash heads aimed at the sky.

Always remember that the *total* distance the light must travel—up to a ceiling and back to the subject, or out to a wall or reflector and back to the subject—

must be calculated whenever using bounce flash. If the total distance that the light must travel is greater than the range for the flash/film/aperture combination, your pictures will be underexposed. Top-of-the-line flashes indicate underexposure with a red or green signal that blinks rapidly after a shot. (To extend flash range, use the A mode.)

Finally, shortening the distance that the light must travel was the reason the white card for bouncing flash was invented—and is the reason why you should use one, too. When light needs to travel only a few inches to a bounce card, the distance the softened light can travel forward is reduced from the reach of direct flash, but not nearly as much as when you bounce flash off a ceiling. Battery life is conserved when a flash can cut off before full power is expended, and the flash recycle time is decreased.

Special Flash Situations

As mentioned earlier, getting good flash shots with clever cameras is easy when your subjects are average in tone without large areas of black or white, when the existing light isn't too contrasty, and when indoor pictures are made from moderate distances in home-size rooms. Sometimes, however, you might be photographing someone against brilliant highlights, such as sun on water, or huge shadowed areas, such as indoor arenas or night skies. The worst-case scenario is when bright light and dark shadow occur together. When this happens, a photographer's best judgments are called for; TTL-metered flash exposures are excellent a great deal of the time, but computers still can't think. In this kind of bright/dark situation, you can try to solve the contrast problem three ways: mount your camera on a tripod for a *time exposure* of several seconds, and add flash to the foreground; work with a supplementary flash; or use nonstandard techniques.

Flash Photography at Night

When using a detachable TTL flash on-camera, you can select the SS mode, which is also called the *night-portrait mode* (NP) and the *museum mode* (MS) if available for bal-anced flash pictures of people against distant, well-lit backgrounds. Such backgrounds can include floodlit buildings or monuments, or big rooms with some bright lights. Foreground subjects can be farther from the camera than with a built-in unit because of the increased flash range.

Whenever making conventional flash pictures outdoors at night or in any big, dark spaces, you should stand as close as possible to people, even with a powerful flash. The reason is subject contrast. There is a big difference between optimal exposure for light-skinned faces, white shirts, and light dresses at a distance in dark nightclubs, and that needed for, for example, closeups in well-lit restaurant interiors. High contrast can fool many computer-controlled flashes, causing light-skinned faces and other light-toned picture elements to be overexposed. By cutting out all or most extraneous background area, you reduce contrast and should have no trouble getting well-exposed pictures with any TTL flash.

But remember, flash can't do everything. At night, turn your flash off, and use the *landscape mode* or time exposures for those distant scenes and dark interiors where there is nothing worth flashing in the foreground. Use a tripod.

I made this shot of a child on a slide with my Nikon N90 camera in aperture-priority mode. I also used a 35–80mm F3.5–4.5 zoom lens set at about 50mm and my Nikon SB-26 flash; I exposed ISO 100 slide film at f/11.

For this shot of the entrance to Sydney, Australia's Luna Park, I mounted my Nikon N90 camera, in manual mode, on a tripod. With a 20mm F2.8 lens and my Nikon SB-26 flash, I exposed at f/4 for 1/2 sec. on ISO 100 slide film.

Dealing with Flash Falloff

When using any single flash, you'll get visible light falloff on totally flash-lit pictures of people or objects that are spaced down a long table or spread out in a big room. But if you use a tripod and the SS mode, and ask people to sit or stand as still as they can—in order to take as much advantage as possible of existing light—the falloff effect won't be so noticeable. Adding one or more small self-slaved flashes to such a scene can help (see below).

Flash Fill with Backlighting

Backlighting occurs when the sun, or sometimes bright water or a bright artificial light, is low or immediately behind a person's head or other silhouetted subject. This illumination can be quite beautiful, but it is often contrasty. Get in as close as possible—to within 5 feet is safest—then make flash-fill shots the same way you do when shooting in overhead sunshine. If your camera offers *backlight compensation*, try using it with flash, too (refer to your camera manual).

Flash Fill with High-Contrast Subjects in Daylight

Adding flash fill in sunlight, asking subjects to move out of areas that are partly in sun and partly in shade, and working close are the most effective ways to deal with high contrast. When using black-and-white films, you can lower contrast by overexposing subjects by 20 percent, as well as by reducing development time by 20 percent. (For more information, consult film makers' technical literature and custom photo labs.)

Flash Fill with Small Self-Slaved Flash

Sometimes using one flash on a camera can't produce the type of lighting or fill effect that you want. An easy solution might be to add one or more *self-slaved flashes* somewhere in a scene. A *slave* is a photoelectric device that is sensitive to light. In this type of unit, it is built-in; the slave fires the small off-camera flash when your flash fires. When positioned at least a couple of feet farther from a subject than the main flash, low-powered, self-slaved flashes don't affect TTL flash exposure controlled by the camera. But they can provide useful accent light. You can hide self-slaved flashes behind flowers or coffee carafes down a long table or tuck them into the dark corners of a room. You can even place one behind a portrait subject's head.

I like and use the Morris Mini Slave Wide self-slaved flash. It has a clear dome and throws a weak-shadowed light in a circle. The flash is small (about the size of a small apple) and inexpensive (the price is about $35). Morris makes a set of dome-shaped color filters for this unit.

Other types of self-slaved flash are available. Some are tiny, but they throw light in only one direction. And there are even some self-slaved flashes that you can screw into light fixtures, replacing bulbs. (Any small flash can be filled with a separate slave and used in the same manner.)

Using Ring Flashes

Ring-flash units fit around lenses and are attached with a threaded retaining ring of the appropriate size. Most ring flashes are low-power units (for information on high-power ring flashes, see Chapter 11 on page 118). These devices make taking closeup pictures with on-camera flash simple. Most top camera makers offer a ring flash as a separate unit, incorporated into a macro-type lens, or both. Sunpak makes modular, dedicated ring flashes for many popular TTL cameras. These ring flashes connect to the camera's hotshoe with an appropriate cord.

Ring flashes were first designed for medical and scientific photography, but you can use them to shoot, for example, portraits, flowers, and insects. Some nature, fashion, and beauty photographers use ring flashes extensively. When you aim them directly, they produce almost shadowless light. A distinctive soft shadow appears all around any subject placed against a wall or seamless paper background. If you want to try a powerful ring flash before buying one, you can rent one at some photo dealers.

Slow sync works in large, low-lit indoor spaces. To photograph these rug vendors in Pakistan, I used my compact Nikon SB-23 flash in TTL mode; my handheld Nikon N90 camera, which was in program-slow-sync mode; a 20mm F2.8 lens; and ISO 100 slide film.

Chapter 5

DETACHABLE FLASH UNITS USED OFF-CAMERA

After you've mastered using on-camera flash directly and with bounce cards and diffusers, your important next step is to learn how to use a flash off-camera. You can use all of the techniques you've learned so far for getting good pictures with built-in and on-camera dedicated flashes with a detachable flash off-camera. The resulting photographs can be just as good—and sometimes better. This is the one indispensible flash technique needed for successful wedding, public-relations, and news photography. Raising a flash high on a bracket and *bouncing*, or reflecting, light down onto a subject is the only way to almost entirely eliminate the unwanted redeye effects of flash reflecting off the retina. Mounting a flash high on a bracket above the lens minimizes reflections in eyeglasses, too.

Handholding a flash unit above your head, at arm's length to one side, or even below the lens are other possible ways to place background shadows where you want them. These approaches usually minimize redeye effects, reflections in glass, and *hotspots*. These are white spots on slides or prints. I often use these techniques when I shoot in zoos and museums.

You can even mount an off-camera flash on a lightstand or tripod, and bounce it out of an umbrella. This produces softened shadows exactly where you want them. Another option is to diffuse the off-camera flash via a soft lightbox for near-studio-quality lighting effects.

Dedicated Flash Cords

To use a dedicated flash off-camera, you must have a *dedicated cord*. Dedicated cords are designed to transmit computerized signals between electronic cameras and *through-the-lens-metered* (TTL-metered) flash units, and must be compatible with your equipment. The coiled cords have a shoe to connect to the flash at one end and a foot that locks onto the camera hotshoe at the other. The foot on the cord has a hole underneath that is threaded for standard *bushings*. These are the 1/4-20 threaded screws used on tripod heads, flash brackets, and lightstands that enable you to easily mount cameras and lights. The thread is standard for equipment sold in the Americas and Japan. Equipment made for use in Europe and some other countries uses a larger bushing; adapters are available.

For this wedding shot, I connected my Nikon SB-26 flash, which was fitted with a Sto-Fen diffusing dome, to my Nikon N90 via an SC-17 dedicated cord. Sometimes I held the flash high, and sometimes I rested it on the camera. The soft fill cheered up the overcast afternoon light. Shooting on Coney Island, New York, with my camera in manual mode and a 28mm F2.8 lens, I exposed ISO 100 slide film for 1/60 sec. at f/5.6.

Flash brackets are attached under a camera body and permit you to mount a detachable flash above or to the side of a lens. The advantage of using brackets is that they almost completely eliminate the possibility of ugly redeye reflections. You can also use detachable flashes off-camera by mounting them on tripod heads, or on lightweight, portable lightstands that are made of collapsible, hollow tubing and can extend to heights of 6 feet or more.

Dedicated cords are pricey (costing a minimum of about $50 and sometimes double that or more). The exact price depends on the brand and model of camera and flash used. Some dedicated cords extend to about 6 feet when stretched out; others are shorter, but you can join two of these if desired.

The ability to get TTL exposures when the flash is off-camera is one of the greatest benefits of electronic cameras and flashes. By all means, buy a dedicated cord if you make any quantity of serious flash pictures. Simply connect the camera and flash with the dedicated cord. Then using TTL-metered flash off-camera isn't complicated. All the camera and flash settings you are familiar with are available, and you still get the benefits of TTL-metered flash exposures. You can even reverse the flash,

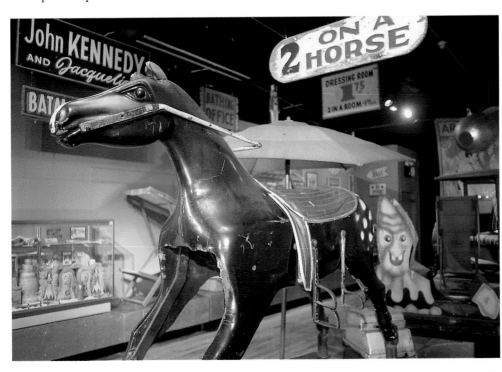

For this Coney Island, New York, scene, I mounted my Nikon N90 camera, in manual mode, and a 20mm F2.8 lens on a tripod. Then I aimed a compact Nikon SB-23 flash at the horse. The flash was attached to the camera via an SC-17 cord stretched to about 6 feet on the left by an assistant. TTL flash fill corrected the warm color. Shooting ISO 100 slide film, I exposed at f/11 for 1/8 sec.

I made this shot of Times Square with a borrowed Canon EOS 1, in manual mode, on a tripod. I held the Canon 540-EZ flash, which was in TTL mode and attached via a stretched Canon dedicated cord, as high as possible and aimed it at the statue. With a Canon 80–200mm F2.8 lens set at about 100mm, I exposed for 1/15 sec. at f/4 on ISO 50 slide film.

bounce it off a suitably placed reflector or a white umbrella, and get TTL-metered exposures (see page 58 later in the chapter). Don't confuse dedicated cords with *sync cords* (also called *sync/PC cords*), which are used to connect off-camera manual flashes—and strobe units—to manual cameras (see Chapter 9 on page 93).

Handheld Off-Camera Flash

For the most part, I use handheld off-camera flash; I don't use brackets much. When I raise a flash high and aim it down on my subject, background shadows are thrown way down, too. They don't show in the picture area even when people are standing close to walls. And, as mentioned earlier, angling a handheld flash onto a portrait or group shot reduces both eyeglass reflections and redeye. By aiming a handheld compact flash down onto flowers or insects, you can make extreme closeup flash pictures that aren't possible with on-camera flash; on-camera flash aims light beyond closeup subjects.

I sometimes use a handheld flash high when photographing at night in order to record street scenes, parades, and fans at sporting events, as well as crowds at dances, discos, fairs, and festivals. You can do the same to shoot community meetings, school events, crowd scenes, and more. Holding flash high spreads the light a little more than using a camera-level flash does, so this method is helpful for illuminating nearby landscape features or architectural elements.

With a little practice, you can learn to operate an autofocus camera plus a moderate focal length or zoom lens with one hand. This leaves your other hand free to aim the flash. If you have a shaky hand or you're using a long, heavy lens, operate the camera two-handed and support the lens to avoid blur. Have a companion hold and aim the off-camera flash for you. Taping a tiny flashlight over the head of a handheld flash might help you to aim it accurately. Practice by carefully pointing the flash head where you want the light to go.

I carry a compact TTL flash and a dedicated cord in my camera bag at all times. They add almost no weight, but they make it easy for me to get pictures that aren't possible even with on-camera flash. In zoos or aquariums, for example, I angle a compact flash by holding it as far as possible to one side. This provides flash-fill illumination without image-destroying reflections on wires or glass. When working in fields and greenhouses or at flower shows, I choose a minimum lens aperture—via the *aperture-priority mode* (A) or the *manual mode* (M)—for maximum depth of field; I aim the flash at my subject, perhaps a flower or butterfly, to freeze motion.

You can also handhold large, adjustable TTL flashes off-camera also. They provide a greater range than a compact flash; however, they get too heavy to hold for long.

Off-Camera Flash Mounted on a Bracket

When you must shoot many pictures with any off-camera flash, you can run into two problems: keeping the flash aimed accurately and fatigue. The solution to both problems is to mount the flash on a good bracket. This will enable you to comfortably center the weight, operate the equipment with both hands, and aim the light consistently. You can wind the dedicated cord needed for off-camera TTL flash exposures around the flash bracket in order to keep it out of the way.

Flash brackets come in many designs, but just about all of them raise the flash well above the lens. You can aim the flash direct, bounce a compact flash, or use an adjustable flash direct. See which technique you prefer. Remember, a flash held high via a bracket almost completely solves the redeye problem in group pictures-though nothing can eliminate it completely. (For my choices of lightweight brackets, see below.)

RECOMMENDED FLASH BRACKETS

I work with flash on a bracket only occasionally. When I need a bracket, I use the Stroboframe Quick-Flip, which is compact and quite light. This device permits me to quickly mount and dismount my camera and flash via thumbscrews. It flips to position the flash for vertical shots and is a bargain (you can find one for about $40). Stroboframe makes brackets for most camera formats. The company also markets the good Lepp double bracket designed for extreme closeup flash photography.

If I used a bracket with my 35mm cameras and flashes at all times, the bracket I would choose is the custom-made Newton. This precision bracket is light, rigid, and beautifully made, and flips over for vertical pictures. It comes supplied with Phillips-head screws for rigidly mounting the bracket to the camera tripod socket and the flash to the bracket. Kirk Enterprises makes rugged custom flash brackets, as well as a heavy-duty, double-flash bracket for closeups.

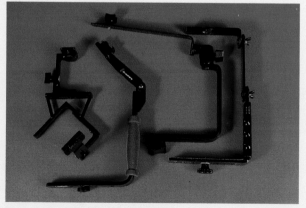

These four flash brackets (from left to right) are the Newton; the Stroboframe Quick Flip, which has been modified for closeups; the Kirk, and the Norman.

Off-Camera Lighting Accessories

If you want to use a detachable, TTL-metered flash off-camera, the first accessory you need to buy is the essential TTL-dedicated cord mentioned earlier. (Currently you can get true TTL-metered, off-camera flash exposures without a dedicated cord only a couple of ways—see Chapter 7 on page 72.) Practice handholding any off-camera flash until you are thoroughly comfortable using it; aim it from various angles at people, pets, still lifes, flowers, and even nearby landscape features. Learn about other versatile off-camera flash and lighting accessories. Don't overload yourself with gadgets—they can't make you a better photographer—but be aware that the best ones can help you solve some flash problems.

Lightstands

Lightstands make getting repeatable lighting effects much easier than handholding a camera and a flash under studio-type conditions. Bogen/Manfrotto's sturdy,

I made this closeup of a purple orchid with a 105mm F3.5 manual macro lens. I handheld the camera while a friend aimed a compact TTL flash attached to a stretched SC-17 dedicated cord from behind and down onto the flower, making it translucent. Working with my Nikon N90 in aperture-priority mode and my Nikon SB-23 flash, I exposed at f/16 on ISO 50 slide film.

lightweight stands lock firmly with quite large plastic knobs, have "stops" that prevent overextension, and come in varying heights. A 6-foot portable model that collapses for travel is fine for a first lightstand. If you use two lightstands, you can hang a reflector opposite your main light in order to control shadows.

American-made PIC lightstands have long been rugged standards, are also lightweight, come with "stops," and lock with small, knurled metal knobs. They are compact to pack, come in many heights, and are now marketed under both the PIC name and those of specialist lighting-accessory manufacturers.

When you want to achieve studio-like lighting with a TTL flash, it helps to mount the camera on a tripod, connect the flash via a dedicated cord, and then mount the flash on a stand, positioned a few feet from the camera. You'll still get the benefits of TTL flash exposures, but you can easily bounce or diffuse light on your subject. Add a lightstand to your kit if you find you need one.

One way to angle a flash on a lightstand is to mount a small *ball head* between the flash and the lightstand. A ball head is a useful locking device controlled by a knob and made by Hama and others. I use Photoflex Shoe-Mount Multiclamps. These lightweight, inexpensive (costing less than $20) devices can be angled; hold a white umbrella, which is used to bounce flash when no white surface is handy; and enable you to attach shoe-mount or threaded flash units to lightstands.

Calumet's comprehensive, photographic mail-order catalog shows pictures and prices of all of the lighting aids mentioned and more. The small Photoflex catalog featuring that manufacturer's own handy lighting aids is useful, too (see "Resources" on page 142).

Tripods

A tripod lets you set slow shutter speeds for flash (and other) pictures for which a long time exposure or a small lens aperture for great depth of field is needed. Using the *slow-sync mode* (SS) with flash fill requires a tripod if you want the landscape, cityscape, or big-room backgrounds to be sharp, and the *ghost*, or double-exposed, effects of moving subjects to be minimized.

A tripod makes composing portraits and shots of interiors and still-life subjects easier. I own four or five tripods, but for the most part I use Gitzos because of their exceptional quality and variety. Gitzo models range from tiny to enormous. I have a useful big Studex, but my favorite tripod is a Tota-Luxe model, which is compact, sturdy, and lightweight and reaches my eye-level with a camera on it (see Chapter 6 on page 62). I also own several tripod heads; my favorite is a lightweight #2 Gitzo ballhead.

Bogen/Manfrotto makes high-quality, moderate-price tripods in many sizes that are popular with both amateur and professional photographers. I own the 3001 model. It is sturdy, not too heavy, and a good height for many people (it costs about $70 without a head). Choose a Bogen ballhead carefully; I find some clumsy. Because the screws attaching tripods and heads are interchangeable, you have an alternative: substitute a Gitzo or any other

For this shot of religious treasures, I mounted my Nikon N8008 camera, in manual mode, and 55mm F3.5 macro lens on a tripod. Then I set the aperture and f-stop to exclude the existing light. My Nikon SB-24 flash, which I connected to the camera via an SC-17 dedicated cord, was at minus .5 and in TTL mode. I bounced the flash down onto the still life from a lightstand-mounted white umbrella. The exposure on ISO 64 film was 1/60 sec. at f/16.

I made this shot of London pub food with my Nikon N90 in aperture-priority mode, a 20mm F2.8 lens, and my Nikon SB-26 flash. I mounted the camera on a tripod and set the f-stop and aperture to record some existing light. I connected the flash to the camera via an SC-17 dedicated cord, selected the TTL setting, and bounced the flash down onto the landlord from a lightstand-mounted white umbrella. Shooting with ISO 100 slide film, I exposed at f/5.6 for 1/8 sec.

brand ballhead you like. Slik makes both solid professional tripods and good, lightweight, budget tripods.

A tripod that you can extend to about 5 or 6 feet high makes a useful substitute for a lightstand, especially outdoors on uneven ground. Of course, you can individually adjust tripod legs. A dedicated remote cord permits the flash to be mounted where the camera ordinarily goes. Then aim the off-camera flash from a close, flattering angle onto a seated outdoor portrait or still-life subject. Handholding the camera frees you to explore different camera angles and foreground/background relationships up to 4 or 6 feet from the subject, depending on cord length. Keep in mind that you can combine two dedicated cords.

Don't be seduced into buying any "just as good" tripod. Be especially careful to avoid inexpensive, flimsy VCR tripods. They aren't strong enough to hold 35mm still cameras securely; you can, however, use them with point-and-shoot cameras or as adequate lightstands.

Umbrellas

These are probably the easiest to use and most versatile light-modifying accessory. Translucent, white *shoot-through* photographic umbrellas are inexpensive and portable, and permit you to bounce or diffuse light anywhere. Get a first umbrella no smaller than 24 inches across; the bigger the umbrella and the closer it is to the subject, the softer the reflected light. Studio and location photographers use 36- and 48-inch opaque white or black-backed umbrellas for bouncing light. Black-backed umbrellas concentrate light to produce for dramatic deep shadows. A 24-inch translucent white umbrella from Calumet costs about $20; big (48-inch) black-backed ones, about $50.

The 1912 book *Flashlight Photography* (author unknown) I own recommends bouncing flash light out of an umbrella for soft, even light quality. This continues to be excellent advice, and today, using off-camera dedicated flash, you can use one-light bounce techniques and still get TTL-metered exposures.

You'll need a TTL camera, dedicated flash, dedicated cord, lightstand, white photographic umbrella, and some form of umbrella "clamp" or mount. First, secure the clamp or mount to the lightstand. Slide the umbrella stalk into the appropriate hole, aim it at about a 45-degree angle, secure the umbrella with a thumbscrew, and then open the umbrella. Join the camera and flash with the dedicated cord. Place the lightstand 2 or 3 feet in front and to the right or left of your subject. (Use a small flashlight taped over your flash head to help you aim the light if you wish.) Adjust the stand height so that the umbrella is about 2 feet over a seated subject's head.

Be aware that the angles and numbers discussed here aren't written in stone, but they are good starting places for many human and still-life subjects. Experiment, but remember always that the larger the bounced or diffused light source and the closer it is to the subject, the softer the light.

When bouncing light from an umbrella, be sure that the total distance the light must travel, from the flash to the umbrella and back to the subject, is well within the flash range. I bounce a single flash from an umbrella placed no farther than about 3 to 4 feet from my subjects, and I often work with the umbrella as close as 2 feet. At these distances, the flash must travel only about 4, 6, or 8 feet, respectively.

Close light is almost always flattering, and allows you to select relatively small *f*-stops, such as *f*/8 or even *f*/11 via the A or M modes. I use an 80mm moderate telephoto lens for most studio-type portraits; when combined with those apertures, this focal-length lens permits good depth of field. If I were to bounce flash from farther away, it would look harsher. In addition, I would have to use wide-open apertures and might not be able to hold the whole subject in focus.

For portraits, start by choosing a lens or zoom range of between 35mm and 80mm. Stand 3 to 4 feet from your subject, and frame the individual through the camera viewfinder. (Take care not to extend the dedicated cord so far that you risk pulling over the flash, lightstand, and umbrella.) Then turn on the camera and flash, check the camera and flash settings, focus, and shoot. Experiment with different stand placements and umbrella angles to vary the light.

A light aimed down and almost directly in front of a subject is called a *beauty light*. This type of light shows every detail and is flattering to the best-looking subjects. A *sidelight*, which as its name suggests is aimed from the side; it emphasizes texture and character lines on faces. A *high three-quarter light*, aimed down from about 2 feet above and 2 feet to one side of the subject, works well for many portraits and still-life subjects.

A white or silver reflector attached to a second lightstand, placed so that it is a mirror-image of the umbrella setup, improves many one-light pictures. By reflecting the flash so that light is bounced into the shadowed side of the composition, the reflector reduces contrast.

Self-Slaved Flashes

In photography, a *slave* is a device that responds to a signal and *fires*, or triggers, any flash or strobe that it is attached to. *Self-slaved* means that the slave is built-in and activated whenever the flash unit is turned on. Self-slaved flashes are low-power, light-sensitive units designed to be triggered by another flash. Because light travels so fast (186,000 miles per second), any slaved flash will appear to go off at the same instant as the "trigger flash."

With bounce or diffused flash as the main light on, for example, a portrait or a still life, you can use one (or more) tiny self-slaved flashes to separate foregrounds from backgrounds. These flashes also provide accent lights and brighten dark corners of rooms. You can use gaffer tape to attach self-slaved flashes under household lampshades to replace low-wattage bulbs, or to attach them to walls in order to add a *hairlight* to portraits. When set farther from a subject than the main flash, a low-power, self-slaved flash doesn't affect the TTL-metered flash exposure. (Any flash with a small separate slave attached can be used instead of a self-slaved flash.)

Portable Reflectors

Reflectors increase lighting versatility, especially when you use only one main light. The most convenient reflec-

I made this portrait in a darkened room using my Nikon N90, an 80mm F1.8 lens, and my Nikon SB-26 flash, which was connected to the camera via two joined SC-17 cords. Shooting ISO 200 film, I chose aperture-priority mode and set *f*/11 on the lens. I bounced the flash, which was in TTL mode at minus .7, into an 18-inch silver umbrella that was about 2 feet in front of the subject. A silver Photoflex reflector positioned 1 foot behind the subject provided flash fill.

tors are round or oblong, collapsible, fabric models in sizes from about 12 inches to 72 inches. I find reflectors that are 24 inches and 36 inches in size to be the most useful, as well as the easiest to hold, to hang on lightstands or tripods, and to pack. Larger sizes work well for full-length figures and small groups. Reflectors made of 24 x 36-inch sheets of white, silver, or gold artists' illustration board are inexpensive. Many fashion and studio photographers use these devices to reflect light. In a pinch, use anything—aluminum foil, a white sheet, or even a newspaper held close—to reflect light into the dark side of a subject and reduce contrast.

Silver reflectors kick back the most light. Gold ones are highly effective, too, but they give a sunset effect to the filled shadow area of color pictures. White reflectors produce subtle fill effects.

I like Photoflex collapsible reflectors. They come in white, silver, and gold to bounce or reflect light, and in several finishes, shapes, and sizes. They are more rigid than some other brands when used in windy conditions.

The California Sunbounce is a rigid but collapsible professional reflector. In some shooting situations, you might want to intensify contrast, such as when you're photographing a white-on-white composition. This is when black reflectors, which are designed for this specific purpose, come in handy.

Clamps and Adapters
Several small A-type clamps are useful for hanging background material, attaching reflectors to stands or tripods, and more. These clamps cost a few dollars each at photo dealers, and less at hardware stores. Photoflex makes my favorite flash-to-umbrella adapter. This device permits bouncing any flash attached to a dedicated cord from an umbrella of any size aimed at any angle (and costs less than $20).

Diffusers
When you aim a flash through any shoot-through, translucent white umbrella, the light is diffused, not bounced. Use the umbrella adapter, and aim the umbrella at the subject. This reflects the umbrella ribs on shiny surfaces, however, and is the reason why some clever individual invented the softbox. I use softboxes for still lifes and many studio portraits (see below).

Diffused light is soft and flattering to many types of subjects. To diffuse a TTL flash mounted on a stand connected to the camera by a dedicated cord (or two joined dedicated cords), aim the flash through white sheets, white shower curtains, or white plastic bags. Diffusing materials from Rosco or Kodak are made specifically for this purpose. Hang or tape up the diffusing material. Black-backed diffusers mounted on special collapsible frames and enclose flash or strobe heads are *softboxes*, or *lightbanks*. These are useful (see below).

Precise diffusion effects always depend on the thickness of the diffuser, whether or not it is backed with black, and the angle and distance of the diffused light to the subject. The thicker the diffuser, the softer the light. Experiment to find which effects please you.

Portable Softboxes. Convenient, lightweight, collapsible fabric softboxes (lightbanks) have been popular for years with location photographers who use professional flash or strobe lighting. All except the largest fold small for travel. Softboxes are mostly black-backed, scattering no light behind them. When you angle them on a bracket or lightstand, the result is a controllable diffused light that looks much like window light. Softboxes even reflect as window-like rectangles on shiny surfaces. Small softboxes

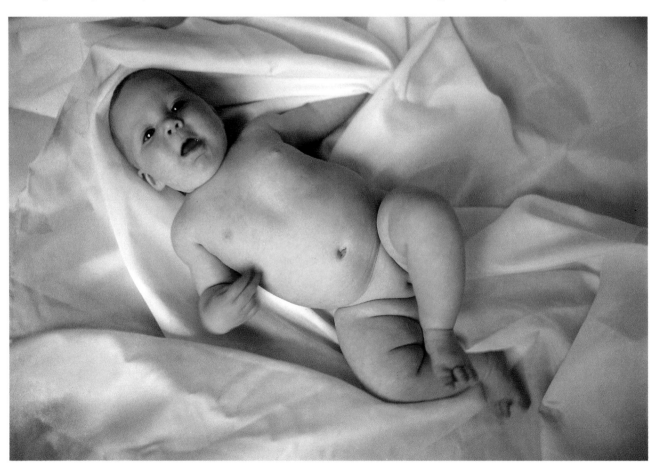

For this shot of a baby on a white sheet, I determined the exposure using a flash meter. I attached my Nikon SB-24 TTL flash in manual mode to my Nikon N8008 via an SC-17 dedicated cord. As I worked, the baby's mother aimed the flash at an angled white reflector to produce a soft bounce effect. I bracketed by varying the f-stops. With a 35–80mm F3.5–4.5 zoom lens set at about 50mm, I exposed at f/8–f/11 on ISO 64 slide film.

that you can use with one flash inside were recently introduced. These are excellent for portraits and still lifes when positioned close to the subject.

I use Chimera softboxes. These are well-priced and sturdy, and diffuse light evenly. They come in on-camera, mini, midi, large, and huge sizes. I find them to be the easiest softboxes to assemble and take apart. In addition, the Chimera softboxes collapse and roll up small, which make them perfect for travel.

With flash, I like the Chimera Midi 16 x 24-inch softbox and use it for many portraits and some still lifes. For portraits, I aim this softbox from slightly above and almost directly in front of my subjects. For easy still-life lighting, I raise the softbox so that the flash illumination shines almost straight down, from about 2 feet above and slightly behind the setup. (You can aim a flashlight through the back of the softbox onto your subject, to help you place the light just where you want it.) The light quality from a softbox is excellent when used close. A distance of 3 to 4 feet from the subject is best. I shot some of the portraits in this book this way.

Retaining Rings. These devices, made by Chimera and other softbox manufacturers, hold lightbanks in an extended position. The manufacturer also offers an adapted retaining ring made especially for small flash units. This accessory enables you to securely attach any TTL flash on a dedicated cord to the ring via a thumbscrew. This ring attaches to lightstands with an adjustable clamp than can angle the softbox. The same ring adapter works for tiny, moderate, and midsized lightbanks (and costs about $65). If desired, you can mount two or even three flashes on the ring.

Gaffer Tape
After the dedicated cord and a tripod, the one lighting aid I would never be without is gaffer tape. This tape, which was invented by a movie electrician, lets you attach many things, including small flashes, to walls. The tape comes in rolls of several widths, generally in its original gray color, although it is now available in black and several bright colors, too. Gaffer tape doesn't take paint off walls if removed reasonably promptly. It is great for hanging backgrounds, reflectors, diffusers, and small self-slaved flashes. I use black gaffer tape for all of the above tasks, as well as to attach small umbrellas to flash heads and to make emergency repairs to cameras, stands, tripods, travel bags, and clothes.

Don't confuse gaffer tape with the inexpensive duct tape available from hardware stores. That tape is quite sticky and can damage fragile surfaces.

Working in Nashville, Tennessee, I mounted my Nikon N90 camera on a tripod and covered my Nikon SB-26 flash head with a Sto-Fen dome. To balance the exposure of the royal blue sky, the bright neon sign, and the couple, I metered off the sky and then bracketed. I varied the shutter speeds, *f*-stops, and flash fill (by using TTL minus settings). The best exposures were at 1/4 sec. and *f*/5.6 settings with TTL flash at minus .3.

Chapter 6
FAVORITE SUBJECTS

By now you've probably noticed that I mostly use wide-angle lenses for my flash pictures. These lenses don't distort much if you hold them level and are diligent about placing people and other favorite intermediate-level subjects, such as flowers and pets, away from the edges of the frame. Wide-angle lenses force you to shoot up close for good-sized foreground subjects, thereby making your pictures more intimate. Wide angles work well for interiors and landscapes, too). Flash up close permits you to use small *f*-stops to ensure good depth of field (which is the zone of sharp focus). Remember the Inverse Square Law? As mentioned earlier, this states that light from any single point source falls off according to the square of the distance from the subject.

In addition to dedicated cameras, dedicated and manual lenses with different focal lengths, compact and adjustable *through-the-lens-metered* (TTL-metered) flashes, and dedicated cords, I use a few favorite accessories on a routine basis when photographing my favorite subjects (review Chapter 5). A tripod is far and away the most important of my flash-photography aids because my technique is to use as much available light as possible, even in low-lit situations. This approach calls for exposing for the background light and adding flash fill in order to improve the quality of the light on the foreground, to emphasize foreground subjects, and/or to correct foreground color.

My favorite Gitzo Tota-Luxe tripod is chipped and battered from frequent use because it goes with me almost everywhere. It allows me to pre-compose the backgrounds of location portraits and arrange still-life subjects from the perspective of the viewfinder. Using a tripod means that I can choose small lens apertures (which usually require slow shutter speeds) for landscapes, and level the camera for distortion-free architectural and interior shots. I can also minimize or eliminate blur when I want slow shutter speeds or time exposures for low-light and night pictures with flash added to the foreground (if any of these options are available). Tripods are a must with long, heavy telephoto lenses.

I also routinely use rechargeable 6V batteries to power my flash instead of disposables. Other essential aids are a Sto-Fen diffusing dome and a LumiQuest bounce card device, and a roll of black gaffer tape. I carry a few filters, including a 30M (magenta) filter used over lenses to correct for average fluorescent lights, and a flash-head-size sample pack of Rosco gels in case I need or want color over my flash. (Gels are pieces of colored gelatin sheets.) For example, a 30M filter on the lens requires a Full Plus green gel on the flash head for correct color of both the foreground and background (see page 67 for more information on color filters and gels).

People in Their Environment

To photograph people in their surroundings, I use wide-angle lenses or zoom settings. I place subjects away from the edges of the composition, so that distortion will be minimal, and expose for the background if it is bright and add flash fill. I like to slightly underexpose a low-lit background.

When shooting location portraits, don't settle for the wrong spot in an interesting area; ask your subject to

For a story about social functions, I exposed to record the existing light in this popular party location in Long Island, New York. I handheld my Nikon N90, which was in manual mode, and 20mm F2.8 lens. An assistant held a Nikon SB-26 flash in TTL mode mounted on a collapsed lightstand and attached to the camera by two joined SC-17 cords. He aimed the flash as I directed. Here, I instructed him to point it down toward the girls. The exposure on ISO 100 slide film was *f*/2.8 for 1/15 sec.

move—politely of course. If someone who is paying you demands a shot be made "right here" and you don't like the place, take the picture the subject wants. Then suggest trying a few more photographs against another background, explaining why you want to try it.

People in Action

When you add flash fill in low light, *ghosting*, or the overlapping of foreground and background images, and blur effects frequently occur. To minimize them, use the highest shutter speeds and widest lens apertures possible. When you use flash fill in bright sunlight or backlight, your camera's top flash sync speed will restrict your *f*-stop options. So in any bright light, expose for the brightest area of the background, stand as close to the foreground subject as possible to maximize flash effectiveness—a wide-angle lens helps—and add TTL-metered flash as fill.

Photographing sports action with a telephoto lens and adding flash fill is possible at distances within the flash range, and can be effective in low light. Expose for the background using the widest lens aperture possible, set the flash in *TTL-fill mode*, and aim it directly at the action. Professional sports photographers use tripods or monopods with long lenses in order to minimize picture blur caused by camera shake. The use of a *teleflash* device will extend the flash range somewhat (see Chapter 11 on page 118).

Formal Portraits

When you shoot formal portraits, mount your the camera on a tripod. This arrangement helps you pre-compose backgrounds, and maximizes the possibilities of taking advantage of any window or existing light when you select slow shutter speeds and use flash as fill. I sometimes reverse my flash and bounce it off a reflector that is either hung or held by someone else close to the flash and aimed down at my subject. At other times, I attach a small umbrella to the flash head using gaffer tape and bounce its light off the subject.

All of these techniques make the light source flattering to most subjects. When using these approaches, you should remember to work close to your subject to compensate for the reduced flash range.

Birds and Animals

Light an animal or bird portrait as you would a human portrait by bouncing flash out of an umbrella if you wish. Use direct flash to add highlights to the eyes and a sheen to the dark fur or feathers of domestic or wild creatures within flash range. Maximum apertures and teleflash devices extend the flash range when you shoot with long lenses (see Chapter 11 on page 118).

I shot this fast-moving backlit subject in slow-sync mode. The in-camera meter was in wide-area mode. The program set the shutter speed, aperture, and on-camera TTL flash fill. Program settings produce creative limitations. This picture is well exposed, but if I'd chosen manual mode and varied the aperture, shutter-speed, and fill settings, I could have reduced or eliminated the man's arm and leg motion. I used my Nikon N90 in manual mode, a 20mm F2.8 lens, my Nikon SB-26 flash, and ISO 100 slide film.

Shooting in New York City's Grand Central Station, I exposed for the existing light, bracing my camera against a balustrade. A TTL flash can't be angled to aim down when attached to a camera hotshoe, but by using a bracket and a dedicated cord I was able to angle my Nikon SB-26 flash. Although the area was huge, the closest people small, and the flash blinked to indicate insufficient range, some fill light did hit the people in the foreground. With my Nikon N90 in manual mode and a 20mm F2.8 lens, I exposed ISO 100 slide film for 1/4 sec. at f/8.

Flowers and Nature Closeups

For extreme closeups of these popular subjects, you must use a detachable flash; a built-in flash will overshoot the subject. You should select small *f*-stops for two reasons. First, small apertures maximize the depth of field possible with a lens of any focal length. This is especially important for closeups because the inherent depth of field with any lens focused close is shallow.

The second and even more important reason to use small *f*-stops for closeups is that the light from a flash used up close is quite bright, and it takes a short but perceptible amount of time for a TTL-metered flash to peak and then turn off. So if you use a wide aperture, the subject might be overexposed before the in-camera computer has had time to signal the flash to shut down.

Landscapes and Cityscapes

At dawn or dusk or in bad weather, foregrounds might be shadowed while skies are bright. An alternative to using a *graduated filter* (which shades from dark to clear and can reduce the light of the sky) is to expose for the bright area of a backlit landscape and add flash fill to the close foreground. Aim the flash at rocks, bushes, flowers, an animal, or a person in the foreground of the landscape. A wide-angle lens helps in this situation, and a tripod is a must in low light.

Adding TTL flash to a close object or person in a street or cityscape or large public space is very easy. Aim an on- or off-camera flash at cars, reflective signs, theater or movie marquees, or people within flash range. Shoot displays in store windows by angling the flash to the glass to avoid hotspots or problems with autofocus. Take pictures in, for example, subways, bus and train stations, and airports.

When shooting at night or in low light, choose slow shutter speeds or the SS mode and expose for the background. Be sure to meter off a sidewalk rather than bright lights. The shutter speeds must be slow, while the apertures

▲ The aperture-priority mode on my Nikon N90 camera selects 1/60 sec. as the sync speed in low light. This setting, combined with the *f*/8 I chose for extensive depth of field, meant that this portrait was illuminated only by flash, freezing any of the child's motion. I mounted my Nikon SB-26 flash, which was in TTL mode and connected via an SC-17 cord, on a lightstand. Then I bounced the flash on the family off a 24-inch white umbrella that was about 3 feet away. I also used a 35–80mm F3.5–4.5 zoom lens set at about 50mm and ISO 100 slide film.

► The wild-fox population of New Jersey's Island Beach State Park approaches close, looking for handouts (even though it is against the law to feed the animals), especially in winter. I mounted my Nikon N90 camera, in manual mode, and a heavy 80–200mm F2.8 zoom lens set at 200mm, on a tripod at the roadside. In low sun, the TTL flash easily reached 30 feet at the moderate aperture selected, thereby filling dark shadows. I photographed this red fox on ISO 100 film for 1/125 sec. at *f*/5.6.

must usually be wide. Use a tripod to minimize background blur and ghost images of flashed foreground subjects moving in front of lit background areas.

Snow and Rain

Use a clear *ultraviolet* (UV) filter to protect your lens. (I keep UV filters on all my lenses instead of lens hoods at all times.) To shoot in snowy and rainy conditions, protect your camera and flash with a clear plastic freezer or dry-cleaning bag. Use rubber bands or tape to seal the bag(s) around camera, lens, and flash if the weather conditions are severe. You should frequently wipe the UV filter with a facial tissue while you work. (I don't worry about dust specks from the tissue, but if you are super fussy, follow up with a wipe with lens-cleaning tissue.)

In severe weather, you should change film only in a protected spot where moisture won't get inside your camera, and dry off the camera carefully before proceeding. In cold conditions, be sure to keep your camera and flash warm inside your jacket when not in use. Once again, remember that batteries lose efficiency in the cold, so carry spares.

When shooting in snow or rain, underexpose the backgrounds slightly and add flash fill to emphasize flakes or drops. The flash will make close snowflakes sparkling white. Effects aren't very predictable, so shoot plenty of pictures. You might also want to do what I often do: bracket background exposures by slightly varying the *f*-stop.

In rain, experiment with different shutter speeds. It is possible to record rain as out-of-focus droplets or as streaks. If it isn't raining hard and you eliminate dark skies, puddles, and reflective ground from your composition, the picture will almost look as if you shot it on a partly cloudy day. For example, flash popped onto a nearby group of flowers in a drizzly English garden can have the surprising effect of brightening up the whole landscape.

When you've finished your wet- or cold-weather shooting, place your camera, flash, and film in containers, inside in a large, plastic, zipper-lock bag. Squeeze out the air and seal the bag before entering a warm room. When you do this, moisture will condense on the outer surfaces, but it won't reach the delicate camera and flash mechanics and electronics, or condense on the film. Wait for the moisture to dry before opening the bag.

Using TTL flash on foreground plants in poor weather is a favorite trick of mine. In this shot of Queen Mary's Garden at Hampton Court Palace, England, the sun is suggested even though it was drizzling. I used clear plastic to protect my Nikon SB-26 flash. With my Nikon N90 in manual mode and a 20mm F2.8 lens, I exposed ISO 100 slide film for 1/30 sec. at *f*/8.

For this shot of the MGM Grand Hotel lobby in Las Vegas, I exposed to record the existing light. I mounted my Nikon N90 camera, in manual mode, and a 20mm F2.8 lens on a lightweight tripod. The Nikon SB-23 flash, which is my favorite compact/backup TTL flash, can't be angled on-camera. But by attaching it with an SC-17 dedicated cord, I can aim it wherever I wish. Here, I aimed it up at the ceiling. The exposure on ISO 100 slide film was f/2.8 for 1/15 sec.

Architecture and Interiors

Once again, the secret to shooting these favorite subjects is to expose for the background and add flash fill to foreground objects or people. Because wide-angle lenses and moderate-to-small f-stops maximize depth of field, you must be very close to an object you're flashing. An old technique known as *flash painting* can light spaces that aren't too big or high. Here, full-power, multiple flash pops are set off around a room by using the test button (see Chapter 11 on page 118 for more information about this technique).

Still Lifes

Any found or created arrangement of inanimate objects is a still life. You can shoot still lifes against plain or colored paper or fabric studio backgrounds. You can also place still-life subjects in an interesting location, which is an approach I like.

It is important to be able to visualize flash effects and the placement of shadows when shooting still-life objects. Do this by shooting in low outdoor light, or darkening an indoor work space and taping a small, flat flashlight over the flash head. With this aid, you should be able to see and adjust flash effects. You can usually create artistic effects by taking the flash off-camera, mounting it on a

While shooting the Treasure Island Hotel exterior in Las Vegas, I realized that a small flash couldn't balance the foreground exposure with the bright backlight at the 30-foot range needed to frame the hotel entrance. So I used a high shutter speed and a wide-open f-stop to record some sky color; this combination underexposed the foreground by a stop. I knew that the flash fill from my Nikon SB-26 flash would be able to reduce the contrast at that aperture and distance. With my Nikon N90 in manual mode and a 20mm F2.8 lens, I exposed for 1/125 sec. at f/2.8 on ISO 100 slide film.

lightstand, and connecting it to the camera with a dedicated cord. Then you can bounce the flash off an angled collapsible reflector, a hanging sheet, or a white umbrella and onto the subject.

Experiment with positioning the flash and reflector or umbrella so that the light falls on the subject at different angles. For the softest possible shadows, keep the flash-to-subject distance small, and use a reflector opposite the main light source.

Glass, metal, and other reflective objects are best photographed with the light source shone through a diffusing device. Commercial softboxes or portable lightbanks often come in handy for these subjects (review Chapter 5, and see Chapters 10 and 11).

Adding Color with Filters and Gels

If you must shoot color pictures in a dreary place or on a dreary day, adding color accents via the use of color gels (pieces of colored gelatin sheet) over a flash might help. For example, throw red light from a gelled flash onto a gray factory wall, or use a pink gel on your flash to highlight a low-lit musician in a club. Blue light suggests police and hospitals.

Other possibilities include working with warm, orange gels to blend flash with household-type lighting. Use a second, self-slaved flash without a gel for a white-light accent if desired. Another option is to use the main flash in the usual way, and a color gelled self-slaved flash as a small bright accent somewhere in the scene. Take a look at an example of the work of Chip Simons, a master of using color gels with flash (see the Gallery on page 129).

When you use gels or filters with flash, keep the following lighting basics in mind. If you put a color filter over a lens, the entire picture will take on the color or tint of the filter. If you place a gel over a flash head that is the sole light source in a picture, the resulting image will also be colored the same as the gel. But if you put a color gel on a flash head, expose for the background, and

To shoot this kitchenware, I used two slaved automatic flashes, mounted on stands, in manual mode and taped yellow and blue gel over the flash heads. I read the exposure with a flash meter; automatic sensors don't give accurate results when two or more flashes are used together. Working with my Nikon FM-2, a 55mm F3.5 macro lens, two Vivitar 283 flash units, and two Wein Peanut slaves, I exposed at f/11 for 1/60 sec. on ISO 100 film.

add flash for fill, only the flashed area will take on the color or tint of the gel.

Accurate color can be important. To achieve it, photographers often use color filters on lenses to correct such problematic factors as fluorescent lighting. Fluorescent lights record green or very green on daylight slide films. In the case of common, cool-white fluorescent lamps, putting a 30M filter on the lens is the standard way to solve the "green" problem. So if you're shooting in an office, hospital, school, or factory in existing light alone, the resulting color slide images will look natural if not perfect.

Suppose that you want to emphasize a foreground person or object in a scene in which you've corrected the overall color by placing a 30M filter on your lens. If you

For this shot of poker machines in Laughlin, Nevada, I exposed and bracketed for the screens showing the cards, using my camera on a lightweight tripod in the dimly lit casino. I taped a blue gel over my compact Nikon SB-23 flash's head. The screens and bright signs were minimally if at all affected by the gelled light, but the shadowed TTL flash-filled areas recorded as deep blue on the ISO 100 slide film I used. With my Nikon N90 in aperture-priority mode and a 28mm F2.8 D lens, I exposed for 1/4 sec. and 1/8 sec. at f/4.

If you use a filter on a lens, you must use the complementary-color filter or sheet of gel on the flash or strobe; otherwise, the flashed area will take on the color of the filter on the lens. For example, placing a magenta filter on a lens requires putting a green gel on the flash or strobe.

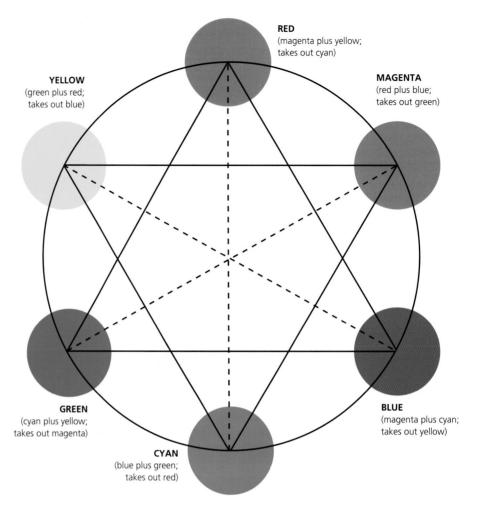

RED
(magenta plus yellow; takes out cyan)

MAGENTA
(red plus blue; takes out green)

YELLOW
(green plus red; takes out blue)

BLUE
(magenta plus cyan; takes out yellow)

GREEN
(cyan plus yellow; takes out magenta)

CYAN
(blue plus green; takes out red)

don't make another correction, the subject or object within flash range will take on the magenta tint of the 30M filter. To correct the color of the flashed area, you must tape a gel that is the *complementary color*, or exact opposite color, of the filter over the flash head. In other words, make the color of the flash the same as that of the fluorescent light. So use a 30G (green) gel on the flash.

Rosco is a well-known manufacturer of photographic and theatrical gels. You can buy its products, which come in 20 x 30-inch sheets at any good photo dealer. Useful, small-flash-head-sized Rosco sample books are often available free from dealers. They are also available directly from Rosco (see "Resources" on page 142).

With the Rosco identification system, the correct gel to balance a 30M filter is called the "Full Plus Green" gel. It is, as you would expect, light green. If you use a 30M filter on your lens and the Full Plus Green gel taped over the flash head to produce foreground fill light, the colors of both the foreground and background will be correct on color slide film.

Similarly, suppose you're shooting under tungsten lights, which are continuously burning lights, and using fill flash on the foreground. Here, you must balance any deep blue filter used on the lens to correct overall color with an appropriate orange gel on the flash head (for more information about filters, gels, and color compensa-

tion for professional flash and strobe use, see Chapters 10, 11, and 12).

Copying Art, Artifacts, and Documents

You can shoot good slides or prints of fairly small, nonreflective pictures and documents that aren't behind glass with a single flash unit. First, tape or hang the subject, whatever it is—a painting, photograph, document, or book, for example—so that it lies flat on wall, easel, or table. You might have to use taped-down, invisible, nylon fishing line filament over a book or album to keep the pages flat. I shoot paintings on an artist's easel. Since few paintings fit a standard photograph format, such as 4 x 6 inches or 8 x 10 inches, I hang small pictures with push-pins tacked into the center of a large piece of hardboard covered by black felt. I lean large paintings against a black background.

The next step is to put your camera and flash in the *aperture-priority mode* (A). This sets a high enough sync-speed/aperture combination to exclude daylight, which can cause unwanted reflections. Then center the lens on the subject. Make sure that the camera is level from side to side and at the same angle as the painting. A small spirit level and a grid drawn in marker or pen on a sheet of clear acetate are both helpful aides if you need to make a number of copies.

Next, bounce a lightstand-mounted, off-camera flash at one of two sheets of white artist's illustration board placed close on either side of the subject. The bounced light will travel back and forth, so the overall lighting will be even. If the subject is important, and especially if it is predominantly white, bracket the exposure. Use the *flash-select mode* if you have one to do this. If not, set a higher ISO speed on the camera, which will transmit this information to the TTL flash, so that the flash will put out less light. Do the reverse if more light is required. For example, if the film-speed rating of the film you're using is ISO 100, setting the camera on ISO 125 or ISO 80 will measurably alter the exposures.

For the best results and even framing, use a tripod. To shoot directly down on your subject, use a tripod boom arm. Bogen makes a good one that fits any tripod that permits using interchangeable heads.

To copy a picture behind glass, you need two flashes, and must carefully angle them at a white reflector to avoid hotspots in the glass. To photograph such objects as sculptures, masks, pottery, small products, and valuables, review the suggestions for lighting still lifes (review page 66). To shoot frame-filling closeups of tiny objects, you might need a *macro* lens. An alternative is to use an inexpensive *extension tube* between your camera and lens. These tubes come in different lengths of about 8mm, 15mm, and 27mm.

The Nikon set of manual tubes I own were inexpensive (costing about $50) and work fine. The extension tubes require using the A or M camera mode, and manually setting a small *f*-stop on the lens. I prefer to use *f*/11 or *f*/16. A 50mm lens and a telephoto or zoom lens in the 70–220mm range accommodate the tubes well. Using this setup and my Nikon N90 and dedicated Nikon SB-26 flash, I am able to get all the benefits of TTL exposure and TTL flash fill without having to calculate exposure formulas.

I simply mount an extension tube between the camera and lens, focus, and take the picture. If a tiny object is too small in the picture area at closest focusing distance for a given tube, I use a higher number tube, or combine two or even three tubes. I almost always use a tripod to ensure the best results. For closeups, depth of field is always extremely limited.

If accurate color is important for the copy work you're doing, you should include a standard Kodak Color Control Strip in the first frame, and possibly in all of the pictures. You can tape this strip, which comes in both small and large sizes, near the top or bottom of any flat, copied work—be careful not to obscure any part of it—to serve as a guide for the color lab, separator, or printer. The strip will be cropped out later (see Chapters 10 and 11 for more information).

I photographed this 18th-century polychrome angel head, which is about 1/4 human size, in a church in Strasbourg, France. I used my Nikon N8008, a 35–70mm F2.8 lens at 70mm, and an on-camera Nikon SB-24 flash in TTL mode. Shooting the angel head from about 2 feet away, I wanted to minimize reflections and achieve good depth of field. So I set *f*/11 in aperture-priority mode with ISO 100 film and used the flash with a LumiQuest Pocket Bouncer device.

Part Three

ADVANCED FLASH

For this shot, made on a Long Island, New York, beach just after sunset, I metered off the sky. Handholding my Nikon N90, complete with a 20mm F2.8 lens and a Nikon SB-26 flash, I exposed for 1/15 sec. at f/4 on ISO 100 film.

*B*ecoming an advanced flash photographer isn't a matter of magic, but of continually honing your skills and sharpening your vision by shooting plenty of pictures and keeping track of what works visually and what doesn't. You don't run before you crawl and then walk, and you don't drive on a busy interstate at rush hour before practicing on quiet roads. Race-car drivers practice all the time and might even get special training. Why should photography be any different? Once you've mastered basic and intermediate flash techniques, acquiring advanced ones will come quite naturally.

Light Quality

When you first shoot pictures with serious flash equipment, you'll be happy to get a well-exposed image. Soon, however, you'll demand more. In order for you to use lighting well, it is critical that you know how to vary highlight-to-shadow relationships, as well as how to achieve hard, soft, sparkling, or other effects. The following basics about working with advanced flash equipment will get you started:

- Hard light, such as that from direct flash, is called *spectral* light. Soft light is called *diffuse* light.

- Hard light casts defined shadows. You can alter the quality of hard light somewhat by the size, shape, and finish of the flash or strobe reflectors you use.

- You can carefully place multiple hard lights to create glamorous effects known as *Hollywood* lighting.

- Silver umbrellas and mylar reflectors are among the surfaces you can use with multiple hard lights to produce sparkling effects.

- *Bare-bulb* or *bare-tube* light casts distinct but weak shadows in a circle around the tube.

- You can concentrate hard light by using black *grids* or *snoots*; these metal or (sometimes) cloth devices, which are made specifically for this purpose, go in front of the light source.

- You can diffuse light by aiming the light(s) through translucent material; you can soften the light by bouncing it off either close or quite distant reflective surfaces.

- The larger any light source, and the closer it is to a subject, the softer the effect.

- A single light bounced from a large umbrella high and in front of a subject is called a *beauty* light.

- When using several manual flashes or strobes of any type or size together, you can alter the *lighting ratio*, or the relationship of one light to another, two ways. Simply move the lights closer to or farther away from the subject or each other. The second technique is to turn the power on individual lights up or down.

- Fashions in lighting change all the time. For the latest look, study the best editorial publications, especially the world's top fashion magazines.

I exposed for this lobster claw flower in low daylight and bounced TTL flash fill out of a LumiQuest device to add sparkle to the raindrops. Here, I used my Nikon N90 in manual mode, a 55mm F3.5 macro lens, and my Nikon SB-26 flash. The exposure was *f*/11 for 1/8 sec. on ISO 50 slide film.

Chapter 7

ADVANCED 35MM CAMERAS, FLASHES, AND TECHNIQUES

Talented photographers who have pushed plenty of film through the camera can make fine pictures with just about any camera or flash. You won't get any argument from me about this. But it is easier, faster, and more fun to work with top-quality gear once you know how. I don't think it matters whether you prefer Canon, Minolta, Nikon, or some other brand of camera or flash. What does matter is that high-end models in each line offer maximum creative options, are designed for heavy use, and—in the case of electronic cameras, lenses, and flashes—have more computer power than entry-level and mid-range equipment.

Enhanced computer power translates into faster camera operation, advanced metering, faster autofocus, and increased flash-exposure accuracy, especially in poor light. It also translates into the possibility of controlling *through-the-lens* (TTL) flash output for special situations and creative exposure adjustment while retaining the basic benefits of TTL-metered flash.

The Benefits of Using Advanced Cameras

By now, so many people are familiar with computers that I probably don't need to explain that the more memory capacity a computer has, the "smarter" it is: the more complex things it can do, and the faster it can do them. It takes a computer with a great deal of memory, for example, to run today's advanced photo-manipulation and retouching programs.

Computerized cameras, lenses, and flashes also depend on memory, and the smartest ones have the most mem-

These are the current Minolta, Nikon, and Canon advanced camera/flash combinations.

ory capacity. For example, I like and use Nikon equipment. My entry-level Nikon N50 is a clever camera—it would have been miraculous only a few years ago—and produces good TTL-metered flash exposures when used with its built-in flash. I can, and sometimes do, use it with my detachable Nikon flashes, the simple, compact SB-23 and the advanced, adjustable SB-26. These flash units work well enough on my N50 camera for average situations. But it can't take advantage of the SB-26 flash's most valuable feature, the user-variable TTL-flash output. The N50 simply doesn't have enough internal memory for me to adjust the output.

The Benefits of Top-Quality Advanced Equipment

Professional assignments are often hectic, so any piece of equipment that saves time and stress is worth having. Advanced amateurs also know that when they shoot fast-moving subjects with flash, a dedicated flash might mean the difference between getting a great shot and missing it. Professionals and advanced amateurs like precise control of lighting, and with a top-of-the-line dedicated camera and TTL-flash combination, they aren't locked into program exposures. Once you learn advanced camera and flash settings, you'll find that it is surprisingly easy to alter them quickly for varied effects.

With my N90 cameras, which are advanced—but not the most advanced—Nikons, I can use the SB-26 flash, and alter, via the *flash-select mode*, the TTL-metered flash output up or down, in 1/3-stop (.3) increments. This means that I can compensate for non-average subjects or contrasty light situations, as well as adjust the flash output simply because I prefer the way that less—or more—flash looks. This also means that I can vary flash and flash-fill exposures, all without affecting the background exposure of a picture. The ability to control flash exposures this precisely is what, for me, makes admittedly rather high-priced equipment well worth the expense.

If you own advanced equipment, take time to sit down with the manuals and thoroughly familiarize yourself with the controls, modes, and settings. I highlight my manuals, make a summary of important settings on a file card when I get a new piece of equipment, and carry the card around until I've learned it. When I travel, I always carry my camera and flash manuals with me. I never know when I might need to refer to them.

Advanced Modes and Settings

Sorting out the jargon describing the features and settings of advanced photography equipment and flash requires some effort. This is because certain expressions derive from nineteenth-century photographic usage, while others require at least a familiarity with electronics or incorporate the latest from Silicon Valley. I am sure that the nomenclature will become clearer, and that in all likelihood you—like me and most other professional photographers—will sooner or later develop a fairly standardized way of operating the equipment. You might never need all the possible features offered. Anyway, here are my best efforts at rendering technical terms into plain American English.

Automatic Flash. A sensor on the front of the flash controls this non-TTL unit (see Chapter 8 on page 84). A thyristor cuts off the light when the sensor determines that enough flash has reached the film. Many top TTL flashes can also be set in automatic mode (see below).

Automatic Flash Mode. When you use an adjustable TTL dedicated flash in automatic mode, you must select an *f*-stop on the lens and an appropriate shutter speed. The chosen *f*-stop is set on the flash used in automatic mode. Flash exposures are read by a sensor on the front of the flash, not through the lens. Exposures are correct within

the distance range indicated on a scale on the flash's LCD screen. Don't confuse this mode with automatic flash units, the program auto settings on point-and-shoot cameras, or the program camera setting on SLR cameras (see Chapter 8 on page 84).

Automatic Mode. This program setting for built-in flashes fires any flash that is turned on or activated when the light is low, even if there is no hope of the flash illuminating the subject. Avoid this setting.

Bulb Mode. The B mode on a camera holds a shutter open as long as the shutter release is held open. This mode is available on some basic cameras and all top-of-the-line cameras.

Flash-Fill Mode. With flash fill, you add flash light to a scene basically exposed by daylight or available light in order to lighten shadows or emphasize foreground subjects (see "TTL-Fill Mode" on page 75).

Flash-Select Mode. This important mode on advanced flash units gives plus or minus values to TTL-controlled flash and flash-fill exposures. Use the flash-select mode (sometimes called *flash-set mode*) in two steps. First, with the flash set to TTL or TTL-fill mode, press the "Select"/"Set" button on the flash (see "TTL-Fill Mode" on page 75).

▲ For this shot of New York City's Central Park model boating pond in winter, I metered off the sky underexposing by 1/2 stop. Then I manually focused on a rock about 12 feet away and panned with the hungry gulls; I didn't expect one to fly within 2 feet. The TTL flash fill from my Nikon SB-26 flash is a bit "hot" but dramatic. With my Nikon N90 in manual mode and a 20mm F2.8 lens, I exposed for 1/250 sec. at *f*/4 on ISO 100 slide film.

◄ People who dress up for public events are almost always willing to be photographed. Shooting on New Year's Eve in Times Square, I exposed off the sidewalk to record some background lighting. Because of the crowds, I handheld my Nikon N90 camera, in manual mode, and 35–80mm F3.5–4.5 zoom lens set at about 50mm. I bounced the flash from my Nikon SB-26 flash in TTL mode out of a LumiQuest diffuser. This exposure on ISO 100 slide film was *f*/5.6 for 1/15 sec.

To make this shot of a wheat field in Dorset, England, I exposed off the sunny sky. Using a 20mm F2.8 wide-angle lens at a distance of about 3 feet from the giant roll of wheat exaggerated its size in relation to the background. At such close range, my on-camera Nikon SB-26 flash in TTL mode was able to fill the shadowed side of the roll, even with a small aperture. Look at the distant rolls for comparison. With my Nikon N90 in aperture-priority mode, I exposed ISO 100 slide film for 1/250 sec. at f/11–16.

Second, when the TTL symbol blinks on the flash LCD screen, press one of two "up"/"down" adjustment buttons to raise or lower TTL flash-fill output. On many flashes, adjustments are in 1/3-stop (.3) increments; on other units, the adjustments are in 1/2-stop (.5) increments, up to plus two or minus three full *f*-stops (see your flash manual).

Hertz (Hz) Mode. This flash setting is used in two steps for multi-mode flash exposures (see "Multi Mode" below). To use it, choose the number of flashes per frame and frames per second.

High-Speed Flash-Sync Mode. This setting is possible with certain advanced camera and flash combinations. It permits multiple bursts of high-speed, low-power flash to synchronize with shutter speeds of up to 1/8000 sec. You must use this mode in combination with a flash set on "manual" at greatly reduced power settings. This mode is used for flash fill with high-speed films and for motion-stopping effects, both at extremely close distances (see your flash and camera manuals). Because of the low light output, the value of both multi mode and high-speed flash-sync mode is to me theoretical; I'm told they have scientific value.

Manual Mode. The M setting on advanced electronic cameras permits you to choose both the camera shutter speed and the dedicated-lens aperture. The results: control of depth of field and blur, as well as being able to choose the background exposure level for flash-fill exposures—all

while still getting the benefit of TTL-metered flash exposures. (Keep in mind, though, that the M camera mode doesn't allow you to set a shutter speed above the maximum sync speed if the flash is turned on.)

Manual Flash Mode. With this mode, TTL or automatic flash units produce maximum output each time they're fired (provided they're fully charged). When you use this mode, flash power can be reduced to 1/2, 1/4, 1/8, 1/16, 1/32, and even lower on some units. Manual flash mode is intended for use with TTL multi-mode and high-speed-mode flash settings, as well as for motion-stopping short flash duration (see advanced equipment manuals for more information).

Manual Flash Units. When fully charged and used on full-power or reduced-power settings, amateur and professional flash and strobe units always put out the same amount of light. (To learn about using manual flash and strobe units, see Chapters 9, 10, and 11.)

Modular Flashes. Independent flash manufacturers make these units, which come with *modules,* or connectors, designed to operate with different brands of dedicated/TTL cameras.

Multi Mode. This mode, which is difficult to use well, is an option on advanced TTL flash units. It sets multiple flash bursts on one film frame to produce repetitive effects. The number of flashes per frame and per second is controlled by the Hertz (Hz) setting (see above). Multi mode requires that the flash be set on flash-manual mode, at low-power output (often 1/32 power). The camera shutter must be set at a slower speed than the total time needed for the repeating flash sequence. Choose only a few flashes per frame and frames per second for the best results. Work at night outdoors or in a darkened room indoors. Average-toned subjects work best. Be prepared for a high number of less-than-good pictures.

Rear-Shutter-Curtain Flash-Sync Mode. This setting, which is also called *second-curtain flash-sync mode,* might be set on either the flash or on the camera (see your instruction manuals). This mode fires the flash at the end of a long exposure rather than at the beginning. The effect is notice-able only when you combine flash fill in low light with slow shutter speeds (below about 1/15 sec.). Then this flash rear-sync mode throws ghosts behind a flashed sub-ject instead of in front of it. (With conventional slow-sync mode, moving ghost effects appear in front of "stopped," or frozen, images caught by flash.) I use the rear-sync set-ting when the subject is moving in a predictable direction only.

Slow-Sync Mode. As mentioned earlier, this SS mode is known on different cameras as *night-portrait mode* (NP) and *museum mode* (MS). This option, which isn't available on all cameras, is the only simple-to-use program mode that I find truly useful. It sets a slower-than-sync shutter speed on the camera so low-lit backgrounds out of the flash range can record on film. The SS mode also quickly calculates how much TTL-metered flash fill you must add

to shadowed or silhouetted foregrounds for a well-bal-anced exposure. Try using the SS mode indoors in low light, too. This setting usually calls for a tripod, unless you want impressionistic sharpness and blur effects.

TTL-Fill Mode. This mode balances TTL-metered flash out-put with bright, average, or low daylight without over-powering the available light. I use this mode whenever shooting with flash in daylight. The "TTL" and "Fill" icons should appear together on flash LCD screens when this option is in use. For subtle fill effects, I often combine the TTL-fill mode with the flash-select/set option, and reduce the fill output by 1/3 stop (.3) or 2/3 stop (.7).

TTL-Flash Mode. This mode signifies all flashes made for use with a dedicated camera. All light, both daylight and flash, reaching the film is metered through the lens (TTL) via a sensor located behind the film plane. A computer in dedicated cameras determines the exposure.

Miscellaneous Camera and Lens Settings
On advanced cameras, a rotating switch, which is some-times called a *focus-mode switch* or something similar, near the front bottom left of the lens permits you to choose manual lens focus over autofocus (see your cam-era manual). The *depth-of-field preview button* on the right front of the camera body, close to the lens, stops down the lens to the taking aperture so that you can see the zone of sharp focus before you shoot. On some advanced cameras, an electronic setting has replaced the depth-of-field preview button.

For this shot of Coney Island, New York, I metered off the twilight sky. Using my compact Nikon SB-23 flash in TTL mode on-camera, I panned with different children, shooting just before they reached me as the ride whirled. With my Nikon N90 in manual mode and a 28–80mm F2.8 D zoom lens set at about 50mm, I exposed for 1/4 sec. at *f*/4 on ISO 50 slide film.

I made this night shot at a miniature golf course in Tennessee with my Nikon N90 camera in manual mode and mounted on a tripod at about 7 feet from the shark. I used a 20mm F2.8 lens. At this distance, TTL flash fill from my Nikon SB-26 flash was able to lighten the shark's black-shadowed jaw, even at the small *f*-stop chosen to produce excellent depth of field. I selected *f*/16 also because using this *f*-stop (or a smaller one) produces a star effect with bright lights. I exposed ISO 100 slide film for 8 seconds.

When you use many advanced autofocus lenses, you must unlock a slide on the lens in order to manually alter *f*-stops. Additionally, a button on some advanced, autofocus telephoto lenses controls focus method and range.

Choosing a Dedicated TTL Flash

You don't choose a flash dedicated to a specific brand of camera without considering the specific camera model you want and the system it belongs to. For example, you can't put a Canon flash onto a Minolta camera, and you must use a Nikon dedicated flash with a Nikon camera. If you already own one or more cameras that are part of a system, your best choice is the manufacturer's flash made to use all the features of the specific camera model. The flashes described here are top-of-the-line choices for three of the most popular advanced and professional camera systems. All are comparable in power, with a *guide number* (GN) close to 120 (measured in feet when used in normal head position and with ISO 100 film). If you aren't committed to a system yet, comparing these flash units might help you decide.

Canon 540-EZ Flash

This is Canon's top-of-the-line flash; it has large buttons that are quite simple to set (see diagram). The Canon 540-EZ also has separate red and green lights that signify flash readiness and correct exposure. The LCD screen is easy to read and indicates the angle of the flash head. The head can be rotated, swiveled, and aimed slightly downward for moderate closeups. Operating this flash unit is straightforward. It offers the TTL, TTL-metered fill, flash-set, automatic, manual, reduced-power, and multi modes. Canon's dedicated cord needed for this flash is shorter than some other makers' cords (and is a bit pricey).

The 540-EZ flash is a solid, accurate workhorse that many thousands of top photojournalists around the world use, but I don't consider this a reason to buy the

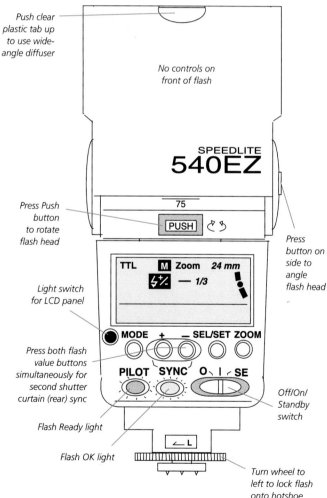

This is the back of the Canon 540-EZ flash.

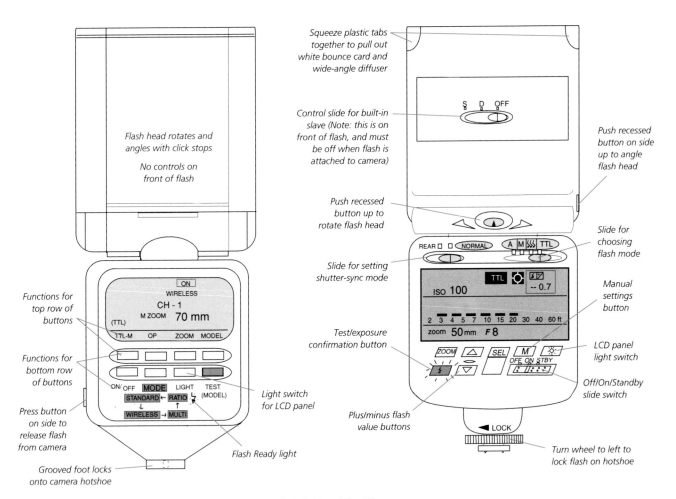

The controls on the backs of the Minolta Program 5400 HS flash (left) and the Nikon SB-26 flash (right) are clearly labeled.

Canon system. I think that the wide variety of easily programmable camera options, great lenses, and superb autofocus are Canon's great strengths. The company also offers a ring flash, a handle-mount flash, and other compact and adjustable TTL-dedicated flash options.

Minolta 5400-xi Flash

Minolta makes excellent cameras and lenses, was a pioneer in autofocus, and is known for its superb professional flash meters. The exposure-metering capability of Minolta cameras is very good. The company makes a variety of 35mm SLR cameras, but the accessory range for the system currently isn't quite as extensive as that of Canon or Nikon. Nevertheless, the Minolta system is one of the most popular on the market with advanced amateurs; some professionals, especially nature photographers, use Minoltas, too.

Minolta's 5400-xi flash is straightforward to use, with TTL, TTL-fill, automatic, manual, multi-, and high-speed flash-sync modes, as well as manual, full-power, and low-power operation. This unit is currently the only flash on the market that you can operate in true cordless TTL mode, triggered by a built-in or detachable on-camera Minolta flash. The light from the on-camera flash must be visible to the remote flash. The light-output ratio between the two flashes is controlled by a radio signal

from the camera, which must be programmed for remote TTL-flash use. *Line-of-sight flash triggering* can restrict the use of the cordless two-flash combination with some light modifiers, but an optional dedicated cord is available. The exposures I made using the 5400-xi flash in tests ranged from very good to excellent.

I didn't find it too easy to read Minolta's manual shutter and lens settings through the viewfinder. Using the Minolta 700-si camera with the 5400-xi flash, the numbers appear as light green superimposed over the picture area.

Nikon SB-26 Flash

Nikon has always made great SLR cameras. The manufacturer is also known for its superb in-camera metering systems and flash units. As mentioned earlier, I've been a Nikon system user for many years, and in my opinion (which, as I've indicated, hasn't been paid for) the SB-26 is the most accurate TTL-flash currently available. I take the two SB-26 units I own on jobs where they get heavy use, and have never had a problem with either.

You select SB-26 flash settings via small buttons and/or a couple of slides. A red "Ready" light goes on when the flash has recycled; this button will also blink rapidly if the flash didn't adequately light the nearest subject in its path. Once you set the flash, operating it is straightforward. It offers TTL, TTL-fill, automatic, manual, and multi modes, as well as manual full-power and reduced-power modes.

The SB-26 flash includes a built-in *slave* unit that can be set to fire the flash off-camera without the use of a connecting cord. The output of the remote flash isn't TTL-metered; instead, you control it in automatic mode by choosing an *f*-stop and a distance setting on the flash LCD screen so that it is weaker than the on-camera flash and doesn't affect the TTL exposure.

Nikon makes an inexpensive compact flash: the SB-23 flash, which has a *guide number* (GN) of 66. I use and like this model. I haven't tried the mid-price SB-27 flash, which permits TTL-metered-flash output adjustment. Nikon also markets a ring flash, a handle-mount flash, and an automatic unit.

Reading and altering shutter-speed and lens settings and adjusting exposure while looking through the viewfinders of Nikons are quite easy. "Plus" and "minus" exposure symbols and numbers appear bold and black below the picture area. This is particularly valuable to anyone who, like me, prefers to combine manual background exposure settings with foregrounds lit by TTL-metered flash fill.

Modular Flash Units

Metz and Sunpak are two well-known independent makers of flash units. Some Metz units are self-slaved; you can used them off-camera similar to the way you use the Nikon SB-26 flash. If you have the appropriate modules (adaptors), you can use these flashes with most popular dedicated 35mm SLR cameras, as well as with many medium-format electronic cameras.

Rechargeable Battery Packs

Disposable batteries are expensive, don't recycle fast, and don't last for much more than one 36-exposure roll of flash pictures. Most serious amateurs and just about all professionals who use flash rely on rechargeable battery packs. Manufacturers offer packs for their brand of flash units, and independent makers market battery packs, too. Although manufacturers invalidate their flash guarantees if you use an independent-brand battery pack, you can't go wrong with one of the following types.

Quantum Battery Packs

The pioneer among battery-pack manufacturers, Quantum makes packs that come in many sizes and power ranges,

Working at New York City's Bronx Zoo, I set a comparatively high flash sync speed in low sunlight at the butterfly exhibit. I wanted to stop the motion of the butterfly on the daisies, but to record some daylight for a delicate effect as well. The program equipment and TTL flash compensated for the light-reducing factor of the 15mm extension tube behind the lens that permitted close-focusing. I used my Nikon N90 in manual mode, an 80–200mm F2.8 zoom lens set at 200mm, and my Nikon SB-26 flash. For this shot, the exposure was 1/125 sec. at *f*/11 on ISO 100 slide film.

from the Bantam, which you can use under a camera, to a 150 watt-second/joule (WS/J) Turbo pack designed for professional flashes. Quantum makes battery-to-flash modules for most brands of dedicated, automatic, and manual flash units. These work for some other battery packs also (and can cost about $50). Perma-Pak, Sunpak, Metz, and Lumedyne packs are recommended also.

Underdog Battery Packs

Lighting guru Jon Falk markets small Underdog 6V (volt) rechargeable batteries that screw under any 35mm camera and are great for travel. I love these batteries; the weight under the camera is hardly noticeable. Adapting the flash to the appropriate Underdog module takes about two minutes (see the Underdog instructions). I use black gaffer tape rather than the supplied Velcro to close the flash's chamber doors. Gaffer tape is removable, while Velcro isn't.

Two Underdog battery packs provide about 300 full-power flashes with a typical GN 120 bounce-head unit, and a higher number of flashes when light output is reduced. A pair of Underdogs costs about $150; the price is slightly more when combined with a dual-voltage (110–220V) charger.

Advanced Flash Techniques

Almost all of today's advanced flash units have heads that you can angle externally or internally, and you can also rotate some advanced flash heads. These features can all be useful at times. But apart from the fact that bouncing and diffusing light reduces flash range, I often like the quality of direct flash aimed straight forward and choose the effect deliberately. All good photographers think a great deal about the effects they want to create with light even before thinking about the techniques needed to achieve them. Using light simply sometimes might be the most advanced technique of all.

Using Adjustable Flash Direct

Use any adjustable flash aimed direct without light modifiers whenever you need maximum light. Bounce cards, diffusers, domes, and color gels placed over flash heads reduce the flash output and range. Obviously, maximum flash power is necessary when you shoot distant subjects and scenes in low light or at night. It is less obvious that you also need all or most of the power of your flash to fill in shadows in bright sunlight at any distance beyond about 5 to 7 feet.

I photographed this young gun seller in the tribal areas between Pakistan and Afghanistan. Working with my Nikon N8008, a 28mm F2.8 lens, and my compact Nikon SB-23 flash in TTL mode, I exposed ISO 50 film at f/5.6 for 1/30 sec.

When working in sun or bright backlight, you must use a small lens aperture. If you don't, the background of your composition will be overexposed. This is true even with an advanced camera that syncs at 1/250 sec. With ISO 100 film, a reasonable exposure on a bright sunny day is 1/250 sec. at f/11 (f/16 on a beach). This means that the flash won't have anywhere near the range it does in low light, when you can use wide lens apertures.

Using the Sto-Fen Omni Dome with Flash
I often use the Sto-Fen diffusing dome on my flash head because of its ability to soften light. I don't angle the flash head but aim it directly at my subject; then the range indicator on my SB-26 flash operates. When I use the Sto-Fen Dome, I deduct a standard 50 percent—and 75 percent in sunlight for safety—from the indicated operating range.

Adjusting Program-Determined Flash Output
Program-controlled, TTL-metered flash exposures chosen even by the most sophisticated equipment (including mine) aren't perfect in difficult lighting conditions, particularly contrasty situations. For example, it is all too easy to overexpose light-skinned faces of people who appear small in flash-lit compositions made outdoors at night or indoors in a big dark space. Knowing this, here you should use the flash-select setting and the "minus" button (indicated by a "-" symbol or an arrow pointing down) to reduce flash or flash-fill output in such situations. I find that the "-.7" setting (2/3 stop, or two taps on the minus button) works well for many such situations.

Suppose that you're photographing dark-skinned people in overhead sun, against white walls, under an awning, or backlit, or to fill a small, close dark area in an otherwise bright composition. Here, you should add to

Working in Peshawar, Pakistan, I grabbed a couple of quick shots before this spice seller waved me away. I set my Nikon N90 on aperture-priority mode, adjusted a 35–80mm F3.5–4.5 zoom lens to about 50mm, and bounced my Nikon SB-26 on-camera flash of a LumiQuest device. I exposed at f/16 on ISO 100 slide film.

For this shot of parade participants, I metered off the paper lanterns and added TTL flash fill at a minus .7 setting. The existing street light was low, and I asked the angels to pose against am almost black background. Not much available light recorded on the film even at such low shutter speeds. The ghost effect is barely evident. I used my Nikon N90 and exposed ISO 100 film for 2 seconds at f/2.

the TTL-metered flash exposure with the "plus" value setting (indicated by a "+" symbol or up arrow). Your experience and preference will combine to determine the exact amount of additional flash desired for these lighting situations. Experiment.

Bouncing Flash Off Your Hand
Once I forgot to pack a bounce card in my bag. I was photographing at a huge, formal ball and wanted the lighting to look subtle even though I was using flash. In desperation, I cupped my left hand over my on-camera, angled flash head, while operating the camera with my other hand and relying on autofocus. The resulting pictures had pleasant flash fill in the foreground, which was warmish in tone (from my pink palm). I've often used this technique since then.

Using Handheld Off-Camera TTL-Flash
With a dedicated flash connected to a camera by an appropriate dedicated cord, you can aim the flash to place shadows where you want them, avoid reflections, or lighten dark corners while still getting the benefits of TTL-metered flash or flash fill. To photograph large groups or crowds, stretch the cord as far above your head as possible and aim the flash head down. You can even tape a flash to a pipe, fence, or tree branch so it hits your subject from the side; you can also mount the flash on a tripod or lightstand. Dedicated cords are about 3 to 5 feet long, depending on the brand. Remember, you can join two dedicated cords if necessary.

When you must photograph crowds or groups, the farther your flash is from the people, the more area it will cover. Have an assistant (or friend) stretch a flash on a dedicated cord as far as it will go to enable you to get TTL-metered flash with maximum light spread (of course, you mustn't exceed maximum flash range). You can even mount a flash on a cord on a lightweight stand or light pole designed for this specific purpose in order to raise the flash high above a crowd.

Combining Wide-Angle Lenses and Flash
As mentioned earlier, wide-angle lenses are invaluable for flash work. They force you to stand close to your subject when you photograph in order to get a decent-sized image in the frame, and offer great depth of field even when used at wide apertures. Both of which maximize flash effectiveness because the distance from the subject and the lens aperture determine flash exposure (review the Inverse Square Law in Chapter 1).

I like the look of wide-angle pictures, too. Wide-angle lenses are great for location portraits, still lifes, and landscapes with interesting foreground features—and flash fill can enhance all of these subjects. Remember, to avoid distortion, place people or recognizable shapes in the center of a wide-angle composition, not at the edges of the frame.

Working with Flash at Maximum Range
A great deal of information has been written about flash falloff on the sides of images when you use flash from a

distance with wide-angle lenses. I don't think that you need to worry about this. If light falloff is visible, it is subtle and gradual, not a hard, defined line.

A lightweight *Fresnel screen* with concentric grooves increases the flash range by bending light rays so that they aim forward. This capability is useful with telephoto lenses. (Augustin Fresnel was the Frenchman who invented lighthouse lenses.) Today's advanced TTL-metered flashes have zoom heads that incorporate Fresnel screens. Cameras used with dedicated lenses set dedicated flash zoom heads automatically. Both teleflash devices with Fresnel lenses and special reflectors can increase flash range (see Chapters 10 and 11).

For this impressionistic shot of a roller coaster at Coney Island, New York, I attached my Nikon N90 on a tripod via a ball-head mount. My compact Nikon SB-23 flash in TTL mode was on-camera. I tried to create the feeling of whirling on a wild ride by panning and flashing at groups just before they reached me. I had no idea what the results would look like. Using a 20mm F2.8 lens, I exposed ISO 100 slide film at f/5.6 for 10 seconds.

I made this shot of butterflies in New York City's Bronx Zoo. I used my Nikon N90 in manual mode, an 80–200mm F2.8 zoom lens set at 200mm, and my Nikon SB-26 flash set at minus .3. For this shot, the exposure was 1/125 sec. at f/11 on ISO 100 slide film.

For this shot made at Great Smoky Mountains National Park, Tennessee, I metered off the trees across the stream, which were backlit by the low sun. I set a slow shutter speed and small *f*-stop on my Nikon N90, in manual mode, because I wanted to achieve extensive depth of field and to record the water as a blur. I positioned my tripod-mounted camera in shallow water at about 4 feet from the large rock. With a 20mm F2.8 lens, my Nikon SB-26 flash, and ISO 100 slide film, I exposed for 4 seconds at *f*/16.

Combining Manual Camera Settings and TTL/Dedicated Flash-Fill

If you choose to operate your dedicated camera in manual mode and set the lens aperture and shutter speed for creative reasons (as I almost always do), you can still use a dedicated flash in TTL-metered mode and get either full flash illumination or flash fill, without the need for calculations. You can set advanced flashes to adjust program TTL-metered flash-fill effects via the flash-select mode (see above).

Combining Long Exposures with Flash Fill

This technique is entirely possible if a close foreground subject is in near darkness. When faced with this challenging situation, I use ISO 100 film and a wide-angle lens, and I expose for 30 seconds at *f*/22. This approach works well for most night scenes and provides rather extensive depth of field for cityscapes. Be aware, however, that you must use the flash fill extremely close to the subject.

This approach enables me to record New York City's many great fireworks displays. I use 15- and 30-second exposures at *f*/5.6 and add flash fill to light spectators in the foreground. Fireworks pictures are unpredictable, but are often good—especially if you wait for red bursts and choose a cityscape as a backdrop for the fireworks.

By using a time exposure with an off-camera flash set to the M mode and 1/4 power, you can *flash paint* a reasonable-size, low-lit room or unlighted outdoor space with multiple flash pops. (For more information, see Chapter 10 on page 106.)

Options for Using Advanced Flash Off-Camera

As mentioned earlier, depending on the brand of camera and model of flash you own and the range of accessories available, you can connect any advanced flash to a compatible camera via a dedicated cord. You can use two or more dedicated flashes together in a variety of ways, and retain all or most of the benefits of TTL-metered flash exposure.

As of this writing, only several of Minolta's "xi" cameras permit you to use the built-in pop-up flash to fire an off-camera 5400-xi flash without a connecting cord and get TTL-controlled exposure from both flash units. With two 5400-xi flashes, one used on-camera and the other off-camera, you can adjust the lighting ratio (which is the comparative output between lights) from 2 to 1 or 1 to 2. This is because the two Minolta flashes transmit information to each other via a radio signal. You must set the lighting ratios on both the camera and the flash, but this won't seem complicated once you've read the manuals and done it a couple of times.

Any camera with a pop-up flash will fire an off-camera Nikon SB-26 flash (or a self-slaved Metz or any other self-slaved flash) placed at a distance of up to about 15 feet from the on-camera flash. One flash must be in the line of sight of the other. Make sure that you've turned on the slave and that the remote flash is responding by firing a test shot.

You must take care to place a powerful off-camera flash well behind a much less powerful built-in flash. If you don't, the strong flash will fool the in-camera sensor behind the lens, causing underexposure.

If you have two Nikon SB-26 flashes, determining lighting ratios is reasonably simple because the units are of equal power. Set the *aperture-priority mode* (A) on the camera, and select an *f*-stop on the lens. Then set the off-camera flash in the automatic flash mode, with the slave unit on the front on "On." Then set the remote flash at leats one *f*-stop lower than the on-camera flash. The flash is now programmed to put out less light than the main flash. This isn't as complicated as it sounds (and is clearly explained in the Nikon SB-26 manual).

Canon doesn't currently offer radio-controlled flash or a built-in slave device. However, the company's flashes are perhaps the easiest of all brands to set.

Combining Two Types of Flash

Try combining any off-camera TTL flash fitted with a slave unit and used in the automatic mode with the TTL-metered exposure of an on-camera flash unit. Adjust the light output for the remote flash to be less than that of the TTL-metered flash. To successfully use this technique, you must first set the lens in the A mode, and the main flash to TTL mode. Next, set the remote flash in automatic mode to an aperture that is one or two *f*-stops lower than the lens setting. This causes the remote flash to put out less light than the main flash so it doesn't affect the TTL exposure. Refer to camera manuals to learn more about using a TTL flash in the automatic mode). It is also possible to use an inexpensive, non-TTL, automatic flash unit, such as the Vivitar 283 or Sunpak 120J, as an auxiliary to a TTL flash using the above approach (see Chapter 8 on page 84).

You can combine several Canon, Minolta, and Nikon flashes all in full TTL mode. Just make sure that the first flash is connected to the camera via a dedicated cord, and the second flash is joined to the first via a supplementary cord, and so on. This is useful for photographers who like to shoot closeups with two flashes on a bracket, or who need several flashes (up to four) used close for such tasks as lighting products evenly or shooting copy work.

Understanding Lighting Ratios

Light ratios are important in photography because light doesn't record on film exactly as the human eye sees it. Color slide films require the most careful lighting. This is because they can reproduce only about a 3 to 1 lighting ratio, which is a difference of two *f*-stops, between the brightest highlights and the darkest shadows while showing detail in both. If the lighting ratio is higher, blownout highlights or yawning shadows can result. The worst-case scenario is underexposure and overexposure in the same picture. Because negative film can be manipulated during printing, a 5 to 1 ratio (or a difference of three full *f*-stops) is possible with both color and black-and-white print films.

While you can control two-light flash ratios using any of these methods, the professional way to determine strobe or lighting ratios requires a flash meter (see Chapter 11 on page 118). The most precise method of all is to use a flash meter combined with lighting tests made with a Polaroid camera (or back) and Polaroid film. This enables you to preview the exact lighting effects before you shoot (see Chapters 9, 10, and 11).

On a heavily overcast day, this young gorilla in New York City's Bronx Zoo was about 60 to 70 feet away from me. This is the extreme range for my flash, even at the widest possible *f*-stop. A Lepp teleflash device pushed over my Nikon SB-26 flash's head extended the flash range; the TTL flash fill reached far enough to add a highlight to the gorilla's deep-set eyes and give some detail to its coat. With my Nikon N90 in aperture-priority mode and an 80–200mm F2.8 zoom lens set at 200mm, I exposed ISO 100 slide film for 1/125 sec. at *f*/2.8.

I made this shot of a fireworks display with my Nikon N90 camera in aperture-priority mode, a 20mm F2.8 zoom lens, and my Nikon SB-26 flash. The exposure on ISO 100 slide film was 30 seconds at *f*/5.6.

Chapter 8
AUTOMATIC FLASH

If you always use a dedicated camera with a built-in or detachable TTL-metered flash, never shoot with a manual camera, and never feel the need for at least one quite powerful but moderately priced flash that you can attach a *slave device* to so that you can use it *remote*, or not connected physically to the camera, and set it off via a flash or some other "trigger" on the camera, don't read on. But to find out more about this technique—and to become a more complete flash photographer—you should learn to use automatic flash. Traditionalists who use manual cameras, as well as those who often make pictures calling for more than one light, should find this chapter immediately useful. And if you don't need the information now, it might come in handy later.

What are automatic flash units? They belong to the technical generation before dedicated, *through-the-lens-metered* (TTL-metered) flashes and were first introduced in the 1960s. A sensor on the front of the automatic flash controls light output. After you set an automatic flash unit and an appropriate *f*-stop on the lens, the unit gives good flash exposures without your having to reset it unless the flash-to-subject distance changes out of set range. This type of flash is still used with all manual cameras, and is popular with news photographers.

Because of the fact that automatic flash units are rugged, inexpensive, and quite easy to set, and, importantly, most can also be set to *repeatable manual mode*, they are frequently used in photography schools and courses to teach flash basics. (Don't confuse automatic flash units with the auto settings on program cameras and flashes.) Three man-

ufacturers known for quality automatic flashes are Metz, Sunpak, and Vivitar.

How Automatic Flash Units Work

Automatic flashes incorporate a built-in or removable sensor on the front. A *thyristor*, which is an electronic switch, controls the flash output. The thyristor causes the flash to cut off when the sensor judges that sufficient light has reached the subject for a good exposure. As always, flash range is determined by a combination of the power of the flash, the film speed, and the *f*-stop selected.

With an automatic flash, first you set the chosen film speed on the flash, and then select an *f*-stop and/or a distance range from the options offered. Next, set the lens aperture that matches the chosen distance range. Then you must set *sync speed* on the camera. Sync speed is the shutter speed that synchronizes with the flash. If you don't do this, part of the picture will be dark or blacked out because the flash didn't reach the film.

Maximum camera sync speed is marked with an "X" on manual SLR cameras, medium- and large-format cameras, and some large-format lenses. Sync speed might be as high as 1/250 sec. on current mechanical SLR cameras, such as my Nikon FM-2, but it can be lower. Sync speed is most often 1/60 sec. on vintage SLR cameras with focal-plane shutters. (Cameras and lenses with leaf shutters sync at around 1/500 sec.) You can never use shutter speeds that are higher than the sync speed with flash, but you can use shutter speeds that are any speed lower than the flash sync speeds for special effects.

Knowing that automatic flashes overexpose light-skinned faces against dark backgrounds, I cut the flash output here by 50 percent by setting "200" on the flash ISO scale with ISO 100 film. Shooting in New York City's Chinatown, I used my Nikon FM-2 manual camera, a 28mm F2.8 lens, my Vivitar 283 flash, and an *f*/8 automatic setting, exposing for 1/30 sec.

For this rainy-day shot, I reduced the flash output by setting "50" on the flash ISO scale with the ISO 25 film I was shooting. I use this trick to cut the fill effect with automatic flash. With my Nikon FM-2 manual camera, a 20mm F2.8 lens, and my Vivitar 283 flash at the f/4 automatic setting, I exposed for 1/30 sec. at f/4.

I aimed my Vivitar 283 flash, powered with a 6V battery and mounted on my Nikon FM-2 manual camera, direct for this Chinese New Year impression. The flash's 4- to 15-foot automatic exposure range with ISO 100 film called for an aperture of f/8. I tried slow shutter speeds, in the 1/15 sec. to 1/4 sec. range to show movement. In automatic mode, the flash provides good flash fill even in low daylight. I shot two rolls of film while panning at the speed of the dancing dragon, thereby achieving both sharpness and blur effects. This shot was probably exposed for 1/8 sec.

Automatic Flash Operation

With any automatic flash, you can work within the distance range you've chosen without having to reset the *f*-stop unless the flash-to-subject distance is significantly altered. Automatic flash exposures are good for most average light situations. You can bracket the flash output for special situations two ways: either by using a variable-power option on the flash, or by changing the film speed set on the flash.

Automatic flashes work well for flash fill in sunlight or on gray days, and even for slow-sync flash fill at low shutter speeds in low light. In these situations, though, you must carefully select an appropriate lens aperture;

use a small *f*-stop in bright light, and the largest possible *f*-stop in low light. You must also be sure to set the sync speed (or any speed below sync) and work well within the distance range indicated on the flash unit.

You can use slaved, remote automatic flashes to lighten dark corners of rooms or the backgrounds in photographs illuminated via TTL-flash. These flash units sometimes come in handy even in large studios. When you use them as accent or main lights, you must operate them in *manual mode* (M) (review Chapter 9).

You can use an automatic flash unit with a 35mm SLR program camera. Set the camera to *aperture-priority mode* (A) or the M mode. Recent-model automatic flashes have a hot foot with one retractable receptor. This slides and locks onto standard SLR camera hotshoes, and doesn't harm the camera. I don't recommend using old automatic flashes on a dedicated camera; they might harm its delicate electronics. (If in doubt, ask your camera manufacturer or dealer for advice.)

Advantages of Automatic Flash

I own six automatic flashes. They are classic, off-the-shelf Vivitar 283 units. I also have an NVS double-powered Vivitar 283 modification with a round, removable reflector, so this unit can be used "bare -tube." I sometimes use two or more Vivitar 283 flash units (as I did for the cover shot, as well as for most of the formal portraits and equipment illustrations in this book). Metz and Sunpak are long-established brands that offer automatic flashes in more configurations and a wider price range than Vivitar. All three flash manufacturers have top-of-the-line automatic flashes that are comparable in power to the advanced Canon, Minolta, and Nikon TTL flashes (shown in Chapter 7).

Select an automatic flash that comes with a head that angles, that you can use in the M mode, and that has a built-in or accessory variable-power option. From compact to handle-mount models, you'll spend much less than you might think (prices start around $80). Good automatic flashes:

- Offer maximum flash power for the money

- Allow moderate change of the flash-to-subject position without changing the settings

- Work well for flash fill in bright and low light

- Permits manual power reduction for bracketing exposures or high flash speeds

- Can be used on program cameras set in aperture-priority mode or manual mode

- Can be used as an off-camera adjunct to a dedicated/TTL-metered flash

- Can be used with manual cameras, and in the manual mode

- Can be combined with strobe units as accent lights

- Are widely available for rental, which is great when you need several flashes.

Dedicated Flash in Automatic Mode

You can use most high-end dedicated/TTL-metered flash units in automatic mode. (Remember, never confuse this mode with an auto program camera setting.) When operated in automatic mode (via a switch or a mode setting—see your flash manuals for specifics), TTL flashes work in the same way that automatic units do. A sensor on the front of the flash controls the flash exposure.

To operate a dedicated flash in automatic mode, you must first load the film in the program camera and check that the ISO setting is correct. Then set the lens aperture in A or M camera mode. Turn on the flash, and verify the automatic mode on the flash LCD screen. The sensor on the front of the flash will then control the flash output, and you'll get good exposures as long as you stay within the range indicated on the flash LCD screen.

One advantage of the automatic-flash option is that if you own both a program camera and a manual camera, you can use the TTL flash in automatic mode on the manual camera. So you don't need to buy a second flash. Another benefit is that you can use a TTL flash on, or close to, a dedicated camera as the *key light* (the main light source) and combine it with an inexpensive automatic flash unit fitted with a slave device.

To do this, place the second flash, which is often called the *fill light* and which you've fitted with a slave, on the dark side of a portrait or still-life subject. The fill adds light and lowers contrast. Carefully directed down, a

The blue automatic setting on my Vivitar 283 flash permits working between 4½ and 15 feet with ISO 100 film. For this wedding shot, I pushed ISO 64 film to ISO 100 and exposed at f/8 for 1/60 sec. Here, I used the flash on a bracket, connected to the camera by Vivitar's SC-1 remote cord via a sensor on camera. The subtle fill opened up the facial shadows.

second flash can illuminate and give a shine to hair. This flash is called a *hair light*. When you aim a slaved flash so that the light bounces off a ceiling or background wall, it can brighten any dark corner in a large space.

Operating an Automatic Flash

Learn how to use an automatic flash in the same way as you would learn to operate any other piece of equipment. It isn't hard, but you do have to use a specific sequence of settings. First, study the flash manual. To make the necessary adjustments, you might have to use color-coded dials, as you do with Metz and Vivitar flashes, or color-coded slides, as you do with Sunpak units. When you use an automatic flash on manual cameras, it is good practice to adhere to the following sequence:

1. Set the film speed on the camera.

2. Set the desired shutter speed. Use the maximum flash sync speed (or any shutter speed below sync if desired).

3. Set the film speed being used on the flash.

4. Select and set the lens aperture you want. Note the minimum/maximum working-distance range indicated on the flash via the color-coded dial or scale. (Another option is to choose the distance range first, and then set the indicated lens aperture.)

You must use dedicated/TTL program cameras in the M mode with automatic flashes whether they are on the camera or they're connected with a PC/sync cord. Here, the flash won't control any camera or lens settings. You must set the desired camera shutter speed (never above maximum flash sync speed, of course) and the lens aperture. Then you must work within the chosen distance range that the flash indicates. Don't worry—all of this is easier in practice than it sounds.

Combining TTL Flash and an Auxiliary Automatic Flash

When you use a dedicated/TTL-metered flash with either an off-camera automatic flash or a dedicated flash in automatic mode, you can control *light ratios*, or the relative brightness of the two flashes, in several different ways:

- By choosing a setting for the off-camera automatic flash that is one-half (or one *f*-stop) less than the lens aperture chosen on the main TTL-metered camera-flash combination

- By increasing the film speed that is set on the off-camera background flash by 50 percent or 100 percent, thereby causing the flash to put out less light

- By using the auxiliary flash in the M mode and increasing the flash-to-subject distance—to 50 percent or 100 percent farther from the subject than the main flash is a safe bet.

Experiment to vary fill light and highlight-to-shadow contrast. Interestingly, both Nikon and Metz seem to promote some *self-slaved* TTL models as off-camera TTL-flash units. But, in fact, these flashes are used remote in

I photographed this bodybuilder in a darkened studio. I set the flash to blue automatic mode and bounced it out of a 42-inch black-backed umbrella from about 4 feet to the right, and down onto the model. I made this portrait with my Nikon FM-2, a 28mm F2.8 lens, and a modified NVS-1 Vivitar 283 flash. The exposure on ISO 100 film was 1/60 sec. at f/8.

automatic mode. You must set the *f*-stop on the remote flash to give at least one stop less light than the flash connected to the camera. If you don't, the TTL metering of the main flash can be fooled, and underexposure will result. You can program an equally powerful (for example, 120 GN—see below), slaved Vivitar or Sunpak flash in the same manner for much less money than it costs to buy a second (120 GN) top-brand TTL flash.

Vivitar 283

This rugged unit, the first automatic flash introduced, was revolutionary. It is still made and is now an inexpensive classic. With ISO 100 film, the Vivitar 283 has a *guide number* (GN) of 120 (based on ISO 100 film, and measured in feet); this is very close to the GNs of top-of-the-line Canon, Minolta, and Nikon flashes that are used with zoom flash heads in the 50mm position.

Vivitar also makes a 285 model, which isn't quite so classic as the 283 but has a built-in, manual *power variator* (which is an optional extra on the 283). Vivitar's automatic flashes require setting the film speed on a dial, selecting an *f*-stop and a distance range from four color-

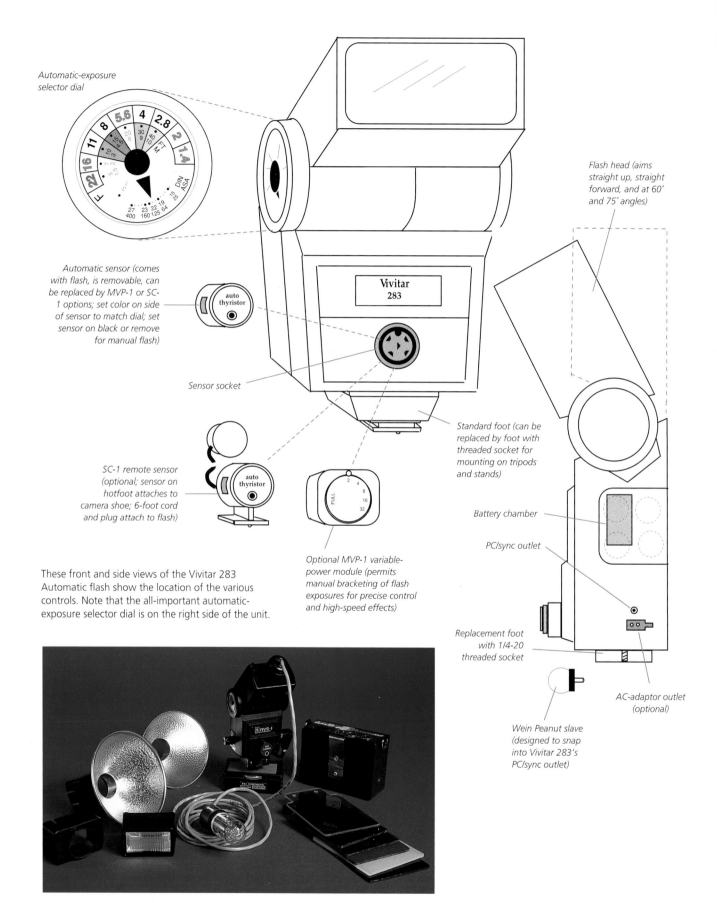

Automatic-exposure selector dial

Automatic sensor (comes with flash, is removable, can be replaced by MVP-1 or SC-1 options; set color on side of sensor to match dial; set sensor on black or remove for manual flash)

auto thyristor

Vivitar 283

Sensor socket

SC-1 remote sensor (optional; sensor on hotfoot attaches to camera shoe; 6-foot cord and plug attach to flash)

auto thyristor

Flash head (aims straight up, straight forward, and at 60° and 75° angles)

Standard foot (can be replaced by foot with threaded socket for mounting on tripods and stands)

Battery chamber

PC/sync outlet

Replacement foot with 1/4-20 threaded socket

AC-adaptor outlet (optional)

Wein Peanut slave (designed to snap into Vivitar 283's PC/sync outlet)

Optional MVP-1 variable-power module (permits manual bracketing of flash exposures for precise control and high-speed effects)

These front and side views of the Vivitar 283 Automatic flash show the location of the various controls. Note that the all-important automatic-exposure selector dial is on the right side of the unit.

The NVS-1 custom double-powered Vivitar 283 flash modification and accessories make shooting in special lighting situations easier.

▲ This NVS-1 is attached to Newton's custom flash bracket.

◀ I made this portrait of a baby on white seamless paper with my Nikon N50, an 80mm F1.8 manual lens, and two Vivitar 283 flashes. The exposure on ISO 64 film was 1/60 sec. at f/8.

coded options, and setting a color-coded sensor to match the color on the dial. When you work within the chosen distance range, automatic-flash exposures are good to excellent. Both the 283 and 285 come with easy-to-understand manuals, as well as short PC cords for use with cameras that don't have a hotshoe.

The Vivitar flashes are widely used by newspaper photographers, photography students, and photographers who are manual-camera users. In fact, the Vivitar 283 flash is so popular that professional modifications of it have been made for years. The only problem with the 283 is that it is difficult to get information from the company that distributes Vivitar flash units in the United States.

Accessories and Modifications. The Vivitar SC-l remote cord enables you to use the 283 flash up to about 6 feet away from a camera while still retaining automatic operation. The Vivitar MVP-l power variator permits reducing flash power in manual steps, from 1/2 power to a minimum of 1/32 power. The minimum-power setting produces a very short flash duration of about 1/20,000 sec., which is useful for closeup nature and scientific photography of fast-moving subjects.

Wein makes a tiny Peanut slave that is designed to snap into the PC/sync socket on either the side of 283 flashes or the foot of 285s. Wein's hotshoe slave works on any flash. Paramount makes 6-foot-long coiled PC cords with Vivitar tips. Holly's replacement foot for the 283 and 285 units accepts any twin-bladed sync cord or slave unit and has a standard 1/4-20 threaded socket for mounting the flash on a tripod or lightstand. Sto-Fen domes come in models for the 283 and 285 flashes, and you can use LumiQuest bounce cards with either unit.

Photographer Philip Leonian's Cougar Design Company makes plates that replace intentionally fragile Vivitar 283 and 285 flash feet. Cougar plates have a threaded socket for mounting a flash on a standard tripod or lightstand, or joined in pairs on the company's T-Bar device. This accessory, plus an umbrella mount, makes it easy to balance and aim two flashes out of one umbrella. Holly and Paramount make replacement flash feet that accept slaves with two-prong blades.

NVS-1 Vivitar Modification. Stuessy Associates of New Jersey makes the NVS-1 unit, a great double-powered conversion based on the Vivitar 283. The NVS-1 offers full

To photograph champion juggler Tony Duncan under the Brooklyn Bridge, I worked with my tripod-mounted Nikon N90, a 20mm F2.8 lens, and ISO 100 film. I took in-camera reflected meter readings off the sky and flash-meter readings off Duncan. For additional lighting, I used two Vivitar 283 flash units mounted on lightstands, equipped with 6V battery packs and Wein Ultra Slave units, aimed directly at the juggler's head from 5 to 6 feet on opposite sides. A light red gel covered one flash head, and a deep blue gel covered the other. An on-camera Wein SST infrared trigger fired the flashes, which I'd set to manual, 1/2 power. I adjusted the flash-to-subject distances, lens apertures, and shutter speeds to balance the sunset light and the flash. I couldn't predict the pattern of the balls, so I shot several rolls of film, varying my angle to the bridge. The best exposures were made at about 1/4 sec. at f/5.6.

automatic operation with precisely repeatable power reductions down to 1/64. Options include a head with a removable flashtube for bare-tube flash that casts soft-shadowed light in a circle. NVS also makes a mount that accepts teleflash reflectors. A *strobe on a rope* for hanging a bare flashtube and snap-on white, black, and color bounce-light devices also come in handy. When used with a Norman 2-D reflector, the NVS-1 accepts honeycomb grids and a snoot—helpful light modifiers—made for portable Normans (see Chapter 9 on page 93).

With the appropriate flash-to-battery module, the NVS-1 operates with Dyna-Lite Jackrabbit battery packs, Quantum battery packs, Underdog battery packs (my favorite), and even photographer-made 6V battery packs. The NVS-1 flash comes with instructions and tip sheets for special lighting situations.

I opt for my NVS-1 when I want to create *bare-bulb effects*, in which light from the flash is spread around in a circle. I also use the NVS-1 as background lighting for portraits and still-lifes, and even for accent lighting in large rooms.

Sunpak Automatic Flashes
To the best of my knowledge, Sunpak markets more different types of flash units than any other company. The Sunpak flashes come in handle-mount, bounce, compact, ring flash, and even underwater models. The GNs for the units (based on ISO 100 film and measured in feet) range from about 15 for ring flashes, 28 to 40 for small manual units, 56 to 66 for compact flashes, 80 to 120 for adjustable bounce units, and 160 for professional handle-mount units. Some people prefer the Sunpak 120-J to

Vivitars because setting its color-coded sliding scale is uncomplicated.

Most Sunpak units offer a choice of three *f*-stops and/or distance ranges. As with all automatic flashes, you must set the film speed, *f*-stop, and distance range on the flash, as well as set the lens to the indicated *f*-stop and the sync speed on the camera. (If desired for creative reasons, you can use almost any shutter speed below maximum sync speed, too.) You can use most Sunpaks with program cameras or combined with other flashes (as described above).

Sunpak's automatic bounce flashes are popular with photography students because they are easy to operate and easy on the wallet. A busy wedding photographer I know loves her Sunpaks, too; she says they never quit. Sunpaks are sold just about everywhere, and the manuals are perfectly adequate. The United States distributor puts out a brochure listing all the units and is helpful in answering inquiries.

Automatic Ring Flash. A small ring flash has a circular tube set in a lightweight metal or plastic housing. The battery chamber might be under the ring or in a separate housing that attaches to the camera hotshoe. A supplied adapter screws in the ring setup so the flash tube surrounds the lens. The resulting low-power light is almost completely shadowless, which is good for many closeups and extreme closeups. Most ring flashes are automatic/manual models; Sunpak makes a couple of modular TTL units. Frankly, for closeups I prefer exposures I get manually with the aid of a flash meter.)

Doctors and dentists use ring flash. A surgeon friend is happy with the results he gets with a dedicated Sunpak ring flash, which he keeps on a Minolta camera in his operating room. Fashion and beauty photographers like ring-flash shadow effects. The units cause a narrow band of shadow to spread evenly all around faces or figures placed close to a background. (Large professional ring flashes operating off battery packs or strobes are in vogue from time to time for fashion and beauty photography.) If you combine a tiny ring flash with fast film, you can get good ring-flash effects for portraits, fashion shots, and more.

Metz Automatic Flashes

German-made Metz flashes have a fine reputation for quality. In fact, users of German and Swedish cameras favor Metz over all other flash units. The company is perhaps best-known for its powerful, handle-mount professional flash units (see Chapter 11 on page 118), but it offers compact flashes, too. Some of these have heads that rotate internally for bounce flash. In addition, you can use Metz's modular dedicated/TTL flashes in automatic and M flash modes. Some are self-slaved. The company puts out a good catalog that is available from most quality photo dealers.

Nissin Flashes

Nissin isn't a well-known name, but the company makes flashes for many camera manufacturers. If you can find a Nissin, you'll be getting a reliable flash at a good price. Nissin offers various automatic and manual units, from handle-mount to ring-flash units.

I made this setup shot of Sunpak flash units in a low-lit studio to control unwanted reflections. I bounced my Sunpak Auto 383 Super Flash out of a 42-inch, black-backed white umbrella that was about 4 feet from the subject. I bracketed by varying the *f*-stop from *f*/6.3, to *f*/8, and *f*/8–11. For this frame, I used my Nikon FM-2 manual camera, a 28mm F2.8 lens, an *f*/8 automatic setting, and ISO 100 film.

Battery Packs and Accessories For Automatic Flashes

As mentioned earlier, when you get tired of buying sets of disposable batteries or tired of slow flash-recycle times, you should invest in a rechargeable 6V battery pack. This purchase will save you a great deal of frustration. Top-of-the-line camera/flash system marketers imply that you must use only their packs, but don't believe them: the battery packs the top independents make often offer more value than the major manufacturers.

Quantum, for example, the best-known battery-pack manufacturer, has been in business for years and makes several different styles and sizes. Quantum packs are thoroughly tested and are guaranteed not to destroy an expensive TTL flash when used with the correct module; different brands and automatic/manual flashes use different modules. Thousands of demanding photojournalists and meeting and wedding photographers use Quantum

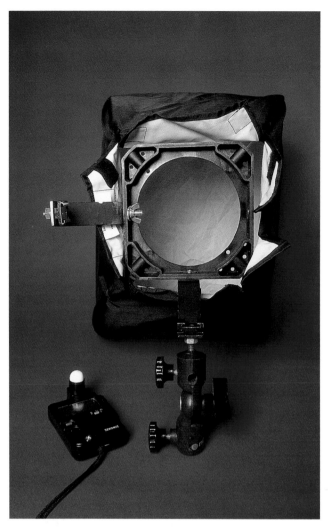

These are Wayne Fisher's homemade flash bracket for a small Chimera softbox, and a Sekonic Digi-Lite F flash meter.

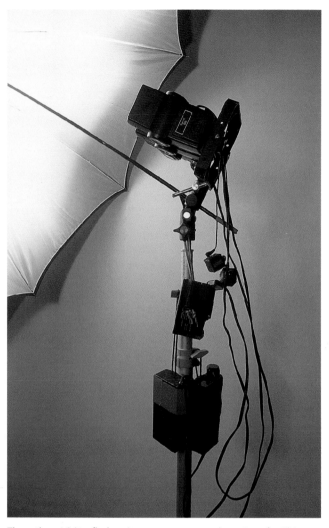

These three Vivitar flash units are on my own adaptation of a Chimera double bracket and ring, bounced out of an umbrella.

packs, which have winking lights that indicate charge status, on a daily basis. Dyna-Lite, Lumedyne, Metz, Perma-Pak, and Sunpak make reliable packs, too, for many TTL or automatic/manual flash units.

I use Underdog custom-made, rechargeable battery packs. An Underdog is cigarette-pack sized, screws to tripod sockets under cameras, and weighs about 11 ounces. It frees me from shoulder straps and trailing cords. Underdog battery packs come in pairs and give about 300 full-power shots. With the exception of a dual-voltage charger, these units don't have any bells or whistles.

Commercial Battery Packs
Quantum makes commercial battery packs of various sizes with battery-to-flash modules for most Metz, Sunpak, Vivitar, and other automatic flash units. You can use Underdog batteries with the appropriate module with many automatic flashes. Commercial battery packs come with chargers; dual-voltage (110–220V) chargers are available for travelers.

Slaves
Slave units are attached to remote, off-camera flashes not connected by any type of cord, and respond to a light or some other signal, thereby firing the slaved unit. Calumet, Quantum, Sunpak, and Wein offer inexpensive to moderate-price light-sensitive slave units for remote, automatic-flash use. Sunpak's basic slaves work well in low light at fairly close distances, as does Wein's Peanut unit, which snaps into the sync outlet of Vivitar flashes. (For information on types of advanced slave units, see Chapters 10 and 11.)

Brackets
Stroboframe makes flash brackets that fit just about all automatic flashes (review Chapter 6). I have two lightweight Quick Flip brackets, one of which has been modified for closeup work. Stroboframe also markets the George Lepp double-flash bracket for nature closeups. Kirk Industries make several custom brackets, including a double-closeup bracket.

Chapter 9

MANUAL FLASH UNITS

When manual flashes, or dedicated/*through-the-lens* (TTL) or automatic flashes set on *manual mode* (M), are used on full power and are fully recycled, they put out the same amount of light each time they fire. This capability permits repeatable effects whether made with a single flash or several flashes used in combination. Small manual flash units have been around for nearly 50 years and aren't at all obsolete. All professional and many advanced photographers learn to manually set camera and flash combinations in order to achieve control of three essentials: depth of field, flash range, and precisely repeatable effects. Learning to use manual flash will improve your skills with setting both electronic cameras and dedicated flash units; it will also serve as preparation for shooting with high-power, professional flashes and strobes.

If you now shoot only with TTL-metered flash, be aware that you can use a low-powered, self-slaved manual flash, or any inexpensive manual flash with a slave unit, as an accent light without affecting TTL-metered flash exposures.

A good reason for students and the "financially challenged" to use manual flashes is that these units are much less expensive than dedicated/TTL and even automatic units. So you can try flash without making a big investment. Some small units cost as little as $10 or $20.

(Photographers who are content to point and shoot can safely skip this chapter.)

Manual Flash and Manual Cameras

You must use an automatic or manual flash with a manual camera. In order to consistently expose color transparency films with manual flash (or AC-powered strobes), owning and learning to use a flash meter is almost a must. This also applies to making pictures with any TTL or automatic flash used in the M mode. If you shoot color print films, you can safely expose by using the scales printed on the back of tiny flashes, traditional *guide-number* (GN) formulas, or the "expert method."

Photographers with professional ambitions should know that most high-power, portable flashes and all professional strobes currently made are manual units. So by learning about manual flash, you're also preparing to use professional equipment. (For formulas and information on flash meters, see page 95.) You can set all advanced dedicated/TTL flash units to full M mode. You can use the Vivitar 283 and 285 flashes, and the top-of-the-line Metz and Sunpak automatic units in manual mode, too. Most of these advanced flashes have built-in or optional manual "power variators" that cut power for precise lighting control.

The Nikon SB-E automatic flash, which is no longer made, doesn't operate as such with any camera I own, but is tiny and reliable. To use it as a manual unit, I tape over its sensor. In manual mode, the SB-E has a GN of 40 with ISO 100 film. For this shot of a gallery opening, I handheld my Nikon FM-2 camera with a 28mm F2.8 lens. I metered for the room light and added flash fill; my choice of *f*-stop, *f*/5.6, was based on my years of experience. I exposed ISO 64 film for 1/4 sec.

For this Times Square "tiltscape," I exposed off the midtoned sidewalk. I aimed my Nikon FM-2 manual camera and tiny flash up at the neon street sign from about 10 feet away, aware that it was highly reflective. With a 20mm F2.8 lens and my Phoenix flash, I exposed for 1/15 sec. at f/4 on ISO 100 film.

Basic Manual Flash Units

The least expensive flashes made (costing less than $20) are low-power manual units. Smaller in size than cigarette packs, these flashes have an "On/Off" switch, a "Ready" light, a "Test" button, and a GN range between about 28 and 45 (based on ISO 100 film and measured in feet). Today's basic manual flashes have a hotfoot; some also provide a short PC/sync cord for off-camera use with cameras without a hotshoe. Paramount makes long, coiled PC/sync cords with tips for all flash types. These cords are useful for holding flash high or off to the side.

When you work with an inexpensive manual unit, like the $12 Phoenix shown in the diagram on page 95, you can calculate good exposure by using the scale on the back of the flash. This scale lists ISO 100, 400, and 1000 film speeds down one side of the unit, and several distance choices in both feet and meters at the top. To use this scale, note the film speed being used and then set the camera shutter to *sync speed* (or to less than sync speed if you're shooting in low light). Estimate and stand at the desired distance from the subject. Next, set the *f*-stop indicated on the scale for the chosen ISO and distance. (You can also choose the *f*-stop first, and then move to the correct distance.) Then shoot.

You can vary flash effects by moving closer to or farther from your subject without changing the shutter speed or *f*-stop. If you judge distance well and the flash is fully charged when you fire it, you should get good exposures.

Exposing Manual Flash

Today, the professional way to expose manual flash of any power is to use a flash meter. Nevertheless, sometimes knowing the traditional way to calculate manual flash exposure with GNs might still be helpful. And being acquainted with the method will certainly reinforce your understanding of fundamental flash principles. These are that flash falls off according to the square of its distance from the subject (the Inverse Square Law), and that the combination of the lens aperture, the film speed used, and the flash's power and distance from the subject determines flash exposures.

Shutter speeds aren't an exposure factor when flash is the primary light source and the shutter is set at sync speed. Slow shutter speeds do, of course, affect long exposures when flash is used on dark foreground subjects against bright backgrounds. But (to the best of my knowledge) in the days before dedicated/TTL cameras and flashes, slow-sync flash-fill techniques weren't used.

Although I could have made this shot of a striped wall without flash, I often just like the effect of fill light. Here, I used my Nikon FM-2 manual camera, a 28mm F2.8 lens, and my Phoenix flash from a distance of about 4 feet. The exposure on ISO 50 film was *f/6.3* for 1/60 sec.

Guide Numbers

GNs are mostly used to compare the power of different flash units. But if you know a flash's GN, you can use it as a basis for determining a manual-flash exposure (see "The Quick and Expert Way to Use Small Manual Flash" on page 99). Flash manuals use ISO 100 film as the standard when listing GNs. So you'll have to increase or decrease GNs accordingly if you shoot a faster or slower film. For example, to determine the right GN for an ISO 200 film, you must double the GN indicated for the ISO 100 film. Similarly, for an ISO 400 film, you must double the GN for the ISO 100 film twice. For an ISO 50 film, you must halve the GN for the ISO 100 film, and so on.

Determining *F*-Stops for Given Distances with Guide Numbers

To get the correct aperture for a specific distance, divide the chosen flash-to-subject distance into the GN. For example, when you use a manual flash with a GN of 66 and the distance scale on your manual lens, you find that standing 10 feet from a large group of people results in a good composition. Dividing 12 into 66 tells you to set *f/6.6* (which is just past *f/6.3*) on your lens for correct flash exposure. Move in and out to adjust exposure.

Determining Distances for Given *F*-Stops with Guide Numbers

This technique calls for dividing the chosen *f*-stop into the GN in order to find the correct distance you must stand from the subject for a good exposure. This comes in handy when you must use a small aperture because of low maximum sync speed for flash fill in bright sun.

Here, the f-stop indicated for 10 feet is between f/4 and f/5.6 (or f/4.5 with ISO 100 film). This means that the guide number (in feet) is 45; verify this with tests.

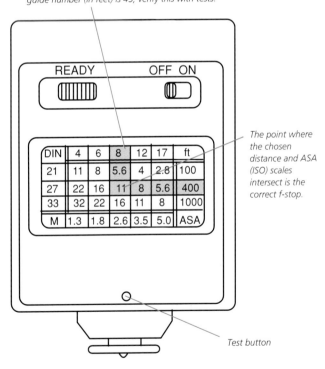

DIN	4	6	8	12	17	ft
21	11	8	5.6	4	2.8	100
27	22	16	11	8	5.6	400
33	32	22	16	11	8	1000
M	1.3	1.8	2.6	3.5	5.0	ASA

The point where the chosen distance and ASA (ISO) scales intersect is the correct f-stop.

Test button

The back of the Phoenix manual flash contains a chart of film-speed, flash-to-subject distance, and aperture combinations.

Shutters, Sync Speeds, and PC/Sync Cords

Learn your camera's maximum sync speed (there is no minimum sync speed). Before shooting, you should always check to see that you've set your manual camera to maximum sync speed if you're working in bright daylight or in a studio where you don't want any low-level ambient light to record on film. (To try slow-sync flash with a manual flash in low light, you can set any low shutter speed you want, but the results will be unpredictable.)

When you shoot in bright light, the need for any camera shutter to be *in sync* restricts the *f*-stops you can choose with any flash. An *out-of-sync* shutter that closes too fast prevents part of the flash from reaching the subject, and a black or dark, underexposed stripe will run across or down one side of the picture area. Learn your camera's sync speed.

Older manual 35mm SLR cameras with *focal-plane shutters* typically have a maximum sync speed of 1/60 sec. This forces you to use apertures of around *f*/11, *f*/16, or even *f*/22 in bright light with ISO 100 film, so you must work very close for flash fill.

PC/sync cords are covered wires that connect off-camera manual flashes (or strobes) to cameras. Using these cords is an interference-proof method of firing manual flash anywhere. The cord transmits an electronic signal that fires a flash when you press the shutter release. You can *hard-wire*, or join together with long PC/sync cords, multiple flashes (or strobes). It is wise to carry a spare PC/sync cord.

Bracketing Manual Flash Exposures

Even experienced photographers using correctly functioning equipment bracket exposures when they don't know exactly which exposure will work best for a particular subject. This is true for flash pictures made outdoors, indoors, and even in the controlled conditions of a studio. You might want to try different exposure effects for the same shot. Sometimes the exposure changes the entire mood of an image.

A *normal* exposure, of course, is whatever you feel most comfortable with. In photography, the term *high-key* means light and bright. This effect, which many fashion and beauty photographers like, is also flattering to mature people. A *saturated* look means either that color transparencies or prints have rich, glowing hues or that black-and-white shots have good detail in highlight areas.

When you light all the pictures on a roll of film exactly the same way, you might not need to bracket but to have *clip tests* made. Here, you expose color or black-and-white film normally, take the film to a professional lab, and have two or three frames "clipped" from one

Once in a while, I still use Kodachrome film, which has very fine grain but is very contrasty. For this shot of a marathon, I exposed off the sunlit grass; flash fill lit the foreground runners, who were about 4 to 6 feet away. With my Nikon FM-2, a 20mm F2.8 lens, and my Phoenix flash, I exposed ISO 64 film at *f*/5.6 for 1/250 sec.

My experience told me to cut the flash back to half power for this shot of children on the beach. "Over-filled" shadows can result when you use a powerful flash, even in exposures based on sunlight. With my Nikon FM-2 manual camera, a 20mm F2.8 lens, and a Metz handle-mount flash, I exposed for 1/250 sec. at *f*/8–11 on ISO 50 film.

end and developed. You or the lab can then judge if the exposure of the balance of the roll is what you want, or needs to be adjusted via a development-time increase or decrease. You can use this professional method when shooting action, nonrepeatable events, or critical studio subjects.

Varying Manual Flash-to-Subject Distance. Moving closer to or farther away from a subject will increase or decrease, respectively, the amount of flash reaching the subject. It won't affect the background of a scene that is out of flash range.

Diffusing a Flash with Translucent Material. Using one or more layers of white plastic, paper, or cloth over a flash head reduces the flash output without affecting the background of a scene that is out of flash range.

Turning Down the Power. A manual flash or an automatic flash with a manual *power-reduction switch* makes bracketing flash effects easy. Reducing the flash output increases the speed of the flash burst, which is useful for motion-stopping effects. Once again, this approach doesn't affect a background that is out of flash range.

Varying the F-*Stop.* *Opening up*, or adjusting a lens aperture to a lower number, increases the flash range, as well as the flash effect on a subject. Opening up also lightens the overall exposure of a scene. Conversely, *closing down* an *f*-stop to a smaller number reduces both the flash effect on a subject and the overall exposure of the background. It is perfectly practical to use the aperture setting to vary flash exposures when manual flash provides all or almost all of the light in a scene.

Practical Manual Flash

In order to become an expert with a manual flash, you might want to rely on some tried-and-true habits. At first, use one lens at a time to find which lens apertures and flash-to-subject distances work best for your style. For example, when I use the old Nikon SB-E flash that I own in the M mode (which I did for some of the pictures in this book), I tape over the automatic sensor; the flash then works manually. The SB-E flash has a GN of 40. With a 28mm or 20mm lens used at *f*/8 and ISO 100 film, I get consistently good exposures between about 4½ and 5½ feet. There is a slight margin for error even with color transparency film. (Although Nikon no longer makes SB-E flashes, you can find used ones.)

Using Small Flash as the Sole Light Source

When you want to use a small manual flash unit as your single light source, always set sync speed (or below) on the camera. To determine exposure, you can rely on either the flash scale, the GN system, your experience, or the easiest way-measurement with a flash meter.

Estimating flash-to-subject distances accurately is critical for manual-flash exposures. You can do this several ways: by using the indicator lines on manual-focus lenses, by pre-measuring your footsteps or outstretched arm, or by carrying a carpenter's tape or a 6-to-10-foot piece of string knotted at 12-inch intervals.

Using Small Flash as Fill

You can use any manual flash, including a ring flash, for flash fill. Always set the shutter speed and f-stop needed for a good background exposure. In sunlight, use slow-speed films and set the shutter to the highest possible sync speed. This will permit a moderate f-stop. When you combine a small flash, a manual camera with a maximum sync speed of 1/60 sec., and ISO 100 film, you must use an aperture of f/11 or f/16 and stand within 2 or 3 feet of your subject in order for the fill flash to be effective. At a shooting distance of 4 to 5 feet, you'll get little flash fill.

My Nikon SB-23 flash has a GN of 66 with ISO 100 film. For this shot of a veteran, I set manual mode on the flash; it delivered enough fill for this basically sunlit portrait, which I shot from a distance of about 6 feet. Using my Nikon FM-2 manual camera, a 70–210mm F4–5.6 lens set at 210mm, and ISO 100 film, I exposed at f/11 for 1/250 sec.

Shooting in Yulara, Australia, I metered off the outback campfire, which called for a long exposure. To illuminate the man, I based the exposure on the flash-to-subject distance, which was about 5 to 6 feet. The background was completely dark, so the final image, lit by the fire and the flash, is without ghosts. With my Nikon FM-2 manual camera, a 28mm F2.8 lens, and my Ying Yang flash, I exposed for 1/2 sec. at f/6.3 on ISO 100 film.

THE QUICK AND EXPERT WAY TO USE SMALL MANUAL FLASH

Specialists who shoot hundreds of manual flash pictures in an evening at clubs, parties, meetings, weddings, and on cruise ships and come up with a good exposure every time, have a secret. They use the same technique that old-time news photographers did.

These specialists always use the same flash with the same film, and the same lens set at the same f-stop, and they stand at the same distance from the subject—for each and every picture they take! If you do this on a regular basis, you'll soon learn how to make the small variations that produce good exposures with most subjects.

When I spotted this Santa Claus taking a short break from his duties, I asked him to pose. The day was overcast, and I shot from a distance of about 6 feet with my Nikon FM-2 manual camera and a 35–80mm F3.5–4.5 lens. The fast shutter speed I used, 1/250 sec., made the picture look as if it were shot at night and eliminated an ugly background. With my Ying Yang flash I exposed ISO 50 film at f/4.5–5.6.

To achieve flash fill at night or in low daylight, you have to set a wide-open aperture and a slow shutter speed. Measure the light with a built-in camera meter or a handheld reflected-light meter and set the lens and shutter to slightly underexpose the background. Underexposing by 1/2 stop is often a good choice. Stand at a distance that provides a pleasing amount of flash fill on dark objects in the foreground. Use a tripod in order to avoid blurred backgrounds.

Using Small Flash for Closeup Photography

You can choose any small manual flash unit to shoot closeups. Use a flash meter to measure exposure. The flash should be used off-camera, otherwise you risk having the illumination from the flash overshoot your subject. *Closeup brackets* can be useful. And remember, ring flashes, which are used on the camera around the lenses, produce shadowless light.

Use a PC/sync cord to attach an off-camera manual flash to the camera's PC/sync outlet. For old flashes or cameras that don't have PC/sync outlets, you can use tiny Hama adapters; these devices incorporate a PC/sync socket or cord, and are available at photo dealers.

Flash Meters

Using a flash meter is the best way to measure manual flash or strobe exposures. And investing in one will save you money on film in the long run. Almost all flash meters are *incident-light meters*, which means that they measure light that falls on the subject. They come with a white dome.

For a simple lighting setup, you just turn the meter on, then set the film speed and the desired shutter speed on the meter. Make sure that the sync speed set on the meter never exceeds your camera's sync speed. To take a flash-meter reading, press and then press and release a button on the flash meter, just before a test flash is fired. The flash meter then indicates which *f*-stop to set. If you change the flash-to-subject distance, take a new exposure reading.

Top-of-the-line flash meters have rotating heads, so you can easily compare the light outputs from complex setups with several different flashes and/or strobes. In addition, you can adjust *lighting ratios*, which are the differences in output between lights, and, therefore, the relative brightness of highlights and shadows. (For more information, see Chapters 10 and 11.) Be sure to get a flash meter that reads daylight and existing light plus flash at different shutter speeds (see below).

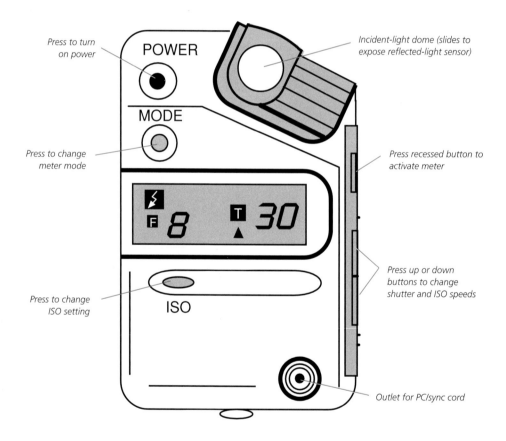

The Sekonic Flashmate meter is simple to operate. Note that the incident-light dome on the top of the meter slides to expose the reflected-light sensor.

Press to turn on power

POWER

Incident-light dome (slides to expose reflected-light sensor)

MODE

Press to change meter mode

Press recessed button to activate meter

Press up or down buttons to change shutter and ISO speeds

Press to change ISO setting

ISO

Outlet for PC/sync cord

▶ To use this gray-card substitute, meter carefully off the 18-percent gray area only, then include this page in a photograph. The different shades of gray, white border, and black must all be separated in tone to ensure accurate exposure, in both color and black and white.

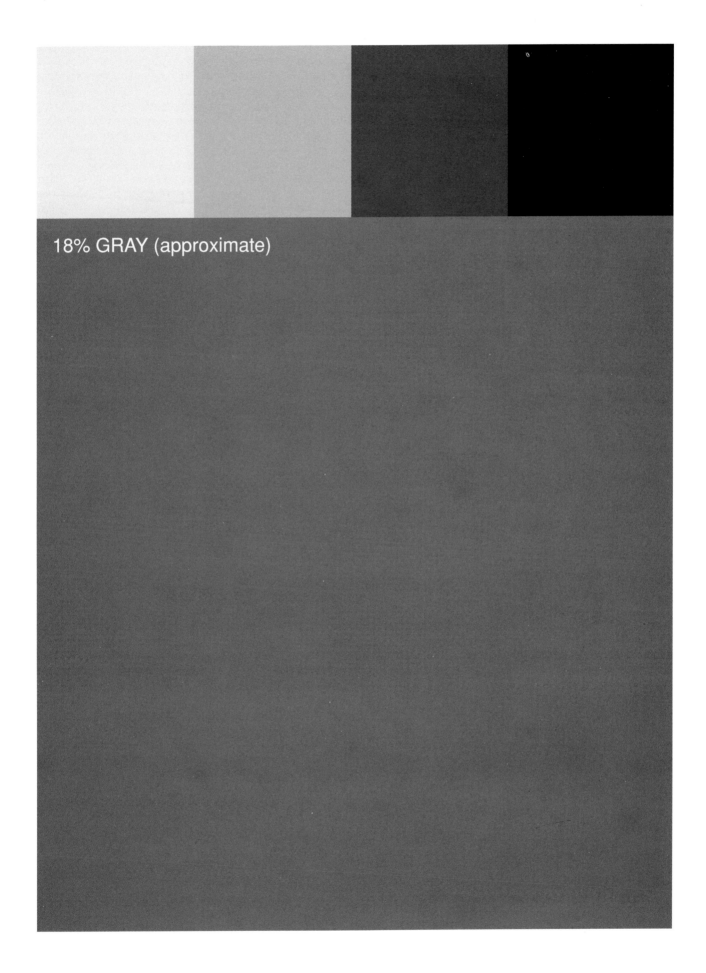

18% GRAY (approximate)

Choosing a Flash Meter

To go beyond the techniques discussed up to this point, you need a flash meter. Today, the best flash meters offer readings that establish and help adjust brightness relationships between light sources. These *lighting ratios* affect contrast on film.

Flash meters can measure ratios between flash and daylight, two or more flashes used together, flash and strobe together, or any number of strobes combined.

Flash meters also measure the cumulative flash pops that photographers sometimes use with still-life subjects to permit smaller *f*-stops and more extensive depth of field, as well as for daylight- or available-light-only exposures.

All of this calls for the highest shutter speeds, the top flash sync speeds, and long time exposures. Even moderate-price flash meters of the major manufacturers are quite accurate and versatile. If you are a serious photographer who shoots studio-type pictures, owns a manual camera

My Phoenix manual flash has a GN of 40 with ISO 100 film. Working at Hampton Court Palace, England, I metered off the sky and underexposed by 1/2 stop. I knew the flash would brighten the gate's gold-painted seal. I used my Nikon FM-2 manual camera and a 55mm F3.5 macro lens. The exposure was 1/60 sec. at f/6.3 on ISO 50 film.

and flash or strobe, and/or has professional ambitions, you'll find that a good flash meter will soon earn back its price in terms of the money saved on bad exposures. Despite wonderful TTL flashes, I doubt that there is hardly a professional photographer around today who doesn't own a flash meter.

Sekonic Flashmate. This neat little meter is easy to set, measures flash with a wide range of shutter speeds, and works well for both combined flash/daylight exposures and all-daylight exposures. (This meter costs about $200.)

Minolta V. This model, from the company that many experts rate as tops for flash meters, offers a wide range of settings. I consider the meter's best feature to be its ability to compare the percentages of daylight/available light and flash in a scene. The unit costs more than $500, but the options make it good value for professional users.

For this shot made near New York City's Flatiron Building, I metered off the dusk sky. I knew that my Phoenix flash would reflect off the sculpture's polished metal, but I wasn't sure exactly how the metal would look on the ISO 50 film I was shooting. I bracketed several frames, varying the *f*-stop between *f*/4 and *f*/2.8 from about 10 to 12 feet away. This lighter image, exposed at *f*/2.8 for 1/30 sec., was the best of the shots, which I made with my Nikon FM-2 manual camera and a 28mm F2.8 lens.

Part Four
SPECIALIZED AND PROFESSIONAL FLASH

Knowing that flying sparks would record as streaks at long exposures, I bracketed with shutter speeds of 1, 2, and 4 seconds to vary the streak effects. The fluorescent lights caused the background's green tone. With my Nikon N90 and a 28mm F2.8 lens, I exposed ISO 100 film at *f*/4 for 2 seconds here.

*I*f you currently aren't too experienced a photographer and read this book casually, you might find this section of the book a bit daunting. Don't worry. Just look at the pictures, and store whatever strikes you most into your visual and knowledge banks. You can always refer back to these chapters at a later time as you gain expertise.

If you are now at that most difficult intermediate stage of photography, and have plenty of enthusiasm, ideas, vision, and ambition but your skills still need polishing, use these chapters as a goal. When you do sooner or later break through the "wall"—as usual, it takes shooting many, many pictures—and can get what you want onto film most of the time, you'll have not only your present pleasure in the act of taking pictures but also the satisfaction and recognition that comes from creating anything good. But everyone makes mistakes, including professionals. You aren't getting worse, just more demanding of yourself.

Advanced photographers can exhibit work in juried shows and earn some money from photography if that is what they want. (Note that I don't say exactly how, where, or exactly how much. I think that books that promise to teach these things aren't completely realistic. You'll find your own unique way.) Going to the next level involves aesthetics as well as gadgets, mechanics, electronics, and business skills. Make the time to look at great photographs and art as often as possible.

To most beginning and established professional photographers I know, the game is often about money! To my professional readers, I say that I hope that at least a few topics covered here are new to you and useful. If you learn one fact or trick that helps you land or complete a successful assignment, or you're inspired to try one new technique because of a picture or suggestion, the book should be worth the money. The master photographers' work in the Gallery section will give you to standards to shoot for (see Chapter 12 on page 129).

For this photograph of traditional British Christmas food, I bounced a Dyna-Lite 500 WS/J strobe out of a 42-inch white umbrella. I determined exposure by using a flash meter supplemented by a Polaroid film test; I bracketed the exposure, varying the f-stop. With my Nikon N90 and a 50mm F1.8 lens, I exposed this shot on ISO 64 film at f/8 for 1/60 sec.

Chapter 10

SPECIALIZED FLASH

To move from advanced to professional lighting and achieve just about all of the outdoor lighting effects illustrated in this book, and many of the indoor ones, you must have several items. You'll need an advanced camera, at least one dedicated lens, and an appropriate TTL flash and remote dedicated cord. You'll also need one or two automatic/manual flashes, one or two slave units, a tripod, a portable reflector, a flash meter, a couple of lightstands, an umbrella and umbrella mount, and some gaffer tape (electrician's tape, sold at professional photo dealers). Add a roll of aluminum foil; a white sheet or silver space blanket (available at camping stores); a moderate-size, portable *softbox*, which is a large, folding, fabric diffuser; a roll or two of white and colored seamless paper; and some color gels for more versatility.

Of course, some effects (like many of those shown in the Gallery section of this book) are possible only with large flashes or strobes with high power and fast recycling times. Also, when you work with small flash units alone, you can't previsualize effects. (Strobes have built-in *modeling lights*, which are continuously burning, low-wattage tungsten hot lights.) If you invest in a Polaroid camera, a Polaroid back, and Polaroid film, and shoot lighting tests as most professional photographers do. The cost will be offset by the money you'll save on reshoots.

If you can't afford powerful lights, connect two or more automatic/manual flashes and "slave" them in order to obtain small *f*-stops. You can also make snoots for small flash units out of aluminum foil, or build a softbox from artboard with the front covered with tracing paper. Most photographers who are good at lighting develop their own techniques and lighting aids.

Location Lighting

"Going on location" means shooting outdoors anywhere, indoors in offices, factories, arenas, airports, restaurants, hotel lobbies, libraries, hospitals, schools, stores, and malls. Most locations are large spaces that you can't completely illuminate with small flash; however, you can augment long exposures in big spaces with flash fill—unless the main subject is fast-moving. Critical factors for location shooting are packing, transporting, and setting lights up quickly, as well as dealing with the light that exists at the site. A good assistant (or even unskilled assistance) is invaluable.

If you must brightly light a large or high room with low-level existing light, you'll probably need to use strobes since the light will have to travel some distance. You might need to use strobes when you add color gels to any subject at a distance. This is because deep-toned gels absorb a great deal of light (see below). A good tip: if you somehow land a job that is beyond your current lighting abilities, my best advice is to hire a good lighting assistant along with your rental strobes. Get names from professional photography associations in your area, check professional photo labs (where many assistants advertise), or ask other photographers for recommendations.

Color and Location Light

Existing lights aren't designed for color photography. Within lighting types, you find variants. Fluorescent lamps, for example, don't come in just one color; three are routinely used, and each records as a different shade of green on daylight transparency films. Continuously burning

For this shot, made in a drab classroom, I placed honeycomb grids and a red and a blue gel on two strobe heads, and then aimed the strobe heads at the wall behind the subject. I used a third head with a snoot plus black Cinefoil aimed at the student, so it emitted a narrow beam of white light that illuminated only his face. I balanced the lighting ratios by using a flash meter and Polaroid film tests, and by adjusting the power of the strobes. Shooting with my Nikon N50 camera and a 50mm F1.8 lens, and two slaved Speedotron 1200 WS/J strobes, I exposed at f/8 for 1/60 sec. on ISO 100 film.

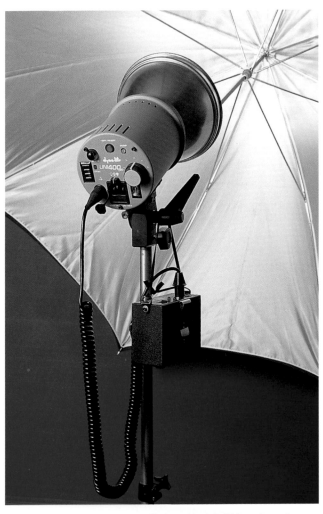

This is the Dyna-Lite Uni 400 Jr. flash and Jack Rabbit pack, and an umbrella.

The Norman 400B flash, battery pack, teleflash reflector, and assorted grids come in handy for on-location shooting.

I shot this picture of the lead guitarist for a rock group with my Nikon N90, an 80–200mm F2.8 zoom lens set at about 150mm, and an on-camera Nikon SB-26 flash. On a shelf to the left, a Morris Mini-Wide self-slaved flash added some fill light. The exposure on ISO 100 film was f/2.8 for 1/2 sec.

tungsten lamps, which are also called *hot lamps* and *household lamps*, burn at different wattages and record as different warm shades of orange. Similarly, industrial lights and streetlights look either slightly or intensely green or yellow on daylight-balanced, color transparency films.

How do you solve these problems? Combine flash use with time exposures. Carry basic filters, and use them over lenses to correct background lighting. When adding flash or strobe to "fill" foreground subjects at the same time as using filters to correct the color of existing light in a large space, you must add the appropriate *complementary color* gel over the flash or strobe head(s). If you don't, the subject or object that the flash hits will record on film the same color as the filter.

Filters, Gels, and Flash

If you shoot color transparency films and want professional-quality results, learn to use color filters with complementary gels on flash (see below). As mentioned earlier, daylight-type color films are balanced for use with all types of film. You can use any flash or strobe with critical-color films to provide flash fill to lighten shadows or emphasize the foreground. The flash will also correct the color of existing-light sources.

I photographed the popular rock group Big Head Todd and the Monsters posed on an amusement-ride car at Coney Island. Shooting with my Nikon N90 and a 20mm F2.8 lens, I set my Nikon SB-26 flash in TTL mode. I exposed ISO 100 film for 1/60 sec. at f/5.6.

IS ACCURATE COLOR IMPORTANT?

The simple answer to this question is yes—unless the picture is a fine-art image or is intended for use by a rock group. The deeper answer is that pleasant skin tones matter tremendously for corporate, fashion and beauty, portrait, stock, wedding, and meeting photography. Food, interiors, and products shot on transparency film absolutely must have accurate color. For other subjects, some variations from "normal" color are generally acceptable as long as they're pleasing to the eye.

For this shot I mounted a Norman 200 WS/J professional flash on a lightstand and bounced the flash out of a 42-inch white umbrella down onto the scene from about 4 feet away. I determined the correct exposure via a flash meter and Polaroid tests. With my Nikon FM-2 manual camera and a 20mm F2.8 lens, I exposed at f/4 for 1/30 sec. on ISO 100 film.

I correctly exposed this party shot by reading the existing light. Minimal fill from my Nikon SB-26 flash in TTL mode was needed; it added sparkle to the piano. I mounted my Nikon N90 and 28mm F2.8 lens on a lightweight tripod, and exposed at f/4 for 1/15 sec. on ISO 100 film.

In a room lit by neon fixtures, a person in the foreground lit by flash will look correct on color slide film. The unfiltered background out of flash range will record as greenish, but the effect probably won't be objectionable. I often use this quick, easy method of obtaining good-looking color in difficult light. Tests are always required for extremely accurate color under difficult mixed lighting; some photographers use *color-temperature meters* (see Chapter 11 on page 118).

Kodak established standard filter designations years ago, which both Tiffen and Hoya filter makers adhere to. Both manufacturers will send helpful leaflets about their products and filter use in general upon request. Rosco and Lee make gels, and will send booklets of gel color samples, which fit exactly over small flash heads. You can also find gel samples at professional photo and lighting dealers for a dollar or two.

Using color gels on flash heads really isn't my style, but professional photographers who shoot industrial subjects often use bright-color gels in order to enliven boring backgrounds or to add mood to an image. Some "people" photographers like color gels, too. Chip Simons, for example, has made a career with his witty, gelled-flash images that are mostly of people. Theo Westenberger is known for her celebrity portraits, which often incorporate the use of gels. (See the Gallery section of this book on page 129 for examples of their work.) To learn more, read photographer Bob Krist's *Secrets of Lighting on Location* (see "Resources" on page 142).

Two Basic Color-Filter/Gel Combinations

When you use color-filter/color-gel combinations under appropriate lighting conditions when on location, both background color and the flash-filled foreground will be rendered as very acceptable on daylight transparency film. When you combine a filter on the lens with foreground flash-fill, you must use the complementary gel on the flash head. If you don't, the flashed area of the picture will take on the color of the filter.

Morris Mini-Wide self-slaved flashes, color covers, Polaroid film, filters, gels, gaffer tape, and a gray card all come in handy for on-location shooting.

The Tiffen FL-D, or a similar Kodak 30M (magenta) CC filter, corrects the color of common, cool-white fluorescent lights. The complement of either the FL-D or 30M filters is a Full Plus Green gel. An 80B (deep blue) filter corrects for 3200K "hot" photo lights. It also does a pretty good job of correcting for the low-wattage, household-type lights found in homes, stores, and restaurants, on daylight color-balanced transparency films. If you don't use a filter, these household lights will look orange on these films. The complement to the 80B filter is the Full CTO (deep orange) gel.

▲ For this shot of a restauranteur in Nova Scotia, Canada, I used a flash meter and Polaroid film tests to balance the ratio of foreground flash and existing light. I put a Rosco 1/4 CTO pale orange gel on a Dyna-Lite 500 WS/J strobe, bounced the strobe out of a 42-inch white umbrella, and aimed the strobe at the man in the foreground. The gel blended the fill light with the color of the existing light. Working with my Nikon N8008 and a 20mm F2.8 lens, I exposed ISO 64 film for 1/30 sec. at f/11.

▶ This picture was well exposed by a flash meter; however, the color is bad because a magenta filter was used on lens to correct the color of existing fluorescent lights, but no complementary color (green) gel was placed on the flash head. As a result, the technician's face, lit by bounce strobe, appears magenta on film. Here, I used my Nikon N8008, a 20mm F2.8 lens, and a Norman 200 WS/J battery-powered flash. The exposure on ISO 100 film was f/5.6 for 1/15 sec.

To photograph this refinery technician, I used a Comet 1200 WS/J strobe at 1/4 power and bounced out of a 42-inch white umbrella. The color in the image is correct because even though I used a 30CC magenta filter on the lens to compensate for the fluorescent lighting of the background, a Rosco Full Green gel on the flash head balances the light on the technician. Note the slight ghost of the moving arm. With my Nikon N8008 and a 20mm F2.8 lens, I exposed for 1/8 sec. at f/5.6 on ISO 100 film.

Flash and Closeups

Shooting moderate closeups with flash and advanced cameras is technically easy because *through-the-lens metering* (TTL metering) takes into consideration all light and all light-reducing factors. These include variable-aperture lenses, filters, closeup rings, extension tubes, even the bellows units used for extreme closeups. You don't have to make any exposure calculations. It is, however, wise to bracket exposures when you shoot light, dark, or contrasty subjects.

The only caution when using TTL-metered flash for closeups is that you must choose a small *f*-stop, otherwise the flash won't be able to shut down quickly enough to avoid overexposure. To use manual flash for any critical work, use a flash meter and bracket (vary) exposures slightly by adjusting the *f*-stop. I use *f*/16 or *f*/22. To use manual flash for closeup work, get a Polaroid back for your camera. If you rent or buy a Polaroid back, you can shoot Polaroid film tests and preview the results. (NPC makes a Polaroid back for most advanced/professional-level cameras.)

Low-power, dedicated, automatic/manual ring flashes are available from top camera makers, as well as from Nissin, Sunpak, and Vivitar. All of these ring flashes are fine for creating almost shadowless renditions of objects within a few inches. Frame-filling portraits are even possible to about 3 to 4 feet from the ring flash.

Some photographers like to work with two flashes when shooting closeups. The way to control the two TTL units is to mount both on a double flash bracket. One flash is connected to the camera via a dedicated cord, and the second flash is connected to the first via an auxiliary dedicated cord. Kirk Enterprises makes a double flash bracket; Stroboframe offers the Lepp Double Bracket. If you decide to try this approach, be aware that double brackets plus two flashes are heavy. (I'm not a

To make this closeup of a ladyslipper orchid, I handheld my Nikon N90 and 105mm F4 macro lens. I used my Nikon SB-26 flash off-camera via an SC-17 cord and bounced the flash into a LumiQuest device. The exposure, chosen to achieve maximum depth of field and to exclude any existing light, was f/22 for 1/60 sec. on ISO 50 film.

closeup specialist; I use one flash for closeups. This is either a compact model handheld and connected to my camera via a dedicated cord, or an adjustable flash mounted on a Stroboframe Quick Flip Bracket that has been modified so it tilts forward.

High-Speed Flash
Small flashes are used at low-power settings for motion-stopping closeups of insects and similar subjects. All flashes with the power turned far down emit a weak light, and must be used extremely close to a subject. You can shoot high-speed film at moderate flash-to-subject distances. Use a flash meter to measure exposure. The speeds that you can obtain with a small flash unit with its power turned down won't completely "stop" hummingbirds in motion or flying bullets. For these subjects and certain special effects, you must use custom-made, ultra-high-speed flashes and strobes.

Turn Down the Flash Power
The easiest way to achieve short flash duration for motion-stopping effects with a flash is to set an adjustable TTL or automatic flash to *manual mode* (M) and turn the power down. The precise flash duration varies depending on the unit and how far you've turned down the flash. Typically, the light from a flash with a *guide number* (GN) of 120 (based on ISO 100 film, and measured in feet) and set on full power lasts for about 1/350 sec. When the flash is set on 1/2 power, the duration drops to about 1/1000 sec. At 1/32 power, the flash burst can be as short as 1/20,000 sec., even with an inexpensive Sunpak or Vivitar unit.

Flash duration can be measured precisely, but these measurements can be, and are, interpreted in different ways. Manufacturers' claims might be optimistic if only "peak" flash output is measured and "tail" light, which comes after a flash burst has peaked, is excluded. To be safe, make your own tests.

A practical way to visualize effective flash stopping power is to photograph a fast-rotating wheel attached to an electric drill. I attached a pie-shaped, multicolored wheel and small letters to my 1/4-inch drill's polishing

attachment (see below). When a flash can separate colors and letters at about 2000 r.p.m. (revolutions per minute), it is fast enough for my purposes.

Short flash duration is used to "stop," or freeze, water droplets, bursting balloons, and the "spills" and "pours" so popular with advertisers of wine and liquor. Short flash duration is also used for photographing such subjects as insects, birds, and industrial processes. Human reflexes might respond more slowly than a high-speed flash, so you might need triggers that fire the flash when a light-beam is broken. Specialists often shoot stop-motion effects in virtual darkness.

High-Speed TTL Flash-Sync Settings
Advanced flashes, notably those made by Canon, Minolta, and Nikon, sync at a shutter speed of 1/8000 sec. when you manually set the flash to 1/32 power, and you select the *high-speed sync mode* (HS) on the flash. I consider the advantage of this approach to be theoretical; it might come in handy when you want to stop the motion of fast-moving insects. (Consult your flash manufacturer's technical department for more information.)

Ultra-High-Speed Flash Units
True high-speed flash units that can achieve a flash duration as brief as 1/50,000 sec. or 1/100,000 sec. are custom-made professional tools. If I needed to use one, I would call a store that rents this equipment and/or consult specialists (see "Resources" on page 142).

Speeding bullets, seltzer squirting, exploding light bulbs, golf balls distorting as the club hits, hummingbirds hovering-all of these actions can be *stopped*, or frozen, via ultra-high-speed flashes. For the most part, advertising, nature, and scientific photographers need this equipment. Turning down a portable flash like a GN 120 Canon, Nikon, or Vivitar will result in low power and brief flash durations (as short as 1/20,000 sec. at 1/32 power).

High-Speed, Sequential, Motion-Stopping Techniques
Photographers often use *light-beam* and *sound-activated* triggers for high-speed subjects; the flash fires when a

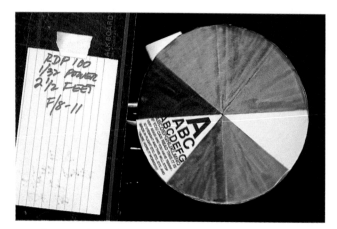 

To make a speed test of a flash unit, I mounted a homemade color wheel on the buffing attachment of a drill. Then I clamped the drill to a lightstand and photographed with the drill turned on. I did a speed test of the Vivitar 383 flash at 1/32 power (left) 169 and a Ying Yang manual flash (right).

beam is broken. Crossed beams are often used to increase accuracy and to reduce the chances of a flash being fired accidentally. You must aim the beams carefully.

Because camera and lens shutters have slight but perceptible delays, photographers often shoot high-speed flash images of bullets penetrating objects, champagne corks popping, wine being poured, and other similar effects in complete darkness, with the camera shutter locked open (see below). Special shutters are made for outdoor high-speed flash use; one expert who uses them is Stephen Dalton, the great British nature photographer. To learn more about these various high-speed techniques, consult the equipment manufacturers. These include Kapture Group, Prestoflash, and Woods Electronics (see "Resources" on page 142).

Multiple Flash

You can combine two or more small flash units when more light is needed. You can effectively light still lifes with cumulative flash or strobe "pops" (see below). You can also use multiple flash or strobe units in order to produce "Hollywood," television, or dramatic theatrical-type lighting effects. The multiple-flash approach also can separate portrait subjects from backgrounds and adds hair light. Multiple flashes and strobes, perhaps gelled, can add bright or color accents to dull scenes, create the illusion of window light where none exists, and light large spaces evenly.

Be aware that the different light sources must record on film the way you intend, and the overall exposure shouldn't be too contrasty. If you don't use multiple flash skillfully, the final images could be awful. For example, you might end up with an emphasis in the wrong place; unacceptable, burned-out hotspots; yawning "black holes"; or crossed shadows.

Using Multiple Flash Units

When you use several manual flash units together, the easiest way to establish a *lighting ratio*, or the relative brightness of one flash or strobe light to another, is to use a light meter. This device can measure the brightness of each light separately. You then move each unit toward or away from the subject in order to control brightness. Some professional flashes and strobes have built-in *power variators* (see Chapter 11 on page 118; for ways of combining and controlling several TTL flashes together, review Chapter 7). And, as mentioned earlier, setting high-power flash or strobe units to operate sequentially requires special equipment (see above).

Ikelite Lite-Link

Ikelite, best known for its underwater flashes, makes the Lite-Link, a clever device that enables you to use an off-camera Nikon dedicated flash in cordless TTL mode. The Lite-Link incorporates a slave unit and a hotshoe. Simply attach your Nikon TTL flash to the Lite-Link, which "sees" the light from the on-camera TTL flash. The device turns on and shuts down the off-camera unit simultaneously with the on-camera flash. And as long as the remote flash is farther from the main subject than the main camera-controlled flash, the TTL exposure won't be affected. I found the Ikelite Lite-Link to work well, both aimed direct and bounced. You can vary the precise lighting ratio by moving the off-camera flash.

Morris Self-Slaved Flashes

The Morris Company makes several tiny, low-power manual flashes with built-in slaves. These are easy to use as accent lights that can be triggered by any flash. I like and own several of the domed Mini-Slave Wide-Plus models (each costs about $30). These flash units cast a light in a circle and accept orange, blue, red, and green covers for color film effects.

You can conceal one or more of these weak lights on a set, as well as use them as accent lights without affecting the overall TTL-metered flash exposure—provided that they're positioned at least 3 feet back from the main light

A fluorescent fixture shed light on this pool table. I bounced a Vivitar 283 flash on a lightstand at full power out of a 24-inch white umbrella to the left of the player. Next, I spaced two Morris Mini-Wide Ultra self-slaved flashes along the left rim of the table. A third Morris Mini-Wide self-slaved unit was on the green baize on the right. While shooting, I rested my Nikon N90 and a 20mm F2.8 lens on the pool table a few inches from the balls; an infrared trigger set off the flashes. I shot a roll of pictures, changing the shutter speeds between 2 seconds and 1/8 sec. I rated the ISO 50 film I was using at ISO 40. I think that this image, exposed at *f*/4, is the most effective variation.

Working in an art collector's apartment, I reversed my Nikon SB-26 on-camera flash and bounced it into a small silver umbrella taped overhead, I also used a remote Ikelite-slaved SB-26 and Morris Mini-Wide flashes. Shooting with my Nikon N90 and a 20mm F2.8 lens, I exposed ISO 100 film for 1/15 sec. at f/5.6.

on the subject. I use Mini-Wides in dark corners of rooms, or hidden on sets, and sometimes even taped to a dough-nut-shaped board to serve as a homemade ring flash. With their low GN of about 28, individual Morris flashes placed a few feet from the camera, don't affect TTL-metered flash exposures. You can use any other low-power manual flash fitted with a slave unit in a similar way.

TTL-Flash in Multi-Mode

The *multi-mode* setting, which is available on most advanced TTL flashes, produces several overlapping moving images on one frame. You must use multi-mode in darkness against a nonreflective black background. Be aware that getting good results isn't easy. (I haven't experimented with multi-mode much. So far I've had success only when my subject was medium-toned, and I set a low number of flashes per second and per frame (Hertz). (For directions on how to set this mode, review Chapter 7 and your camera and flash manuals. For information on professional repetitive flash, see Chapter 11 on page 118 and photographer Ken Regan's comments in the Gallery on page 134.)

Multiple Flash and Strobe Pops

Sometimes achieving the desired small *f*-stops that produce good depth of field requires more flash power than you have available. If you're shooting in a darkened stu-

dio or outdoors at night—still lifes, interiors, nearby landscape features, in fact, any subject that doesn't move—an old technique can help. Combine a long exposure with multiple flash pops.

You need a flash meter that reads cumulative exposures to do this; the Minolta V is one such meter. Your camera must be on a sturdy tripod, your TTL camera and flash set in the M mode, and any flash you're using must be fitted with a fast-recycling battery pack. For example, if one flash gives an exposure of f/8, two flash pops will double the light and give one extra f-stop, or f/11. Four pops will double the light again, thereby permitting f/16 exposures. This is the maximum number of pops required for most purposes, but when necessary eight pops will give three extra f-stops, or f/22. I've actually used the technique, with an AC-powered strobe, for up to 32 pops when shooting spread-out, still-life subjects in a darkened studio. The reason for doing this is to have enough light to shoot at very small f-stops, such as f/22, f/32, f/45, or higher), thereby achieving great depth of field.

Painting with Flash

This old photographic technique, which is also called *flash painting* or *light painting*, involves large spaces, mounting your camera on a tripod, and using a fast wide-angle lens. Adapted for flash, the technique involves aiming the flash head around during a long exposure in a large room. Since you use multiple pops, you must also use a battery pack with the flash so the recycling time is very fast. You'll often obtain the best results when you turn down a 120 GN flash to 1/4 power.

To try flash painting, set a 30-second exposure, and walk rather quickly around a big space, popping off the flash at walls and ceilings to "paint" them with light as evenly as possible. In 30 seconds, with a battery-powered flash with a GN of 120 turned down to 1/4 power, I can get off about 40 flash pops. Try using apertures of *f*/4 or even *f*/2.8 in huge spaces, such as churches, and *f*/5.6 or *f*/8 in average-sized rooms.

The limitation of flash painting is the flash range. Try a few test pops at high ceilings to establish this; you can see if the flash hits. A GN 120 flash won't be able to illuminate the dome of Saint Peter's Basilica, but it will work well in, for example, many caves, unlighted historic structures, and smaller churches. Try light painting in gardens, cemeteries, and woods, too.

Photographer Chip Simons, who uses color gels with his light-painted images, made this technique famous. I've heard Simons say that wearing dark clothes and black gloves minimizes the chances of your "ghost" image appearing in a picture. He also suggests that you take special care to shield the flash head so no light spills onto the lens (see the Gallery section on page 136 for an example of his work and for more information about this technique).

Shooting Buildings and Interiors with Flash

You might be surprised to learn that you can photograph architectural subjects with flash. Shoot large exteriors at dusk when some light remains. Use the fastest possible lenses, wide open, and slow shutter speeds. Add TTL flash. Direct flash probably won't *cover*, or spread to, the edges of a large space shot with a wide-angle lens. However, any available light will be recorded. And the flash falloff will be soft, not hard-edged, and might not be objectionable. Use an adjustable flash head zoomed back to a wide-angle lens setting for maximum light spread. Any other light modifier will reduce the flash range.

Teleflash

As mentioned earlier, the Inverse Square Law states that flash can't travel great distances because of light falloff. Teleflash heads and custom-made devices with Fresnel-type lenses can help. Telephoto reflectors made for professional flashes can throw light forward, too.

The adjustable Fresnel grooved flash heads built into small flash heads extend the flash range somewhat. In my experience, this increase has been up to about 25 percent at the telephoto setting. Custom-made devices that place the Fresnel lens farther in front of the flash head can double the flash range. Teleflash accessories, which can be made of rather flimsy plastic or can be solid and heavy, are popular with wildlife photographers. Highly polished, round teleflash reflectors made for Norman, Quantum, and other professional battery-powered flashes can double the flash range, too.

To maximize flash effectiveness at a considerable distance, you need to use lenses nearly wide open. Powerful

This young brown bear was foraging in a tree not far from a road in Great Smoky Mountains National Park, Tennessee. But at 50 feet, the animal was still at the extreme limit for flash fill at the required *f*-stop. I used a teleflash device on my Nikon SB-26 flash head that I made with cardboard and an inexpensive Fresnel magnifying screen from a stationery store. This extended the flash range; the fill produced an eye highlight and detail in the fur. Shooting with my Nikon N90 and a 300mm F2.8 lens, I exposed ISO 50 film for 1/250 sec. at *f*/4.

strobe units are required for the biggest jobs. Photographer Joe McNally is a flash master and sometimes uses this approach (see the Gallery section on page 130 for an example of his work and his comments on this technique).

Using Flash for Sports

When shooting sporting events with flash, specialists use *f*/2.8 telephoto lenses whenever possible. Long fast lenses used wide open maximize flash range and blur backgrounds. This, in turn, separates the competitors from the spectators. TTL-flash-fill is possible within the flash range; advanced flashes have a signal that blinks rapidly when the flash doesn't reach the subject. It is sometimes worth the risk of flashing at a subject somewhat beyond range because partial or weak flash-fill might be better than none at all.

Those great, tack-sharp indoor sports pictures taken at major-league basketball, hockey, and other arenas are

While shooting at New York City's Bronx Zoo, I came upon this disabled eagle in shadow in its cage. I metered for the bird's head. A friend stretched and held my Nikon SB-23 compact flash in TTL mode used on an SC-17 dedicated cord as far to the left as possible. This prevented the metal wires at the front of the bird's enclosure from being hit by flash. The flash fill from the side provided an eye highlight. Working with my Nikon N90 and a 300mm F2.8 lens, I exposed ISO 100 film for 1/60 sec. at *f*/5.6.

usually made by photographers whose camera equipment is *hard-wired*, or connected by long PC/sync cords, to strobes hung in strategic places from the ceiling. The sports specialists I know started learning their trade by shooting high-school games, which are accessible to anyone. Ken Regan, a great sports photographer, sometimes uses this hard-wired approach to shooting sports motion (see the Gallery section on page 134 for an example of his work and information about his techniques).

Using Flash with Pets and Wildlife

Pets don't like to be flashed from very close, and after two or three flashes they emphatically let you know this by running away. But Roger Tory Peterson, the late ornithologist, author, and artist told me that flash doesn't bother wildlife. He claimed that creatures in the wild are used to lightning, and react to flash the same way.

A teleflash device can help you obtain eye highlights on distant wildlife. It is particularly valuable when a creature's eyes are hard to see because they are small, deeply recessed and the same color as the fur or feather. Aesthetically, an eye highlight makes a creature look alive. But be aware that redeye might show up as "greeneye" with some pets photographed at close distances; this is because their internal eye structure is different from that of humans.

Shooting Through Glass or Bars

By standing at an angle to glass, you can eliminate most unwanted reflections, even with on-camera flash. Pop off test flashes while looking at the glass to see where the light falls. Off-camera flash, slaved or handheld with a stretched remote cord, can provide sidelight on a bird, an exotic fish in an aquarium, or any creatures behind glass, bars or wires without causing reflections. To avoid your own reflection from showing up in the shot, you should wear dark colors,

put black tape on tripod legs, and drape black cloth around the camera.

Remote Setups

Remote flashes are particularly useful in nature photography. Wildlife photographers equipped with long telephoto lenses (300mm, 400mm, and even 600mm lengths are popular) mount one or more slaved remote flashes on stands and place them close to a den or nest when the animal or bird is absent. Naturally, the photographers hide at some distance to avoid scaring the shy creatures. The remote flash is fired by an-on camera flash or some other form of trigger that can be infrared-, radio-, or even sound-activated.

When you put a flash on a lightstand or tripod near a nest or den and trigger the flash from a distance, you can use a long PC/sync cord or a special trigger/slave combination. Nature photographer Leonard Lee Rue III recommends setting up a dummy camera and flash made from wood and cans in order to make timid creatures accustomed to their presence before you start to photograph seriously.

Specialized Slaves and Triggers

Ultra-sensitive, light-activated slaves are the least expensive slaves that work at a distance; they are highly effective when no other flashes are used in the vicinity. Any flash can set them off. I use Wein Ultra slaves, which work well at 100 feet away even in the brightest sunlight. Once again, the only problem is that any flash will set them off, even a stray point-and-shoot camera's flash at a distance.

Infrared Slaves and Triggers

I don't work in crowds much; if I did, I would get a *channeled infrared or radio-controlled trigger/slave system*. Wedding and news photographers depend on these. An infrared trigger used on-camera fires any remote, light-sensitive, slaved flash, without itself emitting visible light that shows up on film. I use the Wein SSR-XT infrared trigger in the studio and outdoors; it fires my light-sensitive flashes without showing up on the film.

You can set *multichannel* infrared slave and trigger combinations to avoid interference from casual amateur or competing professional flash users. Wedding, news, and meeting photographers work extensively with these devices. Wein makes multichannel infrared triggers and slaves (for more information, see page 127).

Radio Slaves and Triggers
Studio photographers, photojournalists, nature specialists, and scientists use radio-controlled triggers and slaves. These can incorporate a timer and a device called an *intervalometer*, which fires the flash at adjustable intervals. Radio slaves and triggers can be fairly simple one-channel, two-channel, or multichannel devices, or programmable via computer-like consoles. Quantum has been well-known for its radio slaves for years; Wizard makes a 16-channel radio trigger/slave system.

Light-Beam, Sound, Sequential, and High-Speed Flash/Trigger Systems
Light-beam triggers are invisible and set off a remote flash when the beam is broken. Crossed light beams mean that the number of poorly composed shots is reduced. Photographers who specialize in closeups of tiny moving creatures ordinarily use "tunnels" that contain the insects (or whatever) that direct them so that at least some hit the crossed beams. The Kapture Group and Woods Electronics make light-beam triggers (see "Resources" on page 142). You can adjust *sound triggers* to varying degrees of sensitivity, while you can program *sequential triggers* to set off a number of flashes or strobe lights at variable intervals.

(For more information about solving problems with these highly specialized professional tools, contact the major camera-system manufacturers. Their technical departments will nearly always produce an expert to give good advice. Special-equipment manufacturers know of lighting consultants available for hire, or hire out themselves. See "Resources" on page 142.)

Basic Underwater Flash
Inexpensive underwater cameras with built-in flash are fun to use on the beach and around the pool. You can also use them in boats and on the ocean, and in rain and snow anywhere and get decent results—if the camera has a reasonably fast, sharp, glass lens. Most disposable underwater cameras have slow, plastic lenses and just won't do.

More than a couple of feet underwater, however, the built-in flashes aren't useful for serious photography. I've discovered that even the clearest-seeming water contains impurities. These show up as white spots when direct flash aimed at a fish or lovely coral first hits sand, mud, or particles of vegetation.

Canon and Minolta are known for affordable underwater point-and-shoot cameras. I have a simple, solid Canon Sure Shot A-1 model. This camera has a 32mm *f*/3.5 medium-wide-angle lens, the essential "Flash On/Flash Off" setting, and a closeup mode to 1½ feet (and costs less than $200).

Light even just a few feet underwater is intensely blue, so you need flash for good color photography whether you're snorkeling or scuba diving. The ideal setup is an off-camera flash mounted on a bracket next to your camera that you can angle at the subject or take off the bracket if necessary. If you go deep, this is a must: it is dark down there.

Nikonos Underwater Flashes, Cameras, and Lenses
I love the water and often snorkel, but I don't scuba dive. If I did go down deep or got a serious underwater assignment, I would use the only single-lens-reflex (SLR) camera that can be used underwater without a housing: the Nikonos RS AF SLR. Nikonos underwater equipment is renowned and used the world over, and is available for rental at many top dive locations. Nikon makes two dedicated underwater flashes, models SB-104 and SB-105, as well as brackets, dedicated cords, and other underwater gear. Nikonos equipment is neither the least nor the most expensive available, but it is lightweight, and the autofocus is accurate. (I'm told that EWA, Sea & Sea, and Sealife are other reliable brands of underwater cameras that are popular with recreational divers.)

Flash doesn't travel a long way underwater. Underwater specialist Robert Rattner advised me that, as usual, you achieve the best flash results when you work as close to the subject as possible. Rattner strongly suggests the use of an underwater wide-angle lens because refraction makes objects appear about 30 percent larger underwater even just below the surface. For example, a 20mm lens underwater is equivalent to a 28mm lens on land. He also says you don't need two underwater flashes for quality underwater pictures; one well-aimed unit can provide excellent lighting. Rattner likes Ikelite underwater flashes when not going too deep.

Finally, be aware that Sunpak makes good underwater flashes. Helix, the Chicago mail-order company, specializes in underwater camera and flash equipment and will send comprehensive information on the subject. For more information, read *Underwater Photography* by Charles Seaborn (see "Resources" on page 142).

Chapter 11
PROFESSIONAL FLASH AND STROBES

Small flash units can't do everything. When you need to light large areas, create daylight effects indoors, throw light a considerable distance, or shoot hundreds of pictures quickly, professional battery-powered flash units or powerful strobe units are a must. Once you've learned how to put these tools together, you'll find that operating them isn't difficult.

Buy or rent such equipment at a professional lighting dealer; this way, you'll be able to get all the help you need to get started working with this gear. Be sure to read and obey all manufacturers' safety instructions whenever you use high-voltage strobe (see "Using High-Power Flash and Strobe Safely" on page 123).

Wedding and school photographers, meeting specialists, photojournalists, among others use professional battery-powered flash units. Industrial, corporate, travel, and fashion photographers in particular use lightweight portable strobes in the range of 200 to 1200 *watt-seconds/joules* (WS/J)—and sometimes more than one at a time. Travel specialists use dual-voltage models. Of course, professional photographers can use all of these units in the studio, too. Photographers who shoot illustration, still life, food, furniture, cars, and interiors ordinarily work with the most powerful portable strobes, usually a number of them at the same time.

Comet, Dyna-Lite, Henschell, Lumedyne, and Norman are all well-known and reliable makers of manual, battery-operated portable flashes that come with various power options. These units range in price from about $700 for a 200 WS/J battery pack and one head, $1,000 for a 400 WS/J unit and one head, and up to $2,500 for a 1200 WS/J to 2000 WS/J battery-pack unit and one head.

Professional Dedicated Flash

Many photographic tools that are now professional standards were originally designed for amateur photographers; these include small flash units with bounce heads and auto-focus modes. Most photojournalists and news photographers who work in 35mm format today use dedicated flash. This type of flash is extremely accurate today. In fact, the best dedicated flashes permit you to increase or decrease TTL exposure to your individual taste or for special effects when desired. You can use top-of-the-line dedicated flashes in M mode or automatic mode any time those particular options suit your purpose better.

Quantum Q-Flash 2

An excellent, professional, fully *through-the-lens-metered* (TTL-metered) battery flash is the Quantum Q-Flash 2, which is a head-plus-battery-pack unit. The Q-Flash 2

For this shot of a Japanese chef, I read for a flareup with a flash meter and set a low shutter speed to record the flames. The chef was additionally lit with a stand-mounted Norman 200 WS/J battery-powered flash head bounced out of a 36-inch white umbrella. I photographed the chef for about half an hour because the pattern of the flames combined with the flash was unpredictable. Working with my Nikon FM-2 manual camera and a 50mm F1.8 lens, I exposed for 1/8 sec. at f/5.6 on ISO 100 film.

offers modules for many TTL cameras. The unit is solid and well-finished and the manual is easy to understand. The reflector is removable for bare-bulb use.

Flash and flash-fill with photographer-controlled "plus" and "minus" adjustments, *multi-mode, automatic mode*, and full *manual mode* (M) with precisely stepped reductions down to 1/125 power are options. Chosen settings and minimum- to maximum-flash ranges in feet and meters appear large on an LCD screen, which can be illuminated, on the back of the unit. An "Options" button permits you to adjust the flash-range indicator for varied reflector positions and/or for Quantum diffusers. Running two units off one battery is possible with an adapter.

I'm excited by the Q-Flash 2 because its TTL-metered flash fill is ideal for photographing wildlife. In addition to wildlife photographers, those who shoot meetings, fashion shows, performances, and sporting events should find the Q-Flash 2 quite useful. With a 150 WS/J pack, a standard reflector with ISO 100 film, and an *f*/2.8 lens used wide open, the indicated flash range is 6½ to 55 feet. The unit meets this claim pretty well. And with Quantum's recently introduced 8½-inch, shallow, parabolic teleflash reflector, used with a spacer between the tube and the flash, the Q-Flash 2's maximum operating range can be as great as about 150 feet with a wide-open *f*/2.8 lens.

Quantum rates its Q-Flash T2 model used with the Quantum Turbo battery pack in two ways: at 150 WS/J, or with a GN of 160 (based on ISO 100 film and measured in feet), which makes it comparable to the largest handle-mount flashes. Quantum's Turbo battery-packs aren't designed to accept modular inserts; a single battery charge produces about 300 full-power Q-Flash 2 flashes. However, the Q-Flash X2 model is compatible with 200 WS/J and 400 WS/J Lumedyne battery packs, 200 WS/J Norman B and C battery packs, and Norman 400 WS/J battery packs. The packs accept battery inserts, so you can carry spares. When you use ISO 400 film with any of these batteries, the flash-range increase is imperceptible, but you do gain two *f*-stops.

Q-Flash dedicated modules are available for 35mm Canon, Contax, Leica, Minolta X and Xi series, Nikon, and Pentax dedicated SLR cameras. Nikons, for example, require module QF-12, and Canons take module QF-13. Modules are also available for most electronic medium-format cameras, including Bronica's ETR-Si and SQ-Ai models; Hasselblad's 500-ELX, 503-CX, 553-ELX, and 205TCC models; and Rolleiflex's 6002, 6003, and 6008 models.

Sunpak 120J-TTL Flash
This portable, battery-operated modular dedicated flash has a removable, round reflector for bare-bulb use; automatic and M modes are also available. Experts have told me that this flash is excellent electronically, but I don't find it too rugged. The model I tested had a head that wobbled slightly when aimed straight forward, which disturbed me slightly. The flash did, however, give excellent exposures. I call it an excellent "semi-pro" unit that is a valid, budget-minded choice (costing about $400 with a Sunpak battery pack). Dedicated modules are available for popular cameras.

Editorial specialist Patricia Fisher uses the Quantum Q-Flash T2, with a Quantum Turbo 160 WS/J power pack, dedicated to her Canons. Modules for other electronic cameras are available. The 2-X version of this professional unit can be used with either Lumedyne or Norman 400 WS/J packs.

Sunpak probably makes more types of flash than any other manufacturer. The line includes automatic flash units; professional/amateur modular TTL units for most brands of 35mm SLR cameras; and professional handle-mount and underwater flash units.

Metz Professional Dedicated Flash

Metz TTL professional flashes have modules dedicated to electronic Bronica, Hasselblad, and Rolleiflex cameras (review Chapter 7).

Professional Manual Battery Flashes

The units discussed below are rugged and reliable, and most are time-tested. They share one advantage: all are more powerful than the units covered in earlier chapters. If you need or want small *f*-stops in placed where you can't plug in to an AC power supply, one of these flashes might be just what you're looking for. However, you must be within reach of "main" power to recharge batteries soon after the end of each shoot.

Lumedyne and Norman Flash Units

Lumedyne and Norman make professional head-and-battery-pack portable flashes. Both manufacturers' brands are long-established and widely used. The equipment has distinct advantages, and come in 200 WS/J and 400 WS/J versions.

Lumedyne's units are manual and modular, consisting of a control unit, battery-pack(s), and base. The three or more components clip securely together. The 200 WS/J and 400 WS/J versions are standard, with the option of higher power by means of additional batteries. I've tested Lumedyne flashes, and I know fashion photographers and big-time wedding and meeting photographers who rely on them. And these professionals push a lot of film through their cameras. Lumedyne's seven-year battery guarantee is the best in the business.

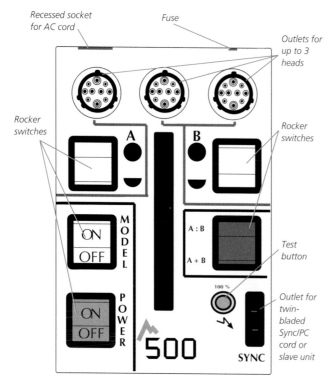

This top view of the Dyna-Lite M-500 strobe I own shows that it can accommodate three flash heads, although I recommend using only two. The other outlet is for a PC/sync cord or a slave unit.

Norman makes two rugged, uncomplicated, manual, portable flash models. Many photojournalists prefer these workhorses. I owned a couple of them for years, and still use some Norman light modifiers. Norman portables are simple to set up and operate. The original models had quirky batteries, but the company has corrected this problem. The battery case, which is quite rugged, accepts inserts.

Both Lumedyne and Norman offer AC adapters. Keep in mind, though, that these increase the flash recycle time. You can use both brands' 400 WS/J battery packs with Quantum Q-Flash 2-X flashes.

The Dyna-Lite Uni-400 Jr.

Dyna-Lite, known for portable strobes, also makes the Uni-400 Jr., a new concept. Unlike Normans and Lumedyne battery flashes, which offer optional AC adapters and heads with 12V modeling lights, this flash/strobe

For this multiple-image shot of a dancer making angel wings, I worked with a custom-made 200 WS/J repetitive strobe courtesy of its creator, A.J. Nye. The strobe tube is built into a 2 kilowatt Mole-Richardson movie spotlight head. I used the setup in a darkened studio; a black-velvet background absorbed stray light. The Nye strobe is capable of up to 100 flashes per second. After doing Polaroid film tests, I tried various effects at reduced output as the dancer made different moves. With my Nikon FM-2 manual camera and a 20mm F2.8 lens, I exposed ISO 100 film for 2 seconds at f/2.8 for this shot.

unit is primarily designed to run on 110V AC current. When used on AC current, the Uni-400 Jr. has a modeling light. When used off an optional Jackrabbit high-voltage battery pack, the Uni-400 Jr. doesn't.

Many Dyna-Lite strobe accessories are compatible. The Dyna-Lite Uni-400 Jr. flash/strobe hybrid is ideal for photographers who shoot indoors in homes or offices, or in a small studio, most of the time, but also shoot outside on occasion.

Comet and Henschell Portable Flash Units

Besides Lumedyne's modular units used with additional power packs, I am aware of two high-power, battery-operated, portable flashes. Comet makes a 1200 WS/J unit, and Henschell makes a 2000 WS/J unit called the "Porty." I haven't used either of these flashes, but a major lighting dealer told me that fashion photographers who work on location love them. The disadvantages of these units are their somewhat slow recycling times when set on full power and, especially for those starting out, high prices. For an example of a Comet in use, see Danny Turner's work in the Gallery on page 138.

AC-Powered Strobe/Studio Flash Units

Giving a course on strobe lighting would require another book, which I don't need to write because so many good ones are already on the market (see "Resources" on page 142). But to get you started, be aware that you can use strobes in almost all the ways you can use flash, such as bounced from umbrellas, diffused through softboxes, condensed via grids and snoots, aimed as accent lights or hairlights, and used bare-bulb. You can, for example, turn down the power on strobes for motion-stopping effects, or attach strobes to hookups for repetitive effects. Various accessories, including interchangeable reflectors, barndoors, snoots, grids, and ring-flash heads, are available for top-of-the-line brands. Lighting accessories and modifiers, and gels work with strobe much same as they do with flash.

You can, of course, mix strobes, professional flash, and small flash units. All flashes and strobes are color-balanced for 5500K daylight, color transparency films. And when you aim strobes direct, you achieve greater range than with small flash units. However, light range is by no means limitless, even with the most powerful single strobe; the Inverse Square Law of light falloff still applies.

The basic flash-lighting rule about "the closer, the nicer the effect" usually applies to strobe lighting, too. But a useful traditional saying relating to studio photography also applies to strobe: "Don't over-light." Translation: Don't use lighting that is too bright, too powerful for a mood, or too complex, or that causes too many overlapping shadows. Learning the possibilities of strobe can take a lifetime of experience and experiments. I expect to experiment with strobe light for as long as I take pictures.

Be respectful of strobes, and follow safety rules when handling them (see "Using High-Power Flash and Strobe Safely" on page 123). But don't be too in awe of them. Once you can light quite well with dedicated, automatic, and manual flashes, learning to plug in, turn on, and use a strobe quite effectively is a matter of practice.

The Lumedyne system is modular, with many accessories; battery packs can be interchanged to vary the power output.

Choosing AC-Powered Portable Strobes

When you make your decision about which strobe to buy, choose a name brand. Well-established companies in the United States and/or Europe and Japan are Balcar, Bowens/Calumet, Broncolor, Comet, Dyna-Lite, Elinchron, Godard, Henschell, Norman, Profoto, and Speedotron. All offer many power and light-modifying options. (I own Dyna-Lites.)

You can expect to pay between $1,500 and $3,000 or so for almost any 1000 WS/J unit with one strobe head. (Most professional photographers use two or three heads.) If you're looking for a good budget-priced strobe, keep the following in mind as you shop. The photography department of the School of Visual Arts in New York City, where I sometimes give lighting workshops, buys two brands of strobe unit. One is the rugged, professional Speedotron Black line. The other is the simple-to-operate Novatron. Although lightweight Novatrons don't have interchangeable reflectors or too many accessories—I call them "semi-pro" units—they stand up well to the rigors of being used by hundreds of students. You can get a 500 WS/J Novatron with one head for well under $500.

Lighting with Professional Flash Units

As mentioned earlier, high light output translates into being able to select small *f*-stops for good depth-of-field, and to have the option of turning down the power for short-duration flash bursts and fast recycling times. High light output also means good—but not limitless—flash range (the Inverse Square Law still applies).

Many photojournalists and busy news, wedding, and meeting photographers use professional manual flashes. You can handhold the lightweight heads or mount them on a flash bracket, tripod, or lightweight stand. A cord connects the flash head to the battery pack, which you can wear over the shoulder or clipped to a belt; you can also hang the pack on a lightstand. The flash is fired either by a PC/sync cord from the camera or remote by a slave/trigger combination. You can aim and use the flash in all the ways you've already learned.

Photographers often use portable flash heads mounted on stands. The light is then bounced out of an umbrella—the larger the umbrella, the softer the bounced light—or diffused through a softbox onto the subject, as described earlier.

Flash Meters

When you use manual flash or strobe, particularly professional units, knowing how to get good exposures is critical. First, get and learn to read a flash meter. Most are simple to set once you've read the manual. Flash meters turn on via a switch on one side. The exposure (*f*-stop and shutter speed) shows on the meter's LCD screen. Press a button, and then an "Up/Down" arrow to adjust the film speed in use. Next, press another button and another "Up/Down" arrow to set the desired shutter speed. Basic flash meters offer two to four shutter-speed options, while top-of-the-line flash meters permit you to set a wide range of shutter speeds.

On advanced flash meters, you have some other choices to make. To read flash illumination alone, set the universal, zigzag "Lightning" symbol on the meter. To read both flash and daylight, set the "Sun/Lightning" symbol, or the word "Combi" (for combined light) on

I photographed this French chef working for a top Tokyo hotel for a magazine article. I used a flash meter to determine the exposure. With my Nikon F3, a 20mm F2.8 lens, and my Norman 200 flash, I exposed ISO 64 film for 1/30 sec. at *f*/8.

the meter. To read daylight alone, set the "Sun" symbol and/or the word "Ambi" (for ambient light) on the meter. Some flash meters read multiple pops; set the *multi meter mode*.

Wherever you work, indoors or outdoors, make sure that you hold the flash meter level. Angling or tilting the white dome biases exposures. Take meter readings every time you move a main light, significantly move fill light(s), or move your subject in relation to the main flash. For a general exposure, aim the meter at the subject. To adjust light ratios, aim the meter at each light in turn.

Reading Exposures

Set the maximum camera sync speed on the flash meter (and the camera) when you want only strobe light. This is usually done in the studio. With advanced flash meters, like the Minolta V, you have the option to set any speed below sync speed on the meter in order to read the exposure for low light combined with flash fill, and adjust the percentages of each.

Metering for Combined Flash and Daylight

My technique is to take an ambient-light reading with the camera, and a flash-meter reading of the flash/strobe light. Then I decide on the foreground-to-background light ratio that I want. The ratio is the amount of flash fill in the foreground in relation to the available light in the background (see page 125). Setting slow sync for a light background means that less fill is necessary, and vice-versa. Experiment. When working with a flash meter and manual flash, use a TTL camera in the M mode and set the shutter speed on the camera and the aperture on the lens, which is also in the M mode.

Firing the Flash

To trigger a flash easily with a meter when you are alone, select the *cord* mode on the meter, and use a long PC/sync

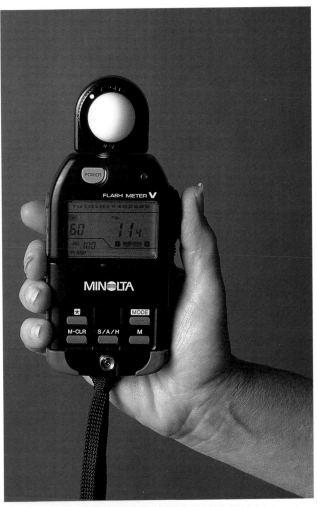

The advanced/professional Minolta V flash meter permits measuring relative percentages of flash and daylight or bright available light within a given scene.

USING HIGH-POWER FLASH AND STROBE SAFELY

When fully charged, high-voltage flashes, strobe units, heads, cords, and strobe tubes contain enough high-voltage current to severely shock you or possibly even kill you when handled improperly. The following basic safety tips might save your life.

- Read the manufacturers' safety and operating instructions before using any strobe or high-voltage flash.

- Don't rent any strobe that doesn't come with an instruction manual.

- Assemble all strobe components completely before plugging the unit in to AC power.

- Make sure that lightstands are tightened and weighted at the bottom before mounting heavy strobe heads on them.

- Use gaffer tape to secure strobe cords to the floor and lightstands for safety whenever you work with models.

- Never change head positions on a strobe without first turning off the power and then discharging stored electricity by hitting the test button.

- Unplug the strobe from the AC power supply and discharge any stored electricity before disassembling the unit. (Today, though, most strobes "self-discharge" whenever you turn them off.)

- Strobe tubes get hot, so let them cool before removing the tube from the head.

- Never, ever use strobes on wet floors or in damp conditions.

- Never, ever let children fool around anywhere near a strobe.

This silhouetted picture of an architect clearly shows how a portrait background is lit separately from the foreground (left). Here, I bounced a custom-modified Vivitar 283 NVS-1 flash with a round reflector off brown seamless paper. This technique silhouetted the subject. Working with my Nikon N50 camera and an 80mm F1.8 manual lens, I

determined exposure by using a flash meter and doing Polaroid film tests. The exposure on ISO 64 film was 1/60 sec. at f/8. The portrait of the architect differs from the silhouetted version in only one way (right). Here, I added two Vivitar 283 flashes aimed through a Chimera Midi softbox at the subject from a distance of about 2 feet.

cord between meter and flash. If you work alone, you might prefer Wein's new, cordless meter trigger, which fires a remote, *slaved* flash or strobe. When you select the *non-cord* meter mode, an assistant—or, if necessary, a model—can push a button on the side of the meter to set it before you hand-fire the flash. The required *f*-stop will be indicated on the meter, usually in 1/10-stop increments.

Testing Exposure with Flash Meters and Polaroids

Today, almost everyone who uses professional manual flash or strobe takes flash-meter readings, makes Polaroid tests, or both, in order to determine exposures and refine light placement. This requires a professional Polaroid camera with adjustable apertures and shutter speeds, or a custom Polaroid back.

Designing Light Ratios That Work

When you work with professional flash and strobe, learn to use light ratios. Light ratios indicate the relative bright-

ness of one light to another. It doesn't matter if the light is hard or soft. Ratios are expressed in numeric terms: 1:1, 2:1, 2½:1, 3:1, etc. So, for example, with two lights, a 1:1 light ratio means that the lights are of equal power and are placed at equal distances on either side of a subject. This is a flat, usually boring and unflattering light that beginners use. Don't make this mistake.

Using lights of equal power in a 1:2, or 2:1, ratio is more interesting. Here, one light is 50 percent closer to the subject than the other, and the subject's light side is one *f*-stop brighter than the dark side.

Color slide films and Scala's new black-and-white slide film require light ratios of no greater than 3:1, or 1:3, when you want to record both highlight and shadow detail. A 3:1 ratio means that the brightest part of an image is no more than 2 *f*-stops lighter than the darkest area. Properly exposed and developed print films can handle higher light ratios. But you shouldn't use more than a 5:1, or 3-stop, ratio if you don't want highlights to be blown out, shadows to turn solid black, or both.

This is a Dyna-Lite strobe and a modified Polaroid 110 B camera.

To establish light ratios using two or more flashes or strobes, shade the meter with your hand (or shut off lights) so that one light doesn't influence another. Aim the dome of the flash meter from the subject at one light source, and take a reading. Then meter from the other light. Compare readings, and adjust the ratios by turning down or increasing the flash power, or moving lights if necessary.

When you set up a classic *three-light portrait*, you can aim a *separation light* from behind the subject onto the background, or a *hair light* down from above. Meter background/accent lights first, and set them so that they won't be stronger than the main light, or *key light*, on the subject. After you set the accent light, turn it off, and then meter the key light and subsidiary foreground fill light in turn. Adjust the light ratio between main and fill lights by turning down the power (if this is an option), or by moving or diffusing lights.

This all sounds complex, and is if you're inexperienced. But you can overcome a lack of experience quickly with practice; looking at the photographs in this chapter should help you get started. Practice will make you feel more comfortable with light ratios. Testing with Polaroids to adjust lighting arrangements will simplify the process (see below). And, as suggested earlier, if you happen to land a job that is beyond your current lighting abilities, hire a professional lighting assistant; many rent their own lighting gear.

Polaroid Testing
To test manually controlled lighting setups with Polaroid film, you must use either a professional-model Polaroid camera with adjustable apertures and shutter speeds, or a Polaroid back that replaces the standard camera back. As mentioned earlier, NPC makes Polaroid backs for the most popular professional 35mm and medium-format cameras. The Polaroid Corporation markets holders for 4 x 5-inch and 8 x 10-inch sheet films for large format cameras.

Polaroid's big 600-SE camera is designed for use with all Polaroid 3¼ x 4¼-inch pack films. If you want less bulk, you have two choices. One option is to use an NPC custom Polaroid back; to find one, check dealers who sell or rent professional photo equipment. The other option is to look for a used Minolta Folding Press camera, or an old Polaroid 110A, 110B, or 195 folding camera that has been adapted to accept pack film. (I use a modified Polaroid 110B camera.)

Choose Polaroid black-and-white or color film whose speed is as close as possible to the speed of the film you'll be using for the final shot. When shooting ISO 100 film in a conventional camera, for example, you have several ISO 100 Polaroid films to choose from—and you don't have to make any exposure adjustments. Polaroid Pro Vivid film produces the best results for critical testing with color transparency films.

To make a Polaroid test, first take a flash-meter reading. Minolta V flash meters permit setting two different film speeds, one for Polaroid and one for final films. You can instantly switch readings from one speed to the other, so calculating changes in *f*-stops isn't necessary. Then adjust the lens aperture and/or shutter speed, and shoot. Next, pull the Polaroid film tab, and ease the film out carefully. Wait the required time for the print to develop before peeling the two layers of paper apart (see the Polaroid film packaging for complete directions).

What you should see is an excellent rendition of lights and darks, or good color, with most Polaroid films. If you don't, adjust the exposure and shoot another test. The Kodak gray card, which reflects back 18 percent of the light that falls on it to indicate midtone or "average gray") is a standard exposure aid. If the slide or print reproduces the midtone accurately, exposure is correct. You can make critical readings by including a Kodak exposure control strip in the shot. If all of the strip's 19 black to white steps are recorded correctly on the film, you have excellent exposure.

Polaroids tests are routinely used to correct mistakes, such as undesired hotspots, unwanted shadows, and glare on glasses. You can use Polaroids to change model positions or object placement, too. Polaroid film is also widely used as a valid commercial and fine-art medium in its own right, as is, or with the popular Polaroid-transfer techniques. The company offers free information on its products and ways to use them (see "Resources" on page 142).

Slaves and Triggers
Slaves can be either occasionally handy devices or essential tools for you. Their prices vary greatly, from less than $20 to hundreds of dollars for models that infrared, radio, or sound signals can trigger. You can switch some slave/trigger combinations to different channels or frequencies in order to minimize interference from other amateur or professional flashes, or stray radio signals. Slaves cut out the need for trailing PC/sync cords on a studio floor when you use several separate flashes and/or strobes together.

Photographers who work on location should be aware that the only completely interference-proof way of triggering, or firing, a flash or strobe is with a long PC/sync cord. In the business, this technique is called *hard wiring* and is often used in permanently wired arenas for sports teams. Then many powerful strobes can be fired simultaneously. News and sports photographers can take turns plugging into such systems.

Basic Slaves and Triggers

As mentioned earlier, you can attach any inexpensive, light-sensitive slave unit to any off-camera flash or strobe, either directly or with a PC cord. Any built-in or on-camera flash, even a flash used off-camera, can then fire the slave up to about 15 feet from the camera by any type of flash, including those on other photographers' cameras. Slaves reduce the number of wires or cords cluttering the ground, which is important when you work around people.

When you use inexpensive slaves, the existing light mustn't be too bright, and the distance between the trigger flash and the slaved remote unit mustn't too be great. The slave must have either the correct PC-cord-type tip,

I used three flash units to make this studio portrait. The hairlight was an NVS-1 custom-modified Vivitar used bare-tube on a lightstand placed about 6 inches behind the seated subject's head; a black NVS "blocker" device behind the Vivitar prevented light from spilling onto the black seamless background. The main light was two joined Vivitar 283 flash units bounced out of a 45-inch black-backed umbrella placed about 2 feet above and to the right of the model. A sheet of silver artists' board clipped to a stand opposite the main light provided fill. Working with my Nikon FM-2 manual camera and an 80mm F1.8 lens, I determined exposure via a flash meter and Polaroid tests. The exposure on ISO 64 film was f/11 for 1/60 sec.

Shooting this double portrait in a darkened studio, I determined the exposure with a flash meter and refined the reading with Polaroid film tests. I lit the background with a custom-modified Vivitar 283 NVS-1 flash used bare tube and backed by NVS's translucent green plastic bounce/blocker device. The main light on the young women was two joined Vivitar 283 flashes bounced out of a 42-inch white umbrella from about 2 feet.

shoe mount, or twin blades, to fit the specific flash or strobe equipment. Basic slaves work well both indoors and outdoors in low light at dusk or at night when other people aren't using flashes close by. Small slave units cost about $20 to $35. Any small flash unit, used direct or bounced, can trigger a light-sensitive slave.

Wein Slaves and Triggers

Photographers use these devices to prevent interference from the lights of other flash and/or strobe users, and to effect long flash ranges. I have a Wein-SSR infrared trigger that sits on the camera's hotshoe but doesn't emit visible light. This unit triggers any light-sensitive, slaved flash/strobe combination within range and costs around $100. My favorite slave is the Wein Ultra-Slave WP-SSL model, which costs about $75. Unlike some other good slaves, it doesn't require batteries. I own four of these units, and have used them in bright sunlight at distances of 100 feet. The Ultra-Slave claims to operate to at least 300 feet from the trigger in low light (I haven't tested the outer limit). Wein makes basic and channeled infrared slave and trigger combinations also.

COMMERCIAL AND HOMEMADE LIGHT MODIFIERS

Light modifiers for professional flash and strobe can be anything that fits over a flash or strobe head and changes the look of the light output. Reflectors with different shapes and finishes; see-through, opaque, and black-backed umbrellas; softboxes; *barndoors*, which are metal flaps that can be attached to shade light; scrims; grids; optical spots; snoots; and Fresnel lenses are some of the modifiers you can choose from. Top-of-the-line flash and strobe systems offer many options. Try modifying light with Rosco's black Cinefoil, wire screening, tin cans sprayed black, a magnifying glass, or anything else you like (see "Resources" on page 142).

Infrared, Radio, Sound, and Light-Beam Triggers and Slaves

News, wedding, and other photographers use infrared and radio trigger/slave combinations when they work in locations where other flashes could set off their slaved lights. A two-channel infrared trigger/slave setup costs about $250, and a basic radio trigger/slave outfit costs about double that amount. Quantum is a good brand. Science and nature specialists are the primary users of sound and beam triggers and slaves, which are mostly custom made. Consult professional lighting dealers for more information (review Chapter 10, and see "Resources" on page 142).

Combining Filters and Gels with Professional Flash and Strobe

In professional color photography, accurate, pleasing color renditions can be critical. As mentioned earlier, testing color and using *color-compensating* (CC) filters and complementary gels when combining time exposures with dedicated flash are essential techniques to master (review Chapters 9 and 10). The same rules and color effects that govern dedicated flash also apply to professional manual flash and strobe—with one exception.

Flash meters take into consideration the light-reducing factor of gels used on the front of lights. However, this type of meter doesn't take into account the light-reducing factor of filters and gels in front of lenses. (Use the camera TTL meter for this.) When using professional lighting techniques with manual flash, it is always safest to make Polaroid tests.

Traveling with Lights

Whether you take portable lighting equipment on location across town or around the world, you should find the following hints helpful:

- Get quality cases that are long enough for your tripod, lightstands, umbrellas, and collapsible, soft lightbox

- Carry spare, fully charged battery packs, and recharge them whenever possible

- Put batteries and battery packs into checked luggage—airport security personnel might remove them from carry-on bags

- Never, ever plug chargers or high-voltage equipment into hotel-bathroom dual-voltage adapters intended for use with small appliances

- Learn the voltage standard in the overseas countries you'll be visiting

- If necessary, carry plug adapters, a dual-voltage battery-charger, a dual-voltage strobe unit, and a portable 110–220V transformer

- Don't trust flimsy, foreign-plug adapters you can pick up at airports; buy them from lighting dealers or at electric stores at your destination.

Bags and Cases

I always hand-carry my cameras, lenses, flash or strobe tubes, and film onto the plane. I use a Tenba backpack if I'm not carrying too much gear. I had this backpack modified so that it takes two cameras, basic lenses, a tripod, and lightstands. I use Lightware and Anvil cases when carrying a great deal of lighting gear.

When you travel by car, any luggage that covers your lighting equipment will do. "The uglier, the better" is my safety rule. Pad lights and lightstands with workclothes. If you're shipping your equipment by air freight, hard cases with reinforced foam dividers are the best choice. My wooden, steel-reinforced Anvil case, complete with a padlock, has protected my strobes well for years (see "Resources" on page 142).

Protecting Professional Film from Hazards

As mentioned earlier, your film is what your photography is all about. So take the best possible care of it. Keep film cool before and after shooting. Process professional films at professional labs only. Never trust Third-World labs; ship your film home for processing if necessary.

To protect my film from X-rays, I put it into doubled Sima lead bags. At airports in the United States, you're currently entitled to hand-examination of film. Arrive early, ask politely, and persist. When you travel between and from other countries, you might find that some airport staff members insist on removing film from your bags and putting it through X-ray machines. So far X-rays haven't damaged my film; I don't know anyone who has experienced this problem.

Chapter 12
GALLERY

I'm honored and appreciative that six great photographers agreed to let me include examples of their work in this book, and that they were so generous in talking about their mental and visual approaches and techniques in detail. I know that I learned some things by reading their words.

Joe McNally, Michael "Nick" Nichols, Ken Regan, Chip Simons, Danny Turner, and Theo Westenberger are all at the top of their profession. All are recognized as

masters of flash photography, and all have different styles.

Expertise alone, of course, isn't the ultimate in photography. Each of these photographers has a passion for photography, as well as a distinctive point of view and great technique. They've become known for their individual styles and specialties, but it is their love of photography that keeps them shooting year in and year out.

I photographed this woman on a deserted beach in Brittany, France, at twilight. Handholding my Nikon N90, I used a 20mm F2.8 D lens and my Nikon SB-26 flash in TTL mode. The subject was virtually silhouetted, so no ghost effects are noticeable. The flash fill both lit her and produced good skin tones. I exposed off the rocks and shot ISO 100 film at f/4 for 1/4 sec.

BALANCING INTERIOR AND EXTERIOR LIGHT

JOE McNALLY

This picture was made with a Mamiya RZ Pro 2 camera with a Mamiya 50mm lens and Fuji Provia (RDP II) film. Exposures ranged from about 1/8 sec. to 30 seconds at about $f/11$; one in the mid-range was used.

The photograph, of a student at New York City's top academic Stuyvesant High School, was made for a *Life* magazine story and shot at twilight. A slow shutter speed combined with both strobe and flash was used. The main strobe lighting the outside wall of the building across the street was a powerful Speedotron 2400 WS strobe with a quad head used bare tube. The interior of the classroom was draped in black. Inside the room one slaved 1000 WS Dyna-Lite was bounced out of an umbrella at the student. All the strobes were gelled Full Green (the color of fluorescence) and that was filtered out at camera with a 30 Magenta filter on the lens. I do this generally when shooting a cityscape as there is so much ambient fluorescent light everywhere you look.

The test beaker is filled with watered-down milk, and the student is holding a Morris Mini-Wide self-slaved flash in the hand that is cradling the beaker. The rest of the exposure is just twilight cityscape.

NINA SABO

JOE McNALLY

Joe McNally spent most of the 1970s shooting for such clients as the New York Times *and news agencies AP and UPI. Then he worked as a network stills photographer for ABC television, specializing in news and sports. In 1981 McNally began freelancing for magazines; he started shooting for* Life *in 1984 and was soon listed on the masthead as a contributing photographer. He then became a contract photographer for* Sports Illustrated *for six years. He is currently a staff photographer for* Life, *the first photographer hired in 20 years in 1994.*

McNally has shot cover stories for Life, Time, Newsweek, Sports Illustrated, Fortune, *and* New York *magazine. He received a Page One Award from the Newspaper Guild of New York in 1986. Pictures of the Year awarded him first place in magazine illustration in 1988, and first place in product illustration in 1993. In 1997, the World Press Photo Foundation awarded him a first prize in portraits. Also in 1997, he won a gold prize in magazine photography from* Photo District News, *and a first prize in general editorial photography from* American Photo.

McNally has taught at the Eddie Adams Workshop for eight years, and lectured at the National Press Photographers' Association Flying Short Course and the National Geographic *Masters of Contemporary Photography series. He shot for numerous* A Day in the Life *books, and was a featured exhibitor at the 1991 Festival of Photojournalism in Perpignan, France.*

American Photo *described McNally as "perhaps the most versatile photojournalist working today" and listed him in its 1993 edition of the 100 most important people in photography.*

INTERPRETING MOTION WITH FLASH

MICHAEL "NICK" NICHOLS

This frame of a charging forest elephant (Loxodonta africana cyclotis) is from a grueling assignment in the Ndoki forest of Central Africa for "Ndoki: Last Place on Earth," *National Geographic*, July 1995. A Canon EOS-1 in TTL mode was set at -1²/₃ stops flash compensation. The exposure was for 1/4 to 1/15 sec. at *f*/2.8.

I spent a total of seven field months over a two-year period in a very untouched and inhospitable place. No Land Rovers here—we did everything on foot.

Forest elephants are the little-known smaller cousins of African Savannah elephants. The females are almost always aggressive, having evolved to protect themselves from the poacher's bullet. Thus, the smell of a photographer can elicit a frightening charge.

I was secretly dreaming of this shot or something like it. To observe the forest elephants, I would groggily rise before dawn, grab the monopod mounted on the camera, and walk down to the river a few hundred yards from camp where we knew they grazed through the night until first light.

I set the ambient-light exposure to a slight underexposure and the flash with a -1²/₃ compensation dialed in, hoping to give that little edge and stopping of action that can create magic. More painting than photography, this technique allows me to bridge the gap between still photography and film.

I waded into the river and started walking toward the elephant, carefully observing her through my lens. When she smelled me and began to charge, I stopped and shot three frames before turning on my heels and running to safety. This shot is the third, shot an instant before my run. The picture fell out of my mind until trip's end when I was poring over the developed film months later and thousands of miles away in Washington, DC. This photo miraculously became the cover of *National Geographic* and got many letters with comments like "Can't your photographer focus a camera?" and "I would have thrown that one in the garbage." It's the one I live for.

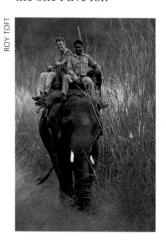

ROY TOFT

Michael "Nick" Nichols is a pioneer in the use of flash mixed with ambient light. Starting as a Photo 101 student in the early 1970s, Nichols strives for photography with an edge that exudes energy and tension. Nichols's projects reflect the disruption of the natural order and the loss of something precious. Nichols is a former member of Magnum Photo and is currently a staff member at National Geographic. *He is the author of* Gorilla: Struggles for Survival in the l *(Aperture),* The Great Apes Between Two Worlds *(National Geographic), and* Keepers of the Kingdom: The New American Zoo *(Thomasson-Grant & Lickle). Once a year, Nichols teaches "The Passionate Image" at the Santa Fe Photographic Workshops.*

MICHAEL NICHOLS

RECORDING A SEQUENCE WITH MULTIPLE STROBES

KEN REGAN

KEN REGAN/CAMERA 5

The rush pre-Olympic-issue assignment from *Newsweek* called for a photograph of a top contender executing a triple axel. It required planning, coordination, and expert technical assistance. I called a good friend, the director of photography at *Sports Illustrated*, Heinz Klutemeier. He suggested I call in tech assistant and lighting expert Jeff Salzer of Wisconsin, one of the best in the business. Then it took many phone calls by my staff to find an arena available for overnight in Boston. The chosen skater was lined up, plus a stand-in who could jump 2½ axels was hired, and 50-foot black velvet backdrop was made by a company that sews curtains for theaters.

New York assistants Gabe Palacio and Ted Carrasco went early to Boston with my gear and collected the rental strobes. We all met Salzer, who brought the custom-made sequencers needed for the job. Everything worked as planned. Starting at 11 P.M. the drape was hung, the stand-in did his job. Polaroid tests enabled us to set marks and place and time the lights so they caught and separated each position of the axel.

I used four Nikon F4 cameras plus two Hasselblads, one with a Polaroid back; if the image was good on the Polaroid, we knew we had it on film on the other five cameras. All were mounted close together on a special bracket and wired to simultaneously fire in sync.

At 4 A.M. we called the Olympic contender who arrived in a limo, warmed up. Then because he was thrown by loss of equilibrium in the total darkness needed for sequential shots, he couldn't make the jump work. He tried over and over but when near exhaustion told us it was "no go."

We packed up to be out by 7 A.M., then began calling. I learned that Olympic gold medalist Brian Boitano was playing an ice show at the Boston Garden. The magazine called Brian's agent in California to find out if he would be willing to do the shot. Boitano agreed, his agent flew in later the same day with clothes for Brian, and we set up again the next night. Boitano arrived on time at 3 A.M. He warmed up, then made 11 perfect triple axels out of 12.

Because the agent brought great pants but no top that worked against black, Brian is wearing my assistant's blue T-shirt in the picture.

GABE PALACIO

Ken Regan, in his career as a professional photographer, has stalked big game in Africa; covered wars in Vietnam, the Gulf, and Bosnia; and documented several Olympic games and presidential campaigns. He studied journalism at Columbia University and film at New York University, and went on to found his own photography agency, Camera 5, with assignments from Life, Sports Illustrated, Time, People, *and* Newsweek.

Over 200 magazine covers later, film director Jonathan Demme asked Regan to shoot stills for "Married to the Mob," "The Silence of the Lambs," and "Philadelphia." Clint Eastwood tapped him as photography consultant and stills photographer for "The Bridges of Madison County," and some of those pictures became the best-selling book, The Bridges of Madison County– The Film. *Regan has made four other successful picture books, two on professional hockey. In 1995-96 he made two wildlife safaris in Africa and returned to Bosnia.*

Regan recently did stills for the films "Up Close and Personal," with Robert Redford and Michelle Pfeiffer, directed by Jon Avnet; "The Devil's Own," with Brad Pitt and Harrison Ford, directed by Alan Pakula; and "In the Gloaming," with Glenn Close, which marked Christopher Reeve's debut as a film director.

PAINTING WITH LIGHT
CHIP SIMONS

I had to photograph new-age drug guru Terrance McKenna for publication. Since I was going to be light painting, I needed total darkness. We used McKenna's "get high" room. I told him to go around his house and find things that made him think about psychedelica. He found his daughter's doll "Grace," a fishing pole (since he was always fishing for ideas), and his opium pipe. He began smoking, and I began shooting. I shot 12 frames, and each one was different: Pantyhose over his face with light painting, drawing rainbows between his fingers, a clown's mask, his head breaking up into sparks. A three-faced head, his face floating in front of the room, and finally one with the multiple arms like the goddess Shiva.

I walked around dressed like a Ninja all in black, changing the color for each flash. I'd flash his arms in one position, change gels, flash again in another position, change gels, etc. I pushed the film plus 1/2 stop. Terrance liked the procedure but was very stoned. After I shot my 12 frames, I flew home.

CHIP SIMONS © 1997

Chip Simons has lived across the United States, spending formative years in Florida, Pennsylvania, and New York. In 1982 he graduated from the University of New Mexico and moved to New York City. Most of his techniques are self-taught. His first success was when his series "I Am a Dog" was published in Andy Warhol's Interview magazine.

Assignments from Esquire, Forbes, Rolling Stone, Spin, and New York magazine followed. For Sony Music, Simons shot album covers for Cyndi Lauper, Grover Washington, Jr., The Radiators, Branford Marsalis, and others. His work has been seen on movie and promotional posters. Assignments have taken him to locations across the United States and Europe, including the former Soviet Union, and Egypt.

Simons continues to experiment. His distinctive style has lead to assignments with such blue-chip advertising clients as American Express, Apple Computer, Coca-Cola, Etonic, Hasselblad, Microsoft, Miller Beer, MTV, Nikon, and "The Tonight Show," where he appeared as a guest of Jay Leno. Simons's work in video can be seen in ID spots for Comedy Central and the BBC.

Articles about Simons have appeared in numerous publications, including American Photo, Popular Photography, French Photo, and Photo District News. He has received numerous awards, and continues to teach workshops and lecture at various schools and media groups. Simons has lectured at New York University, the School of Visual Arts, and for Photo 1990 in Hong Kong. He has also taught seminars at the Art Kane Photo Workshop and the Santa Fe Photographic Workshops. He lives with his family and dogs in New Mexico.

CHIP SIMONS © 1997

USING BATTERY-POWERED FLASH ON LOCATION

DANNY TURNER

This photograph of basketball player Sheryl Swoopes was made on assignment for *Vanity Fair* magazine. In addition to being on championship college and Olympic basketball teams, Sheryl is the only living woman to have a pair of Nike shoes named after her, the Nike "Air Swoopes."

The assignment was to do a portrait of Sheryl and, if possible, show the shoes. My crew, assistant Kris Hundt, hair and makeup artist Kim Pish, and I traveled to Sheryl's hometown of Lubbock, Texas, to make the photograph. I didn't have any ideas about what I was going to do before we went to Lubbock. Sometimes I have the story, or at least a headline to work from or take visual clues from, but not this time. I tend to work in a very simple manner, going to the location and responding to what I find, trying to tell a story about the person by using the environment or props.

Lubbock is a flat and barren part of Texas and except for Texas Tech University is mostly oil fields and tumbleweeds. We looked around for an interesting location but didn't find anything outstanding, so we photographed Sheryl at a city park on the outskirts of town. While trying to find an interesting composition, I had the idea to have her stand on the basketball. Sheryl is a very graceful woman and was willing to give it a try. We placed the ball on the concrete and while my assistant held the ball steady, Sheryl stood in top of it. My assistant then let go of the ball, and Sheryl could actually balance on the ball for about 10 seconds before she fell off. I was amazed! This shot might really work out. We scrounged around the park and found a way to hold the ball steady while Sheryl was standing on it, so we didn't have to worry about her falling.

We shot about four rolls of Fuji RDP 100 film with my Rollei 6006 model 2 (medium-format) camera with a 40mm lens, an aperture of 8 2/3, and a shutter speed of 1/250 sec. This is a mixed-light photograph where I mixed the ambient light with the flash. I used a Comet PMT 1200 watt-second battery flash set at 600 watt-seconds in a medium Chimera lightbox. The flash provides the main and only light on Sheryl. The ambient light illuminates the rest of the scene. By using flash outside, I can control the brightness or darkness of the background scene (ambient light) without affecting the foreground scene (the subject lit by flash). If the flash didn't go off during the exposure, then Sheryl would have appeared as a silhouette because she is lit only by the flash.

I use the Comet PMT for about 90 percent of my work, inside or outside. I especially like not having to look for electricity in the middle of nowhere. It gives me great freedom and one less thing that I have to consider when looking for locations. The PMT gives me five to seven rolls of 120 film and two to three packs of Polaroid per battery. I don't like to shoot a lot of film but just to be sure I have eight batteries (I have four PMTs), but my usual "rig" is one Halliburton case (they are the best!) containing two PMT packs, two flash heads, two battery chargers, and four batteries. Some people say that the PMT's recycle rate is too slow (about 2 seconds at 150 watts, 3 seconds at 300 watts, 6 seconds at 600 watts, 15 seconds at 1200 watts), but I find that it makes for a nice, leisurely pace.

Danny Turner is a successful (but very modest) editorial and advertising photographer who grew up in various parts of the world while his father was in the Air Force, but spent his formative years in Texas. He still travels the world photographing people for editorial and advertising clients. He is a graduate of East Texas State University and has a degree in photography. His photographs have appeared in Texas Monthly, Sports Illustrated, Forbes, Kiplinger's, Outside *magazine,* Bon Appetit, Entertainment Weekly, *and* Vanity Fair, The New York Times Magazine, The Los Angeles Times Magazine, *and (he says) many, many obscure publications.*

CREATING MOOD WITH MIXED LIGHT

THEO WESTENBERGER

The picture of Arnold Schwarzenegger was made on assignment for Carolco to publicize the movie "Terminator II." It was used on the cover of *Entertainment Weekly*.

The company selected the Santa Monica Mall as my location and an unused boutique as my space. I was horrified that I had to photograph "The Terminator" under such circumstances. So I scouted around and found a grim, unfinished corridor leading to the parking garage. This location helped to make an exciting photo. I used a small grid spot on the key light, a 1000 WS/J Dyna-Lite strobe, for the dramatic effect on Arnold's face. Because the space was so narrow and his silhouette so effective, I needed only one more light as a backlight. This was a 2000-watt tungsten light provided by the film company. Barndoors carded off some of the light from the big open head. Additionally, smoke was pumped in to the scene from the rear with a small, rented fog machine.

Shooting with a tripod-mounted Mamiya RZ with a 65mm lens, I exposed Fujichrome 100 RDP film at *f*/8 for 1/15 sec. to burn in the backlight. I got off fewer than 15 frames because the smoke in such a small space was debilitating both to myself and to my subject.

The assignment was a good example of the fact that a photographer should never settle for the given circumstances if there is a better possibility open to him or her.

THEO WESTENBERGER

Theo Westenberger was raised in California, has a Master of Fine Arts degree in photography from the Pratt Institute, and for the last 15 years has worked as a freelance photographer based in New York City. Westenberger's editorial clients include Life, People, Newsweek, Smithsonian, Sports Illustrated, Condé Nast Traveler, Money, Fortune, *and* Entertainment Weekly.

Some of Westenberger's many motion-picture, production-company, and television credits include films from "Terminator II" to "Terms of Endearment" for such clients as Carolco, New Line Cinema, Paramount Pictures, Tri-Star, Universal, and Warner Brothers. She was honored in 1993 by being selected by the Academy of Motion Picture Arts and Sciences to take the group photograph of all the women ever to have received an Academy Award.

Westenberger's work has been exhibited at the Metropolitan Museum of Art, the International Center of Photography, the Smithsonian Institution, the Nikon House Gallery, Wheaton College, Drew University, and private galleries. Her work is also included in many noted photography collections.

Westenberger has received a First Prize in the International World Press Photo Contest; she has also garnered honors from the Advertising Photographers of America, American Photography 11, *the Applied Arts contest,* Applied Arts Award Annual, New York Festivals—International Print and Radio Advertising, *and the* Visual Club.

Westenberger's book credits include Hollywood Legend and Reality, The Best of Life, Life Classic Faces, The Meaning of Life II, The Olympics, A Father's Love, Through Indian Eyes, *and* A Dog's Life. *She teaches a course in lighting at the Santa Fe Photographic Workshops, and a course at the Esalen Institute.*

THEO WESTENBERGER

RESOURCES

Manufacturers/Distributors/Suppliers

Agfa
Division of Miles Inc.
100 Challenger Boulevard
Ridgefield Park, NJ 07660
201-440-2500
Scala black-and-white slide and other films; paper; more

American Photographic Instruments
12 Lincoln Boulevard
Emerson, NJ 07620
201-261-2160
PIC lightweight, compact, and high lightstands

Bogen Photo Corporation
565 East Crescent Avenue
P.O. Box 506
Ramsey, NJ 07446
201-818-9500
Metz/Mecablitz flash units, Gitzo tripods; Bogen-Manfrotto tripods, lightstands, and clamps; more

Calumet Photographic
890 Supreme Drive
Bensenville, IL 60106
708-860-7447
Calumet/Bownes Travelite dual-voltage strobes; PocketWizard 16-channel radio slave system; much more; major manufacturer/distributor of photo products; mail-order house with superb catalog that includes most lighting accessories

Canon USA
1 Canon Plaza
Lake Success, NY 10042
516-328-1809
Cameras; lenses; flash units; accessories

Chimera
1812 Valtec Lane
Boulder, CO 80301
800-424-4075
Portable soft-light banks; adapter rings; accessories

Comet World
311-319 Long Avenue
Hillside, NJ 07205
908-687-8800
Professional battery-powered flash units; dual voltage strobes
See also *Dyna-Lite*

Contax
See Yashica

Dyna-Lite
311-319 Long Avenue
Hillside, NJ 07205
908-687-8800
Dyna-Lite portable strobes; Uni-400 Jr. AC/battery-powered professional flash unit; Jack Rabbit battery packs

Eastman Kodak Company
343 State Street
Rochester, NY 14650
716-724-6970
Film; professional color-correction filters; exposure scales; paper; more

Fuji Photo Film USA
555 Taxter Road
Elmsford, NY 19523
516-789-8140
Film; point-and-shoot and professional cameras; paper; more

Gitzo tripods
See Bogen

Hasselblad USA Inc.
10 Madison Road
Fairfield, NJ 07004
201-227-7320
Legendary medium-format cameras

Helix
310 South Racine
Chicago, IL 60607
800-334-3549
Major photographic mail-order dealer; underwater-flash specialist

Ilford Photo
70 West Century Road
Paramus, NJ 07653
201-265-6000
Chromogenic black-and-white film; conventional film; more

Konica USA, Inc.
440 Sylvan Avenue
Englewood Cliffs, NJ 07632
201-568-3100
Film; cameras, especially point-and-shoots

Leica
156 Ludlow Street
Northvale, NJ 07647
800-222-0118
Legendary cameras; don't overlook the company's point-and-shoots

Lights Limited
P.O. Box 324
Collingswood, NJ 08108
609-854-3848
Under Dog 6V rechargeable gel-cell batteries/accessories

Lightware
141 Platt Street
Denver, CO 80202
303-455-6944
Equipment cases for traveling photographers

Lumedyne
6010 Wall
Port Richey, FL 34668
813-847-5394
Professional high-power, modular battery-powered flash units and accessories

Mamiya America Corporation
8 Westchester Plaza
Elmsford, NY 10523
914-347-3300
Professional 35mm rangefinder and medium-format cameras

Metz/Mecablitz flash units
See Bogen

Minolta Corporation
101 Williams Drive
Ramsey, NJ 07446
201-825-4000
Cameras; lenses; flash units; superb flash and color-temperature meters

The Morris Company
See Speedotron

Nikon, Inc.
1300 Walt Whitman Road
Melville, NY 11747
516-547-4355
Cameras; lenses; flash units; accessories; Nikonos underwater cameras and flash units

Norman Enterprises
2601 Empire Avenue
Burbank, CA 91504
818-843-6811
Professional high-voltage battery-powered flash units; portable strobes

Novatron of Dallas
8230 Moberly Lane
Dallas, TX 75227
214-388-4857
Lightweight but durable portable strobes

Olympus Corporation
Crossways Park
Woodbury, NY 11797
800-221-3000
Cameras, especially good point-and-shoot models; flash units; accessories

Paramount Corporation
720 East 239th Street
Bronx, NY 10466
718-325-9100
Standard, custom, and dedicated PC/sync cords; replacement flash feet

Pentax Corporation
35 Inverness Drive East
Englewood, CO 80112
303-799-8000
Cameras, especially good point-and-shoot models; lenses; flash units

Photoflex Inc.
333 Encinal Street
Santa Cruz, CA 95060
408-454-9100
Collapsible Lite-Disc reflectors; umbrella clamps; other lighting accessories

Polaroid Corporation
575 Technology Square
Cambridge, MA 02139
617-386-2000
Polaroid cameras, backs, and film; macro accessories; more

Quantum Instruments
1075 Stewart Avenue
Garden City, NY 11530
516-222-0611
Professional dedicated Q-flash units; rechargeable battery packs; camera-to-battery-pack modules; infrared and radio slave/triggers

Rosco Laboratories
52 Harbor View Avenue
Stamford, CT 06902
203-708-8900
Photographic gels; black Cinefoil wrap; diffusion material; smoke; more

Saunders Group
21 Jet View Drive
Rochester, NY 14624
716-328-7800
Lepp and Stroboframe flash brackets; Domke accessories and bags; Wein triggers and slaves; more

Sima Products
8707 North Skokie Boulevard
Skokie, IL 60077
708-679-7462
Protective lead-foil bags for film

Sekonic Flash Meters
R.T.S. Inc.
40-11 Burt Drive
Deer Park, NY 11729
516-242-6801
A wide range of good meters

Speedotron/The Morris Company
310 South Racine
Chicago, IL 60607
AC-powered professional portable strobes; Morris self-slaved flash units

Stroboframe Flash Brackets
See Saunders Group

Sunpak flash and slave units
See Tocad America Inc.

Tenba Inc.
503 Broadway
New York, NY 10012
212-966-1013
Camera and light bags and backpacks; some custom work

Tiffen Group
90 Oser Avenue
Hauppauge, NY 11788
516-273-2500
Filters; more

Tocad America Inc.
300 Webro Road
Parsippany, NJ 07054
201-428-9800
Sunpak flash units and slaves; more

UnderDog Battery Packs
See Lights Limited

Vivitar
1280 Rancho Conejo Road
Newbury Park, CA 91320
805-498-7008
Vivitar 283 and 285 automatic flash units and accessories; more

Yashica
Kyocera Group Inc.
100 Randolph Road, CN 8062
Somerset, NJ 08875
908-560-0060
Cameras , especially good point-and-shoot models; flash units; represents Contax in the USA

Specialized Equipment, Slaves/Triggers, Consultants, Repairs

Edmund Scientific Company
101 East Gloucester Pike
Barrington, NJ 08007
609-547-3488
Optical tubing; lenses; much more; for do-it-yourself enthusiasts

Flash Clinic
9 East 19th Street
New York, NY 10003
212-673-4030
Long-established professional specialist; sells, rents, and repairs high-powered battery flash units, including Henschells; strobes; lighting accessories; consultants

Ikelite Inc.
50 West 33rd Street
Indianapolis, IN 46308
317-923-4523
Underwater flash units, and flash and camera housing; Lite-Link slave for Canon, Minolta, and Nikon TTL flash units

Kapture Group
12620 Lamplighter Square
St. Louis, MO 63128
314-525-7135
Ultra-high-speed synchronous and asynchronous flash trigger control systems; more

Kirk Enterprises Inc.
107 Lange Lane
Angola, IN 46703
219-665-3670
Custom flash brackets; custom work; more

LPA Design
13 Shelburne Road, Suite 265
South Burlington, VT 05403
802-864-8572
PocketWizard 16-channel radio trigger and slave units; sequencers; more

NPC (Photo Division)
1238 Chestnut Street
Newton Upper Falls, MA 02164
617-969-4522
Polaroid backs for 35mm SLR and medium-format cameras

NVS-1 double-powered, Vivitar conversions
See S.A.I. Photo Products

PermaPak
Division of Photoco Inc.
4347 Cranwood Parkway
Cleveland, OH 44128
PermaPak snap-in/out modular battery-packs with dual 6V and 9V outlets

Photo Tech Repair Service
110 East 13th Street
New York, NY 10003
212-673-8400
Repairs Vivitar and other flash units, point-and-shoot cameras, and projectors

PocketWizard radio slaves/triggers
See LPI Design; Saunders Group

Professional Camera Repair
37 West 47th Street
New York, NY 10031
212-382-0550
Repairs professional cameras and meters; custom modifications

Quantum Instruments
1075 Stewart Avenue
Garden City, NY 11530
516-222-0611
Channeled infrared slaves and triggers; radio slaves/triggers; more

L.L. Rue Enterprises
Millbrook Road
Blairstown, NJ 07825
908-362-6616
Mail-order catalog of nature-photography equipment; teleflash device; flash brackets; more

S.A.I. Photo Products
126 Somers Court South
Moorestown, NJ 08057
609- 778-0261
Double-powered NVS-1 Vivitar flash conversion with optional bare bulb head; Strobe on a Rope; more

Wein multi-channeled infrared slaves and triggers; slaves and triggers
See Saunders Group

Woods Electronics, Suite 197
14781 Pomerado Road
Poway, CA 92064
619-486-0806
Bean triggers; ultra-high-speed flash units; sequencers; high-speed lighting consultant

Books

Light. Michael Freeman (New York: Amphoto, 1988).

Matters of Light and Depth. Russ Lowell (Philadelphia: Broad Street Books).

Nature and Wildlife Photography: A Practical Guide to How to Shoot and Sell. Susan McCartney (New York: Allworth Press, 1994).

Photographing Buildings Inside and Out, 2nd edition. Norman McGrath (New York: Amphoto, 1993).

Secrets of Lighting on Location. Bob Krist (New York: Amphoto Books, 1996).

Secrets of Studio Still Life Photography. Gary Perweiler (New York: Amphoto, 1994).

The Photographer's Studio Manual. Michael Freeman (New York: Amphoto, 1991).

Travel Photography: A Complete Guide to How to Shoot and Sell. Susan McCartney (New York: Allworth Press, 1994).

Underwater Photography. Charles Seaborn (New York: Amphoto, 1988).

Also worth reading are the following books from the Eastman Kodak Workbook Series, distributed by Silver Pixel Press in Rochester, NY:

Closeup Photography

Electronic Flash

Using Filters

The books contain good theory and are useful for manual/automatic camera users. At the time of this writing, these books haven't been revised yet to include TTL/dedicated flash.

INDEX